IT STOPS HERE

IT STOPS

Standing Up for Our Lands, Our Waters,
and Our People

HERE

RUEBEN GEORGE
with Michael Simpson

ALLEN
LANE

ALLEN LANE

an imprint of Penguin Canada, a division of Penguin Random House Canada Limited

Canada • USA • UK • Ireland • Australia • New Zealand • India • South Africa • China

First published 2023

www.penguinrandomhouse.ca

LIBRARY AND ARCHIVES CANADA CATALOGUING IN PUBLICATION

Title: It stops here : standing up for our lands, our waters, and our people /
Rueben George and Michael Simpson.
Names: George, Rueben, author. | Simpson, Michael (Lecturer), author.
Description: Includes index.
Identifiers: Canadiana (print) 20220429197 | Canadiana (ebook) 20220431450 |
ISBN 9780735242807 (hardcover) | ISBN 9780735242814 (EPUB)
Subjects: LCSH: George, Rueben. | LCSH: George, Rueben—Family. |
CSH: First Nations—Tsleil-Waututh Nation—Government relations. |
CSH: First Nations—Tsleil-Waututh Nation—Socialconditions. |
CSH: First Nations—Civil rights—Tsleil-Waututh Nation. |
CSH: First Nations activists—Tsleil-Waututh Nation—Biography. |
LCSH: Petroleum pipelines—Environmental aspects—British Columbia. |
LCSH: Social justice—Canada. | LCGFT: Autobiographies.
Classification: LCC E99.S21 G46 2023 | DDC 305.897/94—dc23

Book design by Kelly Hill
Cover design by Kelly Hill
Cover image: © Cristina Mittermeier Photography Ltd.

Printed in Canada

10 9 8 7 6 5 4 3 2 1

Penguin
Random
House

ALLEN
LANE

Dedicated to my mom, my dad, my kids, my siblings,
my Tsleil-Waututh family,
my Squamish family,
all residential school survivors,
and all generations thereafter

CONTENTS

ACKNOWLEDGMENTS

The concept of nəċəmat [naut'sa mawt], which I discuss in this book, tells us that everything is interconnected and related. This book could not have been written without all my relations—all the people who have supported me over the course of my life, and who were there for me when I decided to change.

First and foremost, I would like to thank my kids, Cedar George-Parker and Kayah Rose George, who have changed my life in the most positive of ways. Having kids made me want to do better. When Cedar was born, I held him with his head in the palm of my hand, his body resting along my forearm, and as I looked at this little human being who I was now responsible for, I told myself that I better get my shit together. He has now grown up to become a beautiful man, so wise and confident, who travels the world speaking powerfully about protecting the lands, waters, and people. It also amazes me that Kayah, who not long ago was such a tiny baby, is now such a strong, smart, and confident matriarch, standing up for her convictions and always guided by our culture and spirituality.

They both run sweat lodge and pipe ceremonies for me now because they know the teachings and can hold the space. It took me up until my forties to reach the place that they have already reached in their twenties. I love my kids and I couldn't be a prouder dad because of all that they have already accomplished at such a young age, and I just can't imagine how much more they will do for our world over the course of their lifetimes. They are both true protectors of our lands, waters, and people.

My mom, Amy Marie George—Ta'ah—has persevered through horrible things that happened to her, to become an elder and an awesome example of how to do the continuous work of healing. Despite all that happened to her at residential school, she remembered our culture and spirituality, and she passed on those teachings of our ancestors. We may have been economically poor growing up, but she often told us that we were rich culturally and that we had to carry ourselves in a good way. No matter how bad it was for us, she always made us feel special. Today, in our Sun Dance family ceremonies, she tells people, no matter who they are, to call her Ta'ah, or Grandma. She's always there for people, and always willing to open her home and invite people in. We're very close, and we talk almost every day.

My oldest brother Damian has taught me so much. Despite all the chaos around us growing up, with many people medicating with drugs and alcohol due to all the trauma from the colonial system they experienced, he made a choice to create a better life for himself. I've never seen him drink or use drugs, and I think that shows incredible leadership. When we were kids, sometimes we just needed to get away from all the chaos, so he would take us on the bus as far as it would go. We would get off and play around a bit, and then take it home again. Later in life, he taught me how to tap into the ancestors to receive messages and new teachings. We continue to pray together today. My brother's wife, Grace George, is presently the chief of the Katzie Nation. She is a beautiful, strong matriarch. They are a beautiful couple together.

My brother Nathan is such a charismatic guy. Everybody loved him growing up, and they still do. I remember once he was playing soccer and he kicked the ball so hard that his boot ripped right off his foot. And he could sing like Bono of U2. Today, he is suffering from the impacts of the colonial system, but we still have really good visits a couple times a week. We laugh and cry together. If I'm ever having a hard time, he knows it and he'll want to talk it through with me. One time, after he helped me work out some things I was struggling with, I said, "Thank you, brother, you really helped me and you took care of me today," and he replied, "I will always take care of you." Despite his tough situation, Nathan is full of compassion.

My sister Cecily is the best of us all. The Tsleil-Waututh Nation is a matriarchal society, and that matriarchal leadership is exemplified in my sister Cecily. She's always been kind, sweet, strong, loving, and compassionate. She's strong in her convictions. She had three big brothers, but she was never afraid to put us all in our place in a sweet and loving way. And we always listened to her because we loved and adored her so much. Like my mom, she makes us all feel special. She a powerful person, and a knowledge-keeper who remembers our lineage. She's the glue that holds our family together. Cecily married into the Paul family, a beautiful people we respect and admire dearly. Her partner Chad is a strong leader and a spiritual father in our community. Together they are a beautiful, strong couple.

My dad is Terry Baker from the Squamish nation. Unfortunately, he died tragically at a young age. I was just a year old. Whenever I visited my Squamish family when I was very young, they would cry when they saw me because they loved my dad so much. I asked my mom if we could stop going down there because it made me feel so bad to see our relatives so upset. I did stay connected with my cousins Ed and Brad Baker—we grew up together. Eventually, I reconnected with the rest of my Baker family when I was about nineteen years old. My cousins Keith Baker and Bosco Kelly, and many others, have told me good stories about my dad. He was very charismatic and loved by everyone. I pray to my dad a lot, and I can feel him in ceremony. My kids pray to him too, which is beautiful. When I look at my son, I see my Baker family in his face. It makes me think of them, and I send them love and prayers. They are so supportive and loving. I love my Baker family.

Philip Gurney was my mom's partner, who became my stepdad. He and my mom loved each other very much, and he was instrumental in our lives. Philip was Nisga'a, and I still connect with some of our Nisga'a relatives. They take care of me when I'm in their territory.

Mike Simpson and I became beautiful brothers through the process of making this book. He is very patient, loving, caring, intelligent, and humble. Sharing details of your life is a very difficult thing that makes you feel vulnerable, but Mike was a good brother who was there to listen and make these words into a book. It was a long process, and he was very supportive throughout. As we worked on the book, we would do ceremony together, pray together, visit my family, go swimming, and sometimes just hang out. All of that was part of building our relationship to help us work together. As I discuss in the book, when two human beings come together, they form a spirit of love, and that's what we did—we formed a spirit of love and brotherhood. Now we will be brothers for life. It was awesome to be at his wedding with his beautiful wife Celina, and now he has a beautiful son, Cedric. I'm very grateful to have Mike in my life.

I have many, many cousins to thank from the Baker/Squamish side of my family, and from my George/Tsleil-Waututh side. I just love all my cousins—they are all so caring, and at the end of the day, we're always there for each other. My brother-cousin Justin has been instrumental in our lives from the time we were babies, and throughout my whole life. We have always adored each other. We work together and we have lots of laughs and good times, but we also remember the hard times, and we always have our nation and our people in our hearts and in our minds. I also grew up very close to my brother-cousin Gabe, and we work with each other. He is a strong language speaker and the director of our Nation's department of Treaty, Lands, and Resources. Gabe has a big loving heart. My sister-cousin Charlene excels at whatever she puts her mind to. She was a television and movie star from a very young age, and she grew up to become the strong leader in our community that she is today. She is an elected leader, but she also supports and takes care of our community in many other ways. She comes to ceremony, and she works with the Sacred Trust Initiative. She travels far and wide sharing our message, and is an eloquent and compelling spokesperson for our nation. Her presence is powerful, and she is an example of our matriarchal leadership, just like her sister Andrea and my sister Michelle George. Over most of her career, Michelle has been in strong leadership positions. She has strong vision. And like Michelle, all my sisters implement our culture and spirituality into their work. My brother-cousin Will George hung from the Ironworkers Bridge for a day and a half to stop oil tankers from passing through our inlet. He was one of the main people at the watchhouse, which I discuss in chapter five, and he has now been sentenced to prison by the colonial courts for his work protecting our lands and waters. There are many other cousins who I'm thankful for and who I want to acknowledge. I send my blessings to my Tsleil-Waututh and Squamish cousins, and to all my cousins beyond. I love each and every one of my cousins. They are all proud and beautiful people. Our nations dwindled, but we came back from nothing and built our families again. Although I've often been a spokesperson for our nation in our fight against Trans Mountain, all my brothers, sisters, cousins, nieces, and nephews can speak just as powerfully and elegantly as I. I'm proud to be Tsleil-Waututh. I love my people so much, and I love our land so much.

I want to thank all my aunts and uncles. They all helped to raise me, and they always wanted what was best for me. Because I grew up without a dad, I would often go and listen to Uncle Len and Uncle Bob, who were like father figures and gave me very good teachings. Later in life, Uncle Len dedicated time to meet with me every week to talk about things that we wanted for our community. He really invested a lot in me. Auntie Rose was truly a matriarch. She was such a beautiful auntie and she always made sure I was taken care of. I remember once Auntie Rose saw me walking home and pulled over to give me a ride. There was no room in her car because I was a big kid and it was full of stuff. But she said, "You're not walking home," and pulled me in and made me sit on her lap. I would often go talk with Auntie Sue and Uncle Len when I had relationship problems, and they would always help me. Auntie Anne was my god-mother. I would visit her a lot, and she would always take care of me. Auntie Irene and Uncle Joe were my second parents. I stayed with them a couple times for long periods of my childhood and they really looked after me. Auntie Irene was tough but loving. Auntie Cassie and Uncle Bob would always feed us no matter what. Auntie Rose and Uncle Les were just solid. Each and every one of my aunts and uncles are beautiful people.

My partner Olivia and I have had similar lives in many ways. She and her sisters grew up like we did—very poor but rich with love. She went through hell, but still blossomed into the very beautiful person she is today who has a heart that is full of love. She's there for everyone, and everyone loves her, just as I do. She gives so much to everyone, like she does for me and her kids. Her twins, Kin and Teo, are young, very intelligent, and focused on their schooling. Her daughter Moya is strong and confident—she'll stand up for her convictions and morals. She's a protector. They are beautiful, sweet kids.

I want to acknowledge my grandparents, Dan George and Amy George on my mom's side, and Matilda and Dominic Baker on my dad's side. I used to go visit my grandma Matilda as a kid and she made me laugh. She loved me so much. I'm thankful to my grandpa Dominic. I never met him, but I heard lots of stories about how beautiful he was. I was too young to remember my grandma Amy George, but I have beautiful stories of her as well.

Debbie Parker is the mom of my kids and their brother Wetuah Parker Dewey. She does really good work for our lands, our waters, and for human rights. She's always been that way. I love the Tulalip people, and the neighbouring tribes. They have all been very supportive, loving, and caring. I lived in the Tulalip area for ten years, and worked with a lot of kids in the school district while I was there. I still think of them, and I love them all.

Papa Phil Lane Jr., one of my spiritual fathers, is always there for me. Like any father-son relationship, we have some pretty serious conversations, but it always comes back to love. I still go to him for insights into all aspects of being First Nations, and all the things we have to deal with, including our families, our politics, our businesses, but especially our ceremonies. He's always sharing, always helping, always willing, always loving, and always standing by my side. He doesn't let anyone mess with me, that's for sure. Auntie Suthida is such a strong beautiful auntie. She takes care of us all. Their son Tiger, my nephew, is a brilliant young guy.

I'm also very thankful to my spiritual father Chief Leonard Crow Dog Sr. for his dedication and commitment to teaching me. He came to visit our territories multiple times, and we travelled around together visiting different communities. He was so loving, and very humble. Many of the Chiefs and their families down at Crow Dog's

Paradise are my aunties and uncles now, and they helped me grow up. Leonard Jr. is a beautiful brother who is running the Sun Dance now. I look forward to going home.

I have many other spiritual uncles and aunties who I would like to acknowledge. JC Lucas gave me my first pipe, and I love him very much. Uncle Sam George and I travelled all over together, and he came to Sun Dance multiple times. Frank Supernault was the first person to teach me Sweat Lodge. During our fight with Trans Mountain, my late uncle Richard Baker would always call me at the exact moment I was feeling tired and worn out, and say, "You better come sweat. I'm gonna take care of you." Chief Darrell Bob still takes care of me today. My Sun Dance is on his land, and he is loving and caring. The late Carter Camp was the first person who I went to talk to about out Trans Mountain Pipeline fight. His sister, Casey Camp, is one of my spiritual mothers, and I still work with her to this day. She is a beautiful soul. Mary Thunder is another spiritual mother from our Sun Dance who is a powerful woman. Theresa Bob is a beautiful auntie who teaches me so much. I'm very grateful to run the Sun Dance for the Eagle Society. They are all beautiful people. It's a beautiful Sun Dance that I'm lucky to be a part of. The late Calvin Pompana was a beautiful soul. We were friends, and he used to call me "Big Guy." He wanted me to run a Sun Dance and pushed me hard to do it because he really believed in me. In my Sweat Lodge family, I'm very lucky to have very committed firemen, and I'm proud of them. I'm very thankful for my entire Sun Dance family, my Sweat Lodge family, and all my Coast Salish ceremonial families.

Then there are my friends, who have also been my teachers. I talk to Robert Nahanee from Squamish a couple of times per week. We are friends and brothers, but he is also my spiritual teacher for Sun Dance and Coast Salish ceremonies. Guujaaw from Haida Gwaii is a very good friend who I love hanging out with. Jewell

James is a really good friend and teacher who knows so much about the old ways of the Coast Salish people. I love hearing his stories. I've known Mansell Griffin since 1995. We were college buddies, and we are still friends to this day. I love his whole family. Curtis Ahenakew has also been one of my best buds for thirty years—he has been by my side this whole time. We run ceremony together, and he is a strong leader with a big, loving heart. Jimbo is very well known for having a big heart and helping people. He moved away but we still stay in contact. Tracy Nordio is one of my best buds. Katie Grey has been a good friend for ten years. She is very kind, loving, and supportive. Les and Tina Melbon are very good friends. My late best friend, Lacy Morin-Desjarlais, was always the voice of reason to me when I got hotheaded. She accomplished so much. I often think about how much more she would have done if she were still here today. I dedicate a lot of my work to her.

There were many staff at the Tsleil-Waututh Nation who worked with Sacred Trust during our fight against Trans Mountain and I want to thank them all. I would especially like to thank Erin Hanson, Chloe Hartley, and Eugene Kung. They make me look really smart. We work together, but they also come to ceremony, and they are real friends. My brother-cousin Gabriel George is the director of the Sacred Trust Initiative, and my sister-cousin Charlene Aleck is a spokesperson. Ben West was a super-smart policy analyst. He is a very good brother who came to ceremony all the time. He was the biggest supporter of our fight for many years, especially at the start. Carleen and the late Dave Thomas worked with us in the past, and I can't say enough about how wonderful they were to work with. Dave was a wonderful role model for me growing up. Irwin Oostindie was also a big help in all the work we do. The elected Chiefs and councillors from our nation who we worked with in fighting Trans Mountain have shown courageous leadership in standing up for our lands, waters, and people. At the start of our fight, our elected Chief was Justin George, followed by Leah George, then Maureen Thomas, and now Jen Thomas. I want to thank all our Chiefs and councillors for all that they do, not only in supporting our fight against Trans Mountain but for all the work they do for our nation. The CEOs of Tsleil-Waututh who I worked with have also been very supportive: Brenda Baptiste, Andrew Leach, and my brother-cousin Ernie "Bones" George.

We have many allies in our struggle against the Trans Mountain Pipeline, and I'm thankful for how hard they fight. We once called a meeting and had sixty different allied groups show up. There are too many allies to name, but I would especially like to mention a few: Ben West, Rex Weyler, Tarah Stafford, Vandy Savage, Jon Cooksey, Katherine Aubrey and many others were in the very first meeting I attended about Trans Mountain. The Yinka Dene Alliance, who created the Save the Fraser Declaration, were some of the first people we sought advice from. Chief Na'Moks, Freda Huson, and Sleydo' Molly Wickham from the Wet'suwet'en Nation are strong allies, and we visit each other often. Our neighbours and relatives from the Squamish and Musqueam nations always stood by our side. From Squamish, I would especially like to thank Deanna Lewis, Auntie Gail Lewis, and Khelsilem. From Musqueam, I would especially like to thank Shane Pointe and Jeri Sparrow, who were always willing to help. Our Secwépemc relations, and the Manuel family in particular, have always been strong allies. Multiple generations from the Manuel and George families have worked together, from our grandparents, to our parents, and now our kids. Kanahus Manuel is an inspiring warrior. Percy Casper is a beautiful Secwépemc spiritual leader who's always willing to help. Grand Chief Stewart Phillip and Auntie Joan Phillip are also real warriors and such beautiful speakers. They don't bend their morals, values, and conviction for anything and I love them for that. Chief Judy Wilson, Chief Bob Chamberlin, and Chief Don Tom from the Union of British Columbia Indian Chiefs, and all their staff, are always there to stand up for the lands and the waters, and for Indigenous rights. Miranda Dick and her dad Henry are strong Secwépemc warriors. A strong group of sisters who I have worked with over the years are Melina Laboucan-Massimo, Eriel Deranger, Crystal Lameman, Jesse Cardinal, and Sheila Muxlow. They are each strong leaders and powerful matriarchs. Chief Serge Simon and Chief Derek Nepinak are my beloved friends. Gitz Crazyboy and Clayton Thomas-Müller are strong warriors and brothers. Our Coast Salish relatives from Washington State—the Lummi, Tulalip, Suquamish, and Swinomish—were always there for us. Winona LaDuke is a good friend and a good person. I just love being in her presence. My late auntie Lee Maracle came and spoke at some of our events and was a talented Coast Salish speaker who was always willing to help. She was so awesome, and all her kids are awesome people like she was. I have known Auntie Malihatkwa Gwen Therrien almost since birth. She has worked with at least four generations of the George family. I would also like to thank West Coast Environmental Law, Wilderness Committee, Scott and Paul from Gowlings, and many, many more.

At Sacred Circle, the core group of people I work with includes my brother-cousin Justin George, Darwin Douglas, Francine Douglas, Otis Jasper, and Katy Gottfriedson-Jasper. It's been phenomenal to be on this journey with them, using plant medicine to help people heal, and it has certainly accelerated my own growth. We also work with my beautiful friends and angels, Garry and Merissa Turner, Helen and Greg Loshney, Madison Nobbs, Rick Mainers, Turiya Wild Rose, Dr. Rae St. Arnault, and others. These people became more than just friends—we became family.

Finally, I'd like to thank those who helped with the book. Lee Maracle guided us through the publishing process early on, and Victor Guerin and Gabriel George helped with hǝṅ̓q̓ǝmiṅǝm̓ spelling and translation. Phil Lane Jr. wrote a beautiful foreword. Thanks also to our publisher, Nick Garrison from Penguin Random House Canada, Zainab Mirza from Penguin Random House Canada for production, and our agents Stephanie Sinclair and Ron Eckel from CookeMcDermid.

The people I have named here are really the tip of the iceberg. There have been so many other people I have not named here who have impacted my life in positive ways, and who continue to do so. There are countless other friends, cousins, and people in my ceremonial communities who I have not mentioned. I have not said enough about all my aunties and my uncles and grandparents, or other members of my Tsleil-Waututh family, my Squamish family, my Nisga'a family, and my Sweat Lodge family, my Sun Dance family in South Dakota, or my Sun Dance family in British Columbia. Each of these people has had a profound effect on me, and we continue to grow spiritually together. Of the many people who have supported me in my life, I talk more about some than others in this book, because the focus is on our fight against the Trans Mountain Pipeline, but there could be additional books written about my relationships with my cousins and my spiritual aunts and uncles, and about so much more. I thank them all.

by Phil Lane Jr.

As prophesied more than five hundred years ago by Indigenous visionaries, a devastating spiritual wintertime of European diseases and genocide spread across the Americas. By the 1800s, from a population of more than 100 million Indigenous peoples, only 15–20 million remained. The greatest holocaust in human history.

Deputy superintendent of the Department of Indian Affairs Duncan Campbell Scott, architect of Canadian Indian policies during the first decades of the twentieth century, stated in 1920, "I want to get rid of the Indian problem. Our objective is to continue until there is not a single Indian in Canada that has not been absorbed into the body politic, and there is no Indian question, and no Indian Department." To accomplish this goal, more than eighty Canadian government-supported Catholic, Anglican, United Church, and Presbyterian Indian residential schools were implemented across Canada. More than 150,000 Indigenous children were forcibly taken from their families and subjected to the horrors of outright genocide of every form. Eighteen residential schools were established in this "Province of Canada." Since "discovery," up to ninety-five percent of the Indigenous peoples of British Columbia have been exterminated due to this genocidal process.

Despite this genocide, on July 24, 1899, a young boy was born whose words, actions, and family were to have and continue to have a growing spiritual impact across Canada and beyond. I had the great honour of meeting Chief Dan George, a Hereditary Chief of the Tsleil-Waututh Nation, shortly before his passing on September 23, 1981. This blessing led me to meet his son, Chief Leonard George, in 1985, when we made a film together, *The Honour of All: The People of Alkali Lake*, guided and acted by the people themselves. Chief Leonard and I remained spiritual brothers until he passed to the "Other Side Camp" on December 6, 2017.

I visited Chief Leonard George from time to time at his home on the Tsleil-Waututh Nation. The two of us enjoyed having a sweat lodge together, a spiritual healing process that Chief Leonard had brought home from Indigenous relatives in Saskatchewan.

When we prayed together this way, a group of Chief Leonard's curious young sons and nephews would come by to see what we were doing. Little did I know at the time, one of those young boys was going to become my spiritual son, Sun Dance Chief Rueben George. But that is not the end of the story.

As a young boy, Chief Rueben went through every dimension of intergenerational trauma and lateral violence that one could imagine. Full of rage and shame, Chief Rueben would fight at the drop of a hat. Every bar he walked into, he was ready to fight, especially if anyone demonstrated disrespect to Indigenous peoples and his family members. No one really won a fight with Chief Rueben, and in time very few tried. His reputation for violence proceeded with him. He would continue to fight until he had enough. A path I know well.

But rage, shame, and self-abuse can only carry you so far. At the depths of alcohol and drug abuse, a series of life-changing events that are told in this book led Chief Rueben to realize that, unlike his beloved grandfather, he had done nothing to serve the People, and that his life meant nothing. This was when Chief Rueben began his journey to sobriety that eventually led him to begin Sun Dancing with Chief Leonard Crow Dog Sr. and other Indigenous elders who became his spiritual mentors.

Today, after sixteen years of being mentored and made a Sun Dance Chief by Crow Dog, Chief Rueben has conducted seven Sun Dances. Even after he had been given the right to conduct a Sun Dance in his own cultural way, Chief Rueben respectfully waited for some years before he conducted his first Sun Dance.

In whatever Chief Rueben does, he always surrounds himself with elders. One of his primary consultants and elders is his mother, Amy George, the matriarch of the Georges. He always listens very carefully to his beloved children, Kayah and Cedar. His children and extended family are critical in his life. Chief Rueben would give his life for them. It is also remarkable that he and his children's mother have remained friends through thick and thin, holding their children together as most important. A fierce environmentalist and protector of Mother Earth, healer, entrepreneur, and community development specialist, counsellor, entrepreneur, and courageous protector of those less fortunate, Chief Rueben continues the work on himself and serves the People every passing day, no matter what challenges may be in his path.

Hereditary Chief Phil Lane Jr.
Member-Ihanktonwan and Chickasaw Nations

My name is Rueben George, and I am Tsleil-Waututh, səlil̓wətaɬ. We are the People of the Inlet, səlilw̓ət, or the Burrard Inlet, where Vancouver, British Columbia, is found today. Our stories tell us that our First Mother came from these waters. The story of our First Mother is a long story with many important details, not all of which I can share here. But what I can say is that this story tells us that the First Man was raised by wolves, and he was very lonely. He saw that all the other creatures had partners, and he wanted one, too, so he prayed to the Creator. He prayed and prayed for a partner, but the Creator didn't give him one, which made him upset and frustrated. One day, he swam into the middle of the inlet and dove all the way to the bottom. He picked up some sediment from the sea floor and barely made it back up to the surface. After swimming back to shore, he was completely exhausted and passed out on the beach, still clenching the sediment in his hand. While he was asleep, he released the sediment, and when he woke up, it had turned into a beautiful woman. That woman was our First Mother. So, for Tsleil-Waututh people, that inlet is our mother. We are obligated to protect her because she gives us nothing but goodness. That's our law.

In many Indigenous communities, it is our protocol to introduce ourselves by telling people who our relatives and ancestors are. This helps to place who we are, where we're from, and to whom we're accountable. For these reasons, I would like to begin this book by introducing you to some of my relations. My mom is Ta'ah, Amy George, and my dad is Terry Baker. On my dad's side, my grandparents are Dominic and Matilda Baker (née Cole) from the Squamish Nation. On my mom's side, we are descendants of Chief Waut-salk and Chief Kiapilano. My mom's grandfather was Chief George James Sla-holt. Sla-holt is our hereditary name, but after European settlers arrived and forced us into residential schools, they made us adopt Christian names. Many of our people had died from diseases brought from Europe—our families were reduced from many thousands to about seventeen people or fewer. Chief George James Sla-holt tried to protect us, and he told his children to use one of his first names as their family name. That's how we became Georges. Chief Sla-holt's son was my grandpa, Chief Dan George, who became a famous actor.

My grandma on my mom's side was Amy George (née Jack), and she was a descendant of Chief Kiapilano. One day, back in the mid-1800s, Chief Kiapilano's granddaughter, Rowia, found a fifteen-year-old Welsh boy lying on the beach near First Narrows, where the Lions Gate Bridge is in Vancouver today. The boy's name was John William Thomas, and he had just deserted the Royal Navy by jumping overboard from a ship that was out in the inlet. He barely made it to shore because the water is very rough in that part of the inlet. Rowia nursed him back to health, and eventually they married. John Thomas came to be known as Navy Jack, and he was one of the first White people to live amongst us on our territories.

Rowia and John Thomas had four children, one of whom was my great-grandma Christine Jack (née Thomas). At one point during my great-grandmother's childhood, John Thomas had to go away for work and left my great-grandma with a Welsh family. He paid the family lots of money and told them that he wanted them to teach his daughter how to be a fine lady. But when he returned, he found his daughter down on her hands and knees, scrubbing their floor. He told my great-grandma, "Pack your bags. I'm taking you home, and we're never coming back." He took her back to their home on the reserve and told her that from that day forward she was going to follow her mom's way of life. And she did. My great-grandma strictly followed the Native ways after that. She learned to speak all the dialects of Halkomelem, and she also spoke Chinook. She eventually married my great-grandfather, Chief Henry Jack, and they had my grandma, Amy.

Rueben George's grandmother, Amy George, at Indian River, Tsleil-Waututh territory, circa 1942.

Rueben George's grandfather, Chief Dan George, and Rueben's mom, Amy George, at Indian River, Tsleil-Waututh territory, circa 1942.

The two families of my maternal grandparents—the descendants of Chief Waut-salk on my grandfather's side, and the descendants of Chief Kiapilano on my grandma's side—thought that they would be a good match for marriage, and so they were married after my grandma turned sixteen. It was like a royal marriage arranged between two chieftain families. After the marriage ceremony, my grandma started following her mom home. My great-grandma turned around and said to her, "Where are you going? You can't come with me anymore—that's your husband and you have to go with him now." So, my grandma, Amy George, came to live at Tsleil-Waututh with my grandpa, Chief Dan George, and they remained married for over fifty years.

In the pages that follow I am going to tell you the story of how our people took a stand against a multi-billion-dollar company and the Canadian government, which were trying to build a massive oil pipeline across our lands and waters without our consent and in violation of our law. The proposed Trans Mountain Pipeline expansion would result in a nearly sevenfold increase in oil tankers moving through our inlet, each carrying toxic bitumen and other fossil fuel products from the ecologically destructive tar sands. An oil spill in our waters, or anywhere along the pipeline route, would have devastating consequences, and we cannot allow this to happen to our First Mother. As I said, protecting her is our law.

This fight against the pipeline is also part of a much bigger story about who we are and why we fight to protect what we love. The story that I want to tell is the story of our people and our reciprocal relationship with our lands and waters dating back to our First Mother. It's also the story of colonial harm and violence and how that harm continues to impact our people today. In chapter one, I talk a lot about the abuses of residential schools and how those abuses have been passed on intergenerationally and continue to impact our people today. Some of these stories may be triggering, especially for those who have experienced such harm, so please proceed with care and caution, and skip that chapter if you need to. But ultimately this is not a story about our people being helpless victims. This is a story about Spirit. A story about healing. A story about our people taking a stand to protect our lands and waters, to protect the sacred, and to protect what we love, in accordance with our law. This is a story of us stepping up as warriors alongside Indigenous Peoples across Turtle Island and the world. This is the story of our people drawing power from our ceremonies and culture that our Elders held on to, despite all the abuse that they endured, to help overcome the colonial harm that we have experienced in the past and that we continue to experience today in the form of projects like the Trans Mountain Pipeline. This is a story about our people standing up and saying, "It stops here!"

CHAPTER 1

The People of the Inlet

We're sitting at one of our old village sites called Whey-ah-wichen, which means "facing the wind." Today most people know it by the colonial name: Cates Park in North Vancouver, British Columbia. Whey-ah-wichen sits on the shores of səlilwət, or the Burrard Inlet, where our people have lived since time immemorial. My family has an old photo of my grandmother, Amy George, cooking salmon down on the beach here. Back then, the inlet wasn't surrounded by urban development and industrial activity. We are the Tsleil-Waututh people. For Indigenous Peoples, your nation ties you directly to your lands and waters, and Tsleil-Waututh literally means the "People of the Inlet." We are called this because our First Mother came from səlilwət. These waters are our mother.

Our mother, the inlet, has provided us with our ceremonies, our transportation systems, our food, and our medicines. Prior to colonization there were many thousands of Tsleil-Waututh people living along the Burrard Inlet, and eighty-five percent of our diet came from these waters. We had abundance, and our people were healthy. We had sophisticated farming practices and fishing techniques. We had productive orchards and ancient forests full of food. We traded with other nations far and wide. We used the plants that grew all around us to build our homes, to weave rope and clothing, to cook and spice our foods, and to heal our people. We developed medical practices to address any health condition that arose. We had numerous village sites, and we moved around our territory following the rhythms of the seasons so that our resources were never depleted in any one place. We weren't greedy: we took care of what we had and never took more than we needed.

Our people lived with such abundance that we had enough leisure time to make countless works of beautiful art on even the simplest of objects. To give you one example, my brother told me about a maul made by our ancestors. It was a simple stone hammer: it needed to be functional, but it certainly didn't need to be beautiful. Our ancestors could have picked up any old rock, slapped a handle on it, and called it a hammer. But instead they made this hammer perfectly smooth and symmetrical, and then covered it in beautiful art. They could have traded seven canoes for that one hammer. We took time to make art, and that art told us who we were or what clan we belonged to. Our canoes were also works of art. Our homes were beautiful. We made everything by hand. We did things in very special ways. We lived in a reciprocal relationship with the spirit of these lands and waters. It was an extraordinary place that existed in the Tsleil-Waututh territories.

Things aren't like that so much today. Across the inlet from Whey-ah-wichen sits the Westridge Marine Terminal. It is the terminus of the Trans Mountain Pipeline, where bitumen and other fossil fuel products from the Alberta tar sands are loaded onto oil tankers and shipped through our waters. The Government of Canada is now the owner and operator of that pipeline and the terminal, and it plans to expand all this fossil fuel infrastructure extensively in the years to come. This expansion would involve twinning the existing pipeline, tripling the capacity of bitumen shipped here, and increasing oil tanker traffic through our waters nearly sevenfold. We weren't consulted when the pipeline was initially constructed in the 1950s; in fact, we weren't even permitted to hire lawyers or have any legal representation in Canadian courts at that time. And we have resolutely opposed the expansion of the pipeline today. Yet, as we sit here and look across the inlet, we can see that work on the expansion of that port has already begun. Trans Mountain built a twelve-foot-high floating razor-wire fence extending about a third of the distance across the inlet, which prohibits us from accessing that part of our waters. Our nation owns an ecotourism company called Takaya Tours that takes people out into the inlet in traditional canoes, and one day when they were out there in our waters, a security guard from the Westridge terminal screamed at them to get away from the fence and sent police out after them. Even after we won a legal case, which resulted in the courts revoking the pipeline company's permits, work on the port expansion continued and the fence remained in place.

The "Protect the Inlet Flotilla" at the floating razor-wire fence, July 14, 2018. Image courtesy of Greenpeace.

The inlet is our mother, and our law, snəẃeyəł [sno-way-ith], tells us that we have to protect our mother because she gives us nothing but goodness. Everything we take out of her is goodness, and the only thing we should be putting back into her is goodness. All that fossil fuel infrastructure over there across the inlet—the pipeline, the oil tankers, the port, the refineries—that's not goodness. Anywhere in the world where a port is built, the water under that port dies, and our waters are already dying. The Canadian government and the oil companies are causing harm to our mother and violating the laws of the Tsleil-Waututh people. A couple of years ago, we held a ceremony out on our waters. We drifted with the tide in large canoes all along the floating razor-wire fence from the west side to the east. As we drifted, we sprinkled təməł, or red ochre, which is a sacred medicine that we use, along the entire length of the fence to put a wall of love and protection around our waters. We did this to ensure that only goodness goes into the waters, and that only goodness comes back out. We asked our ancestors to help us with this, because the water fed our ancestors just as it feeds us today. We asked our ancestors to block the continued destruction of our mother. And it's been working. We've been standing up to say no to that pipeline for over a decade now, and it still hasn't been built. We've been winning.

A lot of Indigenous languages in North America have words or expressions that signify the interconnectedness of all things. In Lakota, for example, Mitákuye Oyás'iŋ means "all my relations." In our language, həṅq̓əmiṅəṁ, we call this nəc̓əmat, which phonetically sounds like naut'sa mawt. When people are lucky enough to achieve a higher state of consciousness, what they are experiencing is this oneness of nəc̓əmat. To experience nəc̓əmat is to experience the beauty of the Creator. It's to experience the interrelatedness of all beings—the spiritual realm from which everything that has a spirit comes. Some might call this heaven. In our culture, we don't believe in hell or the Devil, but we do have a goal to get back to where we came from. No matter what you do during your life, you're going to end up back there because we are born into this world in a state of spiritual, mental, and emotional perfection, and when we leave, we return to that same state of perfection. When you look a baby in the eye, you can see that they have no prejudice, no hate, no judgment, no anger—they have nothing but genuine unconditional love. It doesn't matter if you are the baby's parent or not; they will love you even if they don't know you. Every single human being is born perfect like that, and it's our dysfunctional society that takes that glimmer from our eyes. People aren't born oppressive: society teaches them to be that way. Some people have learned to be oppressive because they themselves were oppressed. When the violence and oppression of colonial society is modelled to people, they learn to be violent and oppressive themselves. But our teachings are about how to maintain that love that we are all born with, and how to grow from there to become a human being who models respect, honour, dignity, compassion, understanding, truth, knowledge, and wisdom. These are the fundamental teachings of Coast Salish law.

It's sad to think that today we live in a society where many people don't get to experience nə́c̓əmat. People have become disconnected from the spiritual beings of the plants, the animals, the fire, earth, water, and air, and even from other humans. Many people aren't even connected to their own spirit: they don't understand that they have a beautiful spirit inside themselves that needs to be nourished. Our Tsleil-Waututh ceremonies bring us to beautiful places that allow us to experience nə́c̓əmat, and once we have a little taste of this, our spirit craves to be fed this way. Once we experience the reciprocal relation with Spirit, we want to come back to that beautiful place over and over again. As we build our spiritual strength, we nourish our mental and physical well-being so that the strength of our mind and body match the strength of our spirit. Having your spirit fed in this way is a bit like the feeling you get when you love somebody. When you spend time with someone you love very much, you can still feel that love on you when you're apart. Feeling that love is a gift. Having your spirit fed by ceremony is also a gift that sticks with you, and when we receive a gift, it's our responsibility to give back. So, when we leave ceremony with our spirit fed, we have a responsibility to share that goodness, to share that love with others, and to make things better around us.

Prior to the colonization of our lands, waters, and people, life was good here, and it was beautiful. We lived a life of nəc̓əmat, and that's what we're returning to. That's what we want to be, and that's what we are growing back into. I think every human being deep down inside wants that. Nəc̓əmat is our common goal of wanting to be in that beautiful place of our ancestors. But I'll tell you, the beginning of my life wasn't like that, and the reason why is colonization.

ARE YOU RUEBEN GEORGE?

During my teens and early twenties, I was in over 120 fights. I was terrified every single time. But it was sort of like that feeling you get just before jumping off a cliff into water—fear that comes with a huge adrenaline rush. Someone could be on top of me beating me down, and I'd feel this rush of power and strength surge through my body, and then I would throw them right off me. I developed a reputation as a fighter around the city, and that made other people want to fight me too. I guess they were trying to prove something. Guys would come up to me in a bar and ask, "Are you Rueben George?" and I knew right away they wanted to fight. I'd turn to my friends and say, "I'll be right back," and we'd step outside. It was scary because, as a fighter, you know that there's someone in the city who's tougher than you are, someone who can take you down, but you never know who that person will be. I was scared, but I was also really good at fighting. I was stubborn: I could take a real beating and never give up. I only lost three times.

I remember this one time when I was out partying with a buddy of mine, a guy approached me wanting to fight. As soon as I stepped outside, he bashed me in the head with a crowbar. I went down, and he smashed me again, this time in the shoulder. The tendons in my shoulder were torn, and they've felt a little different ever since. While I was down, he stabbed me in the leg with the sharp end of crowbar. I pulled the crowbar out of my leg, got up, threw the guy against a car, and punched him maybe twenty times until he fell to the ground. As I was walking away thinking that it was over, I heard him say, "We're not done yet." I turned back around, and we went at it again. Eventually the cops showed up and everybody fled, but I couldn't get away quickly enough because I'd been stabbed in the leg. I tried to jump over a wall and hurt myself even more. The cops caught up to me pretty easily, pulled me down, and hog-tied me by handcuffing my hands behind my back and then my wrists to my ankles. They threw me into the back of the police car and took me for a rough ride down to the station where they kept me locked up overnight.

The next morning, I looked like a big mess. I was bleeding all over the place. They brought me to the hospital where my arm was placed in a sling and my wounds were sewed up. I think I got about twenty stitches in my head and twenty-five in my leg. After they let me go, I had to find a way to get home on my own because my family was sick and tired of picking me up from jail or the hospital. They just wouldn't do it anymore. Sometimes I'd call them and they wouldn't even pick up the phone because they were fed up with me getting into all these violent situations. I was at St. Paul's Hospital in downtown Vancouver, and I walked down to the bus stop at the corner of Granville and Pender. As the bus pulled up, I caught a glimpse of my reflection in its door and I was a sorry sight. My dislocated shoulder was in a sling and my head was wrapped in a bandage. My white jeans were soaked with blood, some of it from the stab wound in my leg, but some had dripped all the way down my chest from my head. I was standing there looking at my reflection and I thought, What a freaking mess. I looked like a monster.

The doors popped open and I stepped onto the bus, only to realize that I didn't have my wallet with me. I have no idea what happened to it, but I rummaged around in my pockets and all I could come up with was about forty-five cents. I put whatever change I had into the fare box and the driver said, "That's not enough." I looked at him pathetically and said, "I just want to go home." He said, "Today's your lucky day. Go sit down." I sat down, but then I had to go back and ask the driver for a transfer ticket. He was not impressed.

When I finally arrived back at the reserve that morning, I saw that it was Community Day. The entire community was gathered outside and watched me do the walk of shame from the bus stop to my house. Some of the kids were so happy to see me that they came running toward me yelling, "Uncle Rueben!" But as they got closer, they gave me this frightened look, as if they were thinking, What the hell happened to you?

I felt so bad. I already felt bad after seeing my brutal reflection in the bus door, and I felt even worse facing my entire community looking this way. But this sort of thing happened more than once in my life.

COLONIZATION AND RESIDENTIAL SCHOOLS

We were among the last Indigenous people of Turtle Island to be colonized. Infectious diseases from Europe reached us before European people did, and we were still sick when they arrived. It's estimated that even before we saw the first Europeans on our territories, up to ninety percent of the Coast Salish population had already died from smallpox, which had spread from other Indigenous territories where Europeans had already settled or made contact. There's a common misbelief that we are a conquered people, but we were never conquered. We suffered from recurring epidemics of European infectious diseases. We were sick because we didn't have immunity to smallpox or the many other communicable diseases that came with European contact and settlement. We would never have been pushed aside if we hadn't suffered from those diseases. But because we were sick, we were outnumbered very quickly, which made it harder for us to protect what we loved and to uphold our way of life, the rhythm of nətəmat. We are all living the consequences of that now—even those who are causing the destruction.

The settlers arrived with the intention to own the land and extract whatever they could from it. They wanted us to trade our land away, but that didn't really make much sense to our ancestors because you can't give away something you have a spiritual connection with. When you have a spiritual connection with something, you become a part of it, so it would be like giving away a part of yourself. We did have our territories, and we did protect our territories from other nations, but the idea of owning land as private property wouldn't have made sense to our ancestors. Yet suddenly we were being told that other people owned the lands that our people lived on and that it was against the law for us to step foot on our own territories.

Not only did the settlers steal our lands but they also stole our children. In a way, the colonizers were smart because they knew that in order to take our lands, they had to break apart our communities and our cultures. They realized that the most effective way to do this would be to abduct our children and beat into them the idea that our culture and spirituality was evil. And that's exactly what they did. The residential school system was part and parcel of the creation of Canada. It was formally established shortly after the country of Canada was formed. The government forcefully removed Indigenous children from their families and their communities and placed those little children into boarding schools run by the state and the Church, where they were abused by the nuns and priests. They took away children as young as four years old.

I didn't fully register the impact that this had on our people until my son turned four and I imagined what it would have been like to have him taken away from me by the state. This realization hit me again when my daughter turned four. But it's what happened to my parents and to my parents' parents: the government stole them from our family as young children and placed them into an abusive institution. My two older brothers went to residential schools as well, so there are multiple generations of us who had our childhoods stolen and who were forced into these colonial institutions.

Once they were in there, the nuns and priests tried to break their little spirits. They grew up in a place with no love. They were not shown any affection or recognized for any of their accomplishments. They were punished for every little infraction. Those little children were physically, sexually, mentally, and spiritually abused. They were starved, neglected, and killed in those schools. For those who survived and returned home as young adults, residential school was all they knew, and in some cases they raised the next generation with the abuse that they had learned and been subjected to.

The objective of residential schools was to make sure that when our people came out of them, the only thing that would remain Native about us was our blood. Our children were told that they were filthy savages. The nuns and priests forced their religious beliefs upon our people and told us that our culture and spirituality were evil. They told those kids that they should pray for our culture to leave them and that they would go to hell if they continued to practise it. They tried to strike fear into the children by describing how ugly and frightening this imaginary place called hell was. The children were also told that if they prayed, then they would go to heaven. My mom told me that in residential school she prayed to God that she not be abused by the nuns and priests any longer. But the same nuns and priests who told the children to pray for good things were the abusers, so that left the children with nothing to believe in. Their spiritual beliefs were completely diminished.

When my grandfather arrived at residential school, he didn't speak a word of English. Not long after he got there, he said to the nuns "səx̌ʷaʔ," which meant that he needed to pee. They punished him for speaking his language. He was thrown into a cage the size of a doghouse with bars on it, and he was left there overnight. Can you imagine—my grandfather went from living in the long-house with all his relatives, with all the love and warmth of care of nəc̓əmat, to being abruptly torn from that harmonious unity of spirit, forced into this institution designed to break his tiny little spirit, and placed overnight in this doghouse with no blanket, cold and terrified. The next day, when the nuns came to let him out, they saw that he had peed himself. As a punishment for peeing himself, they took away all his clothes and made him spend another night in there naked and alone. They told him, "Don't speak your language, and don't pee yourself!" He got in trouble for telling the nuns that he needed to pee, and he was punished again for peeing on himself after they had locked him up.

When my mom was taken to residential school, she was crying for her parents and a nun told her, "Your parents don't want you. That's why they brought you here. They don't love you. They were the ones that put you here." My mom spent most of her childhood and her young life believing that this was true—that her parents didn't love her and had abandoned her. She also remembers how hungry everyone was in the residential school. She remembers the ugly food and the rotten potatoes that they had to eat while watching the nuns and priests sit at the head of a big table eating a beautiful breakfast with sausage and all sorts of condiments.

She has a story about finding maggots in the oatmeal that she was supposed to prepare for the other children. When she started picking the maggots out of the oats, a nun hit her so hard on the side of the head that her ear started ringing. The nun said, "Leave those in there!" She also remembers being small enough that she could crawl out of a window that was left slightly open and go pick apples from a nearby tree. She would form a pouch with her shirt, fill it up with apples, and then bring them back to share with the other kids. Years later, she was watching *Schindler's List*, and there was a scene that reminded her of all the children's little hands reaching out the residential school window, as they begged her—"Please, please, please, please!"—for an apple because they were so hungry. They were starved and treated worse than dogs. They were treated as though they weren't human beings.

Many children died in those residential schools and were never returned to their families and communities. My mom told me a story about a teacher who kicked a five-year-old girl in the head and killed her. The child fell over dead, and a nun told the other students to step over her and get to class. My mom said that when children died, the little boys would have to bury them. They buried their own cousins and relations. They were woken up in the middle of the night, told to pack the body outside, dig a hole in the ground, and cover it up again. Those bodies were left there in unmarked graves. She also said that in June of each year, when parents would come to pick up their children, they would be told their child "died last winter" and then sent home. No one was ever charged for those murders.

When my mom sued the Canadian government for what they did to her in residential school, I heard her heart-wrenching testimony of the abuse that she endured as a child. I heard her describe some of the absolutely atrocious things she experienced. She spoke of being hit so hard on the hand that she couldn't pick up a pencil, and then she was punished when she couldn't complete her writing assignments because her hand was injured. At one point during her testimony, my mom requested that my siblings and I leave the room because she didn't want us to hear about how she was subjected to extreme abuse over and over again as a child. She didn't want her children to hear how her innocence was taken away by the nuns and priests. Our spiritual father, Alex Paul, stayed with her as she gave her testimony. I don't know how she survived all that. I don't know how she lived through such abuse and still became the beautiful human being she is today. It was horrific.

I remember one time when I was a little kid driving through Victoria Park on Lonsdale Avenue in North Vancouver with my mom and my uncle Bob; we saw this Native guy in a wheelchair whom they both knew. My mom asked why he was in a wheelchair, and Uncle Bob explained that when they were kids, the nuns had whipped this little boy so hard with a leather strap that it broke his back. Imagine even witnessing that kind of violence as a little kid and then being told that this would happen to you next if you didn't follow their ugly dysfunctional rules. Can you imagine the fear instilled in those little kids when they saw nuns beating and killing other little kids and wondered if they were next? That's the message they were given: if you don't believe in God and Jesus, then we're going to break your back, we're going to starve you, we're going to beat you, we're going to molest you, we're going to kill you. They pulled out children's teeth rather than provide preventative dental care because it was cheaper to do it that way. They tested out new nutritional theories, conducted medical experiments, and trialed new drugs on those little children. They were treated like they didn't matter. It was so brutal.

My mom was raised in that kind of abuse, but she was strong enough to live through all of that and heal. My grandfather was also strong enough to heal from what he experienced. But there were many others who couldn't endure that much pain, who couldn't heal, and who didn't survive. Like my dad. My dad went to an Indian day school and experienced many similar forms of abuse, but he didn't have a voice to speak of the injustices he endured. He didn't have a safe place where he could talk about his hurt and pain and deal with his trauma. He didn't get to experience the freedom of ceremony as I did. He didn't have any of that, and he died because of it. What he did have were the nightmares of everything that had happened to him in residential school. It was ugly how they treated him, and he lived through that. But even if you do live through something like that, the trauma stays with you and can be overwhelming. Because he didn't have a proper place to deal with that trauma and express how he felt, he turned to drugs and alcohol to bury the pain. Drugs and alcohol acted as a Band-Aid to cover the hurt and pain so that he wouldn't have to think about the abuse, and in the end, my dad overdosed in the Downtown Eastside of Vancouver, in an ugly stink bathroom at the bottom of a stairwell outside the Carnegie Community Centre on the corner of Main and Hastings. He was young—only twenty-seven years old. I was only a year old. We lost many family members to drugs, alcohol, and suicide. That's how I lost my favourite uncle.

Prior to colonization and residential schools, we had a voice as Indigenous people. We were able to express ourselves and ensure that things remained in accordance with our law, culture, and spirituality. Our ceremonies allowed us to express our hurt and pain as human beings, and they allowed us to hold on to the beauty of who we are. All of that was intentionally stripped away by residential schools in the name of killing the savage and saving the child. The colonizers broke our systems, that harmony that made us stewards of our lands, waters, and people—that beautiful relationship of nəċəmat that we had with everything. Colonization broke us from the ancestors' ability to see the spirit that exists in every little blade of grass. The Government of Canada sought to systematically crush our spirit and assimilate us, and that's why they took these little children and abused them so horribly. They broke the spirit not just of my mom, not just my dad, not just my grandfather, but of Indigenous Peoples right across Canada. This happened to generations upon generations of us. A mental, emotional, physical, and spiritual breakdown occurred in those residential schools. That's what they were designed to do. And what's most sickening about it all is that it was done to little children.

When you think about all that they went through, you realize how amazing it is that our survivors held onto our culture and spirituality the way they did. It's amazing that they kept themselves from being assimilated despite all the horrors they were subjected to. But residential schools and colonization also resulted in a lot of the issues related to addiction, homelessness, and incarceration that our communities continue to deal with today. A lot of our Indigenous communities haven't healed. A lot of our people are much like my dad was when he died all alone, and that's a direct result of what the Canadian government did. We are less than five percent of Canada's population, yet a third of the homeless population in Vancouver is Indigenous. That's a direct consequence of colonization.

When the settlers first came here, we worked with them, we taught them, and we helped them survive on our land. Even though we were sick, we still helped them, and this is what we got in return. From the greed for money, power, and ownership of land came a system that killed, abused, and broke the spirits of little children. My dad could tell you, because that's how he died.

It was the Government of Canada that did this, but it was the people of Canada who allowed it to happen. They knew it was happening, but the society we lived in back then didn't give a shit and they didn't do anything to stop it. All these horrible things were happening to those children, and the government justified it by saying that they were assimilating Native people to turn them into good citizens. Canada claims to be a country of freedom, democracy, equality, rights, dignity, and the rule of law, but there was a price that was paid for Canada's existence, and that price was paid by First Nations. We're still paying that price.

INTERGENERATIONAL TRAUMA AND LATERAL VIOLENCE

Thankfully, I was too young to go to residential school, but my two older brothers were not. The last residential schools in British Columbia closed in 1984, and the last one in Canada closed in 1996. But even once the schools shut their doors, the trauma inflicted by those institutions remained. The legacy of those schools continues to mess with our people. The violence inflicted by the nuns and priests on our parents and grandparents was passed on to my generation. Just as the nuns and priests hit and abused our older generations, a few from the older generations hit us. The oppressed became the oppressors. There were days as I was growing up when I knew that horrific things were going to happen to me. And it wasn't just in my household. Most people witnessed it even if they didn't experience the abuse themselves. Nobody was immune—everybody was affected by it in some way. It happened in Indigenous communities across Canada. That's the cycle of abuse that we're living through.

My mom was in residential school from the age of five to ten years old. During those formative years, she didn't learn from experience how we as Tsleil-Waututh people raise our children. She didn't learn the Tsleil-Waututh ways that give our children the proper foundation they need for the rest of their lives. A friend once told me about a study that found that the foundation laid for a child during the first ten years of their life is what they always come back to. It's from that foundation that a child grows up; it helps them become a beautiful human being connected to all that nature has to offer and to the spirit of all beings that's inside every one of us. My mom didn't have the things that people need early in life—like love, understanding, and the teachings of how to respect humanity—because she and other Indigenous children across Canada were taken away and told that there was evil in them and they were going to hell. When a child falls and is hurt, they need an adult to pick them up and care for them. No one was there to pick my mom up and love her when she was hurt; the adults who were there, the nuns and priests, were the ones who pushed her down. They gave her no love, and they pushed her back down whenever she tried to get up on her own.

Today my mom is an amazing grandma, but many survivors didn't have the tools they needed to raise children and to be a supportive loving parent. All they learned in residential schools was hurt and pain. How are you going to be a good parent and raise children with the spiritual foundation they need when all you knew as a child was violence, starvation, beatings, and abuse? There was a lot of hurt, and the survivors of residential schools didn't always know how to be there for their children. This was the experience of not just our community but also every single Indigenous community across Canada. When successive generations grow up in the horrible conditions of residential schools, how can you expect people to raise children with the teachings of love and humanity? It's amazing to me that many did raise beautiful children despite all that they went through, and they did it by holding onto the teachings of our culture and spirituality.

Even after the children left residential schools, they were still shamed and looked down upon by wider society. My grandma tried moving my mom out of residential school and into Burrard View Elementary in Deep Cove. The parents of students at that school held a community meeting because they were outraged at the idea of a First Nations kid going to school with their children. The parents and community members all said that there was no way this could happen, and they demanded that the Native kids stay in the residential schools where all these horrible things were happening. My grandma went down to that meeting and heard the other parents say terrible things about how her kids were dirty and ugly. She stood up and said, "My kids are clean and healthy." Only one other parent stood up to defend our family. She said that she knew our family and that my mom and her siblings were clean, good kids. Eventually my mom did get out of residential school and went to high school, but there she was picked on almost daily. The Government of Canada was treating us as if we were lesser than people of European descent, and some of the people of Canada treated us that way too.

Things were really hard and painful for my parents' generation, but they did start to fight back. When people tried coming onto the reserve to fight or harass our community, they stood up to protect themselves. It became very well known that if you mess with one Tsleil-Waututh, you mess with all of us. If you mess with one Squamish, you mess with them all. If you mess with one Musqueam, you mess with them all. Our parents' generation fought back in whatever ways they could, because they had to. Someway and somehow they had to put their foot down. They also had to protect themselves from the police. I've heard stories about how no one in our community ever wanted to call the police because of how they treated our people; my uncles and aunties had to police our community themselves.

As in many communities across Canada, a lot of our people dealt with the hurt and pain of colonization through self-medication. They drowned their sorrow by medicating with drugs and alcohol, and what came along with the drugs and alcohol was a lot of physical, mental, emotional, and sexual abuse. My mom and dad both drank to drown out the pain that they lived with. After my dad overdosed, we were raised by a single mom. Then we had a stepdad come into our lives who had also been to residential school. Our house was a party house and with that came abuse, as is the case in many alcohol- or drug-addicted households. On an average week-night, people would be having a beer here and there, or smoking weed here and there, but on the weekend, there would be a party. When the parties started, I knew bad things were going to happen. It would be fun for a bit, until the adults got a little too drunk or a little too high, and then all the terrible things would start happening. I couldn't sleep during those parties, so sometimes I'd just leave. From the age of about four to eleven years old, I would take a blanket and go sleep at the side of the house by the creek. I'd lie on a soft nest of pine needles that had built up over the years, and my dog would snuggle up next to me to keep me warm. When it was too cold to sleep outside, I just wouldn't sleep at all.

By the time Monday came around and I had to go to school, the teachers would be trying to teach me things, but do you think I was able to learn anything when I had barely slept? They would test us on this stuff I hadn't learned because I was exhausted, and when I didn't do well on the tests, they labelled me with a learning disability. I grew up believing I had a learning disability, and back then, there weren't any social programs in schools to help kids who were struggling. I didn't know how capable I was until I went to college; at that point in my life, I found school easy. I didn't have a learning disability—I had sleep deprivation!

There are things I don't remember from my childhood, roughly between the ages of four and eleven. There was so much trauma that I had to block a lot of it out, which is why I struggle to remember certain details. I used to feel like I was robbed of my childhood because there's so much of it that I just don't remember. I do have lots of good memories, like being out on the boats fishing in the inlet the way we did, but in order to remind myself of certain things, I have to ask my brothers and sister. For instance, I remember that sometimes it was just us kids alone in the house while our parents were off partying, but I thought it was about one or two days a month until my brothers told me that it was more like seven to ten days a month. I remember sitting at the window waiting and wondering when my parents would come home, or when an adult would come to check on us. Sometimes when we were home alone with no adults, the abusers would show up at the house, and my brothers would protect me. I remember being about four years old and my brothers hiding me from the abusers or telling me to run away. They were only six and eight years old, but they'd stand there at the door sacrificing themselves to save me. It blows me away. Sometimes I think that of all the people in my life, my brothers helped me most.

Seven to ten days every month, there were no adults at home, so we spent a lot of time fending for ourselves. Back then, the Tsleil-Waututh community may have been rich in culture, but we were poor economically. We were a poor household in a poor community. At times there wasn't a lot of food around. I remember that we sometimes had nothing more than a sack of potatoes at home. It probably would have cost about a dollar for a bag of salt, but we wouldn't even have that. I got really good at making French fries, and I could make them taste pretty good even without any seasoning—I fried them so well that they were borderline potato chips. I also drank a lot of water.

But we made the best of an ugly situation. We went fishing and crabbing a lot. In the winter we'd get in our old boat, or sit out on the booms where the loggers tied up all their logs in the inlet, and we'd tell stories or watch the northern lights as we fished. You could catch Dungeness crab year-round, and I'm grateful that they were so abundant. We also ate a lot of salmon. You'd think I would have grown gills from all the salmon I ate! We ate better during the spring and summer because the orchards and forests were full of food. There were a couple of orchards on the reserve that were full of cherries, plums, apples, and crabapples. One of our uncles would shoo everyone away from the orchards except for me and my brothers; I think he knew we didn't have enough to eat at home. There were also traditional foods, like what we call sθeʔθqəy̓, which is the insides of salmonberry and thimbleberry shoots that you can eat while they're young and rubbery. We ate plenty of that, as well as wild strawberries, huckleberries, and blueberries.

In the warmer months, food was abundant, but things were much harder in the winter when we were no longer surrounded by that abundance. Sometimes family members would bring food over to our house because they knew we were alone. I was only a little kid, but I couldn't help thinking, Why are you bringing us your leftovers? One winter our fridge broke, so we put our meat and frozen things outside in an old bathtub to keep them cold, but my dog came around and ate our meat because he was hungry, too, so my dog was killed. Some days we had no electricity. We didn't have proper clothes either. I had a pair of shoes that were worn right through the soles. I remember having only one pair of pants for an entire year. I'd wash and clean them, then dry them off in the oven. Our basement flooded every year, and you could see right through the walls. It got really cold in the winter. Sometimes Grandpa would send us some money, but the other family members would act funny about that. Childhood was a difficult, difficult time. I remember feeling strongly in favour of abortion and adoption when I was young simply because I thought that children shouldn't be raised in ugly environments, as I was.

As I said, the oppressed become the oppressors. The abuse that some in our community experienced existed because that's what the nuns and the priests and the Canadian government taught our older generations. The violence was transferred laterally, redirected at one another in our community. We all got picked on, and we were all hurt. The abuse was ongoing and daily. I had an older cousin who was abused so bad at home that he became a cowering and fearful person, and then because he was so timid and weak, we bullied him like a pack of wolves. He was five years older than me, but I picked on him too. I didn't know any better. So, our cousin got abused by his family at home, and then he was abused by me and the kids on the reserve, and then when he left the reserve, he was unable to stand up for himself and he was abused again.

It was a violent place where you would be bullied or beaten up if you showed any emotion, which I did—I cried a lot as a kid. But even if you were strong, you still got picked on. We all did. I remember once when I was little, my older cousins cinched a vise grip on my back as a test of strength. They wanted to see if it would make me cry. I was reaching behind me to try to release it from my back, but as I reached back the vise was cinching even tighter, causing me even more pain. I couldn't quite reach it because it was right in the middle of my back. I had to negotiate between the pain of the vise grip pinching my skin and the even greater pain of reaching back as I tried to remove it. When I finally managed to yank it off, I was bleeding. That type of thing was just a normal part of life in the community at the time. Kids growing up in that context didn't know how to be. They felt rage, and they needed to place their rage somewhere. I did too. Sometimes that rage was directed toward animals, like a raccoon or a bear that happened to come into our community. Sometimes it was directed toward other kids. That's what I mean when I say the oppressed become the oppressors. From the Church to our parents, from our parents to our older cousins, and from our older cousins to us. Indigenous communities across Canada were impacted in similar ways.

My older cousins used to try to force me and my brother-cousin Justin to fight each other, but we would refuse because we loved each other too much. To this day, Justin and I have never even been in an argument. One time when we refused to fight, the cousins beat us up really bad and told us that we wouldn't have been hurt so bad if we had just fought each other instead. Another time when they forced us to fight each other, we were crying really hard because we loved each other and didn't ever want to hurt one another. We were only children, between eight and ten years old. I remember sitting with Justin on the beach after they tried to make us fight, and we promised that when we were older, we would put an end to all this abuse. We promised each other that we wouldn't let anybody pick on anybody else like this any longer. We made a pact that we would fix this hurt and make sure that nobody was ever hurt like this again. We were already having those kinds of conversations at such a young age.

I was abused by a few of my cousins on the reserve because we were poor and we didn't have enough food or the right shoes or clothes. But when I left the reserve, it was even worse. It was off the reserve that we really felt the prejudice against us. In the society we lived in, we were the oppressed. Some of Canadian society was still looking down on us. We lived in one of the most economically wealthy parts of British Columbia, and yet we were one of the poor-est communities. On the surface, Vancouver might not seem like a very prejudiced place, but you really feel it when you don't have much. Even going into a store or getting on the bus can be a hassle. People don't want to serve you at the restaurant.

At school, we were treated differently by our teachers, and even by the other little kids, because we were First Nations. Some things really bothered me. I went to school in one of the richest areas of Vancouver, and all my classmates had whatever they wanted, but I didn't even have basic necessities like clothing. Some teachers knew that we didn't have food or proper school supplies. The parents of some kids I went to school with didn't want me to come into their homes, and that felt devastating. The descendants of the people who didn't give a shit about the way little children were being treated in residential schools didn't give a shit about us. Some did try to help though. Sometimes when I showed up to school with no lunch, the teacher would say, "Can everyone please donate something from their lunch to Rueben? He forgot his lunch today." All the other kids would come over and give me what they didn't want from their lunches. I hated it so much that I didn't even eat any of it. I didn't want anyone's donations, and I didn't want their second-hand stuff. It was humiliating and it pissed me off, but I also think it's how my character began to develop.

Early on, I went to a Catholic school where they made us go to church three times a week. They made us get on our knees and pray and then stand up and pray, but despite all the praying we did, they didn't teach us what it actually means to pray or why praying is a beautiful thing. They just told us that if we didn't pray when we were told to, we would go to hell. There was no spirit in any of it. At one point, I was fed up with Catholic school because the nuns were so mean. My mom took me to register for Plymouth Elementary School in North Vancouver, but the principal there said that he didn't want me at his school because there were no other Native kids there. He told my mom to send me to Sherwood Park Elementary because that's where the Natives went. The principal said that straight out, and my mom was shocked.

When First Nations kids start learning history in school, it's not uncommon for their grades to start going down because what they're taught about our culture and our people is degrading. We are taught that our ancestors were hunter-gatherers. What the hell is a hunter-gatherer? We are so much more than that. We had beautiful, sophisticated societies. We had very intricate farming, fishing, and hunting techniques. We had highly effective medical practices. You can compare our cultures with any around the world and they were second to none, more sophisticated in many ways. But within the colonial education system, all of that is boiled down to this degrading notion of hunter-gatherers. All these things added up to create a sense of shame around being Indigenous. I felt that shame. Society told us for so long that we were ugly. Generations of people were told this in residential schools, and it was passed down to me and I also felt ashamed. I was ashamed of being Indigenous because of all the things that Canada had done to make us feel that way. I didn't like who I was; I didn't like how I was raised; I didn't like being poor; I didn't like how I was treated; and I related it all to being First Nations. Carrying that shame was hard. And because I grew up in that racist and abusive environment, I felt like a victim ready to take on more abuse.

My grandpa died when I was eleven, and after that, I tried not to cry anymore because it was just too painful. As a child, I thought my grandpa was one of the few people I was safe with; he would never hurt me. I carried the pain of losing my dad and the pain from all the abuse we'd been through as kids, and I became very rigid. I didn't like being touched, not even a hug on my birthday. As a teenager, I was on my own a lot of the time. When girls started liking me, I couldn't even hug them. I remember that my first serious girlfriend wanted to hold me and cuddle, but I wouldn't let her. Holding hands was fine, but I didn't like anything more than that.

One time she came up to give me a hug, and I put my hands up in front of my chest to keep her at bay. She said, "Why do you do that?" I didn't even realize what I had done, so I said, "Do what?" She said, "You push me away." I denied it. Then she went in to hug me again, and again I put my hands up. She said, "See! All I want to do is hug you and hold you." She told me that I needed help, that maybe I needed counselling or therapy. That's when I started to realize that I had an aversion to physical intimacy. When we were lying in bed holding each other, I'd wait for her to fall asleep, and then I would stealthily pull my arm out from under her and move over to the side of the bed so I could fall sleep without touching her. Sometimes I'd even place a pillow between us. All of that was rooted in the lack of proper affection I received as a child. Instead of all the love and care I should have received, I got physical abuse and sexual abuse. I was beaten. I was hurt. I was abused. All of those things. Sometimes I think I was robbed of the experience of young teenage love because I was too closed off to allow myself to feel it.

I started drinking and using drugs after my grandpa died. By the age of fourteen, I wasn't getting picked on as much anymore because I'd had a growth spurt. By fifteen, I was beating up all the people who had abused me. I think I beat up all my abusers. I started partying around that time, and we were smoking a lot of weed. When I started, we'd get the Acapulco Gold or the Maui Wowie, and all these different strains. Later, hydroponics came in, and then it was B.C. Bud. I'd smoke one joint of that stuff and be ripped, but it made me paranoid. It also made me get into fights. I remember once when I was around sixteen, I was stoned on the SeaBus with my brother-cousin Justin, and this big biker-looking dude starts eyeing me down. I had a baby face that made me look younger than I actually was, and I was also tall and lanky so people didn't think I was very tough. But this guy was eyeing me down, so I said to him, "Fuck you." When we got off the SeaBus, he followed me and we ended up getting in a fight. The marijuana was making me really paranoid like that, so I had to quit.

I think of all the hurt and pain that I experienced. The hurt and pain of being in elementary school and being treated like I was less than everyone else, of being told I had a learning disability when I actually was sleep deprived. Being fearful in my own home and trying to survive as a young kid. Being treated with disrespect by authority figures at school, in the community, or by the police. Even just going into a grocery store to buy something, I would sometimes encounter disrespect. All these things built up and resulted in anxiety, depression, and low self-esteem. When you suffer from those feelings, even simple everyday things are momentous tasks. If I was served food in a restaurant that was burned or not cooked properly, I probably wouldn't have said anything about it, even if it was really bothering me, and that's because I had low self-esteem. And when you have low self-esteem like that, people can tell and they pick on you even more. That's what they did to me.

I didn't think I was going to live past twenty-five, and I behaved as if I wouldn't even when I was sober. I behaved in really risky ways. We'd climb up a twenty-storey building, and I'd walk right along the edge and jump across a six-foot gap in the building. I remember driving over the Second Narrows Bridge in my buddy's car, sitting on the windowsill of the car door and leaning back until I could feel my hair brushing against the road. I had really short hair at the time, maybe two inches long at the most, so my head was nearly touching the road as we drove across the bridge at over one hundred kilometres an hour. If we had hit a bump and my head bounced against the road, I'd be dead or severely brain-damaged. But I didn't care. I didn't think I'd live long anyway, nor did I really want to. I put myself in dangerous situations where I could have been very badly hurt, and I didn't give a shit. It was the same when I was fighting. If someone pulled a knife on me, I'd fight anyway. If they brought an axe, I'd fight anyway. Baseball bats, two-by-fours, all kinds of weapons. That violence was a big part of the drinking period of my life. It was such self-destructive behaviour: I was hurting myself, and the people who loved me had to witness it.

All the ways I was abused as a kid—spiritually, physically, mentally, and emotionally—came out as ugly rage when I was a teenager. Most of the time, I had a calm demeanour; I was soft and easy to get along with. But I could also be hotheaded and explode easily.

I could be super nice one moment and snap the next. That's also how I fought. I was an adrenaline fighter. None of my fights lasted more than thirty seconds. It was my rage that came out in those moments, but that rage was actually an expression of my pain. It was pain that came from not receiving love, respect, dignity, pride, compassion, understanding, truth, knowledge—all those fundamentals of humanity that we need to become healthy and happy. I was still carrying that hurt, and it would explode outward as rage. I needed healing. As I said earlier, I was scared every time I fought, but somehow I enjoyed the fear. It was the exact same fear that I had felt when I anticipated that I was going to be beaten or abused as a child. When I was older, I recreated that fear I'd experienced as a child over and over again by fighting, and I learned to like it. The adrenaline rush that came with that fear allowed me to release the anger I was holding on to from all those years of pain and abuse that my brothers and I experienced.

Some mornings, I would wake up and just feel off. When I woke up with that feeling, I knew I was going to get in a fight that day because I was agitated. But knowing that helped me to keep calm and hold my frustration in: I knew I would have a chance to release it as rage later. Finding a fight was always pretty easy—I'd just go to a bar and look for the bully, because there's always a bully in a bar. Once I spotted them, I'd wait for them to walk toward me and then I'd step in front of them with my back turned to block the way. They'd get pissed off every time and try to push me out of the way. Then I'd turn around and say, "Okay, let's go." Sometimes they'd start screaming and yelling at me, and I'd say, "What are you screaming for? You're bringing attention to us. Do you really want to fight, or are you full of shit? Because if you really want to go, you don't need to yell and scream like an idiot. Let's just step outside and we'll take care of it." Most of the time they wouldn't want to, so I'd have to provoke them a little more.

This kind of thing happened weekly for a couple of years, and I often looked rough during that time. I almost always had a black eye, stitches, or a cut lip. I broke my nose a couple times. I was knifed in my shoulder. I was hit in the head by a crowbar, a two-by-four, and a boulder. I got punched in the head hundreds of times. I'm not sure how many concussions I've had, but it's definitely more than ten and perhaps as many as twenty. I'm still paying for it. Recently I had to get medical tests done on my brain and my ears to investigate the head trauma that I've suffered, because I'm losing my hearing in my right ear. The ringing I hear in my ear reminds me of the intergenerational violence of colonization that I continue to carry in my body every single day.

After that one big fight I was in—when I was all bloody and bandaged and had to do the walk of shame from the bus stop in front of the entire community—I got home and my mom took one look at me and started crying. Then my brother Damian came to talk to me, and he said, "I didn't do a good job raising you. I know why you're hurting yourself like this. It's because I picked on you as a little kid, and now you're trying to prove that you're stronger than me. But you don't have to prove that to me. I already know that you're the stronger one. You don't need to prove anything to me. I don't want you to hurt yourself anymore." My brother cried a little bit, and I'd never seen him cry before.

But I didn't understand what he was talking about. I remember saying, "I don't know why you're so upset with me. I win all my fights! I'm not hurting myself, so you don't need to worry about me." But that's when I started thinking that if I won the fight and I look like this, then how the hell is the other guy's family feeling right now? As I became more aware of the pain I was causing others, I stopped wanting to fight so much, and that started me on my path toward healing. Every time I did something stupid and came home all bloody with a black eye or a broken nose, I saw the hurt in my mom's face. My brother was right—I was trying to prove something. I was hurting myself, and that needed to change.

Today my brother Nathan lives in the Downtown Eastside of Vancouver, near the corner of Main and Hastings, just three hundred feet away from where my dad died in an ugly stink bathroom. For anyone who doesn't know Vancouver, the Downtown Eastside has among the highest rates of homelessness and addiction in all of Canada. One-third of all people living on the streets of Vancouver are Indigenous, even though we comprise just two percent of the population in Vancouver. That's massively disproportionate, and it's a direct outcome of colonization. That's what I see when I'm walking down Hastings. I see people struggling, hurting, and disconnected due to the legacies of colonization.

Some people look at the high rates of homelessness or incarceration among First Nations communities and think it's because we are lazy. That's total racist bullshit. It's not because we're lazy; it's because of the colonial history, the diseases, the taking of our lands, the segregation and relocation to reserves, the residential school system, the restrictions placed on what we can do and how we can do it, and the rights that we were denied, including the right to vote, the right to do business, the right to legal representation, the right to speak our language, and the right to conduct our ceremonies. We were prohibited from practising our culture. We couldn't sing our songs. We couldn't speak our language. If someone was born or died or was married, we couldn't conduct our ceremonies. We couldn't even sell our own land to try to move forward and secure a better way of life. It was against the law for us to do any of those things. We lost so much. We lost part of our identity. That's why so many of my people are homeless and suffering today. All these things weighed down upon First Nations, and yet you have these ignorant people who say we're lazy. The descendants of the people who put my people in residential schools and who stole our lands don't give a shit about the fact that a third of the people living on the streets of Vancouver are First Nations. They don't give a shit about the fact that thirty percent of prisoners in Canada are First Nations. They don't give a shit about the missing and murdered Indigenous women and girls from our communities, and they certainly don't give a shit about fact that there are more Native kids who have been separated from their parents by the child welfare system today than there were at the height of the residential school system.

Being with my brother Nathan comforts me. A couple of years ago, I woke up on Christmas Day and I was feeling sad. My kids said we should smudge to help me feel better, but I told them that I wanted to see Nathan, so I got in the car and went downtown to visit him. When I arrived, I asked Nathan what he wanted to do, and he said he wanted to go get fries and a milkshake, so that's what we did. As we were driving back, I said, "You know, brother, there's a lot of things I don't remember about our childhood. I don't remember a lot of the trauma." He said, "No kidding, you don't remember. When we experience trauma as human beings, our fight-or-flight response kicks in. You fought, but you also fled. You ran deep inside your soul and deep inside your mind. You needed to distance yourself from those traumatic experiences, so you fled far away. You buried those memories deep so you wouldn't have to remember them anymore. That's a defence mechanism we use as little children to cope with the pain." Here's my brother, practically homeless living on the Downtown Eastside with HIV and hepatitis C, saying such profound things. He's fragile like a ninety-year-old man because of the wear and tear from drug use. He broke his arm; he broke his hip; he tore his rotator and then broke his femur. He also had a heart attack. Yet here is this beautiful human being offering me these brilliant and insightful lessons about our dysfunctional lives. What he said was so beautiful that it made me cry. He didn't know that I was crying because he was in the passenger seat of the car

looking straight ahead as I drove. He didn't know that the whole
time he was talking, I was sitting in awe of him, thinking about
what a brilliant guy he is. At the end of that day, as we were parting
ways, I told him, "Brother, you are so wise. I was feeling very sad
this morning, but now I feel better. Thank you for taking care of me
today." He smiled his sweet smile and said, "I always take care of
you, brother. I always have, and I always will."

Nathan remembers a lot more than I do, and maybe that's why
he is where he is and why I am where I am. He once told me that he
can't heal like I have because the memories hurt him too much. He
said the reason he does drugs and drinks is because the life we experienced was too hard for him to cope with; he couldn't face it in order
to heal. He uses drugs and alcohol to push away that pain, just as I
used violence. The life that I'm talking about, which created all my
rage, is the same life that makes my brother use. Sometimes I wonder
if the different directions our lives have taken is a result of Nathan
remembering much more than I do. Maybe the pain of all those
memories is too great. About ten years ago, he was sober for about
eight months. During that time, he told me that he felt like using
again because all the things we experienced growing up were surfac-
ing again and he just couldn't deal with it. He said, "I'm sorry I
can't be like you, brother. I'm sorry that I can't sober up. The life
that we had is too hard for me to think about, and that's why I use.
But I'm very proud of you for being sober and all the things that
you do. I live vicariously through you." A couple days later, he
started using again.

Sometimes I look at my brother and I think, Maybe I'm just one
bad decision away from being where he is, and maybe he's just one
good decision away from being where I am. Maybe it could have
been him writing this book. He sacrificed himself for me. My brothers hid me and protected me so that I wouldn't get hurt and abused
as a little kid. A six-year-old kid and an eight-year-old kid hiding

their four-year-old brother. They stood there and took the abuse so that I didn't have to. I told Nathan that no one is more responsible for the way I turned out than my two brothers because they protected me. He said, "I'm proud of you."

Sometimes I think I hear a collective voice down at Main and Hastings saying, "I can't—it hurts too much." I love everyone down there. They deserve love. Those are my people, and they feel the pain of colonization. And the story of that pain in my family is the story of Indigenous people right across Canada. I know what it's like to be young and want to run away. I know what it's like to be a little kid who believes in adoption or abortion because he thinks it's not fair to be raised the way that he is being raised. I know the hurt and pain that I went through, and I didn't even have it as bad as my mom or dad did when they were kids, or as bad as my grandpa who witnessed entire communities dying. That's why I do what I do. That's why I never give up. That's why I've done ceremony every week for the last thirty years.

I do it for my brother. I do it for my dad, Terry Baker, who died three hundred feet away from where my brother now lives. I do it for my aunties; I do it for my uncles and for my stepdad, Philip Gurney, who also overdosed and died. I do it for my cousins who died. I do it for all of them. They needed a space where they could heal from the pain of colonization and experience a reciprocal relationship to Spirit, where they could connect with the spirit that lives inside them without resorting to drugs and alcohol. I do what I do because they never had that and because there are others who need it still.

The pain of colonization caused by the abuses of the nuns and priests was passed on intergenerationally from my grandparents to my parents, and on to me. I also passed this on to my kids. I wasn't a perfect parent by any means. I wasn't always good to them. I yelled at them. I was an angry person, and they started to adopt some of the ugly characteristics that I modelled. But now they're calling me out on it, and we're healing together. I remember once when they were young, my dog was in my way, and I kicked it away. My kids saw that and said, "Why did you kick the dog? Why did you do that?" I hadn't ever really thought about it before, but I started to ask myself why the heck I would do such a thing. Then I remembered: that's how I was treated. I would just be walking by and I'd get kicked or punched for no reason. Vise grips placed on my back for no reason other than to inflict pain and abuse. People hurting other people. Older teenagers hurting a little kid. My kids are telling me now that I contributed to their low self-esteem and that all they needed was love and safety and all those things that I had also needed when I was a kid. It hurts to recognize what I did, but I'm so proud of them for having the courage to speak out and do something about it. So, now we are healing together. Now we are saying, "Enough!"

SMEŃÁLH: GOOD TEACHINGS

Despite the ugly alcoholism, drug addiction, and abuse that came with colonization, we still had the beautiful teachings of our culture that our Elders fought so hard to hold on to. Whenever we got into serious trouble growing up, our Elders, and particularly Uncle Bob, would sit us down and talk to us about smeńálh [smin-olth], which is a word in our language that means to carry yourself well with good teachings. Uncle Bob was so powerful with his words. He's the only person I've ever seen who could make a room full of people laugh and cry in the same sentence. He spoke our language with so much soul that even non-speakers like me could understand what he was saying. Uncle Bob would teach us about the importance of carrying ourselves with the teachings of our culture and walking in a way that was true to who we are as Tsleil-Waututh people. He would tell us that we must walk with the pride and respect of our people.

Uncle Bob would say that when you're in a canoe, you have to paddle together and pull your weight to win the race. Our nation competes in canoe races that are big community events, and some of those races are over six miles long. If you're watching from the shore, the canoes go right out of sight and come back again. To compete in those races, you have to train as hard as you can to the point that you want to give up. There could be thirty-five different nations competing in the event with eleven paddlers in each canoe, all trying their best and their hardest to win. You have to put your paddle deep into the water and pull it with all your might to move forward quickly. You paddle on one side until the skipper calls a switch, then you have to slide over to the other side of the canoe and, without skipping a beat, return your paddle back to the water in perfect sequence with all the other paddlers. It happens so quickly, and it's a beautiful sight to behold from the shore. But when you're in the canoe, you just paddle, and paddle, and paddle, hopefully to victory. You give everything you've got to try to catch the canoe in front of you while staying ahead of the canoe behind you. Your muscles get sore. Your back gets sore. You feel exhausted. Sometimes you just want to quit, but you keep paddling with your brothers and sisters because you're all in the canoe together. You don't stop because there are ten other people in that canoe with you; you know that they won't stop, so you don't stop. Then the adrenaline kicks in and gives you a boost of energy. You do it together, as one. Uncle Bob would tell us that being in the canoe is just like life. Sometimes life gets hard, and you want to quit. You feel you can't carry on any longer, but you have to push yourself forward anyway. And when you cross the finish line, you've accomplished something together. We start together, and we finish together. We are one together.

Sometimes when I'm lying in bed in a nest of pillows, it feels so good that I want to stay there all morning, but I know that I have to get up. My son will say, "Pop up! It's a good day! It's a beautiful day!" I used to say the same thing to my kids when they were little. That's like life—sometimes you feel like you don't want to get up, but you get up anyway. You feel like you can't move on, but you summon the energy and find a way to do it. These are the strong lessons that you get from the canoe, about working together and encouraging each other when somebody's feeling down. As brothers and sisters, we need to encourage each other, support each other, help each other, and will each other to move forward as one. These were teachings that my Uncle Bob shared when we were young, and I still remember them today. There are many good lessons of the canoe.

I remember a couple times when I found myself in trouble, my aunts and uncles sat me down and shared similar teachings with us about who we are as Tsleil-Waututh people, about the importance of protecting and caring for our lands, of being one with our lands. They also taught us about the importance of giving back. Whenever we caught Dungeness crab, my mom would tell us that we had to bring any leftover bits back to the water for the other animals to use. She told us that you always give back to the water and to the other creatures because they give themselves to us.

My mom would often tell me the same stories about a better way of life. One time I rolled my eyes at her and said, "Why are you telling me this again?" but then I got in even more trouble. At the time, I didn't realize how important it was for her to teach me the same stories over and over again at moments when I needed the lesson. But those words and teachings really stuck with me, and I found myself telling those same stories to my kids as they were growing up. What I realized is that my mom wanted to make sure I got it right. And now she shares those lessons with my kids as well. Despite all the trauma they endured, the aunties and uncles and all the Elders managed to pass on these beautiful teachings of our culture to the next generation. They instilled in us from a young age the importance of walking with our heads held high and sticking up for ourselves.

My aunties and uncles were all like second parents to me as I was growing up. I learned a lot from Uncle Len and also from

Auntie Sue, who was such a good protector of us all. Auntie Sue
was from England, and she was fierce. She wouldn't let anyone mess
with us, but she was also so loving and caring and always there for
us. Whenever I had relationship problems, I knew I could sit down
with Auntie Sue and Uncle Len and that they would help me make
sense of things. My siblings (Damian, Nathan, and Cecily) were
raised right alongside their kids (Justin, Gabe, Zach, and Isaac) like
one big family. In our language, we don't have a word for cousin—
we all call each other brothers and sisters. At times I also lived with
my mom's sister and her husband, Auntie Irene and Uncle Joe Aleck,
who also really loved me and called me their own. Uncle Joe was
a traditional speaker of our language. He would tell each of us,
"You're my favourite." Their kids (Joey, John, Jim, Jeff, Andrea,
and Charlene) were raised as my brothers and sisters as well. I would
also spend time in the home of Uncle Bob and Auntie Cassie, who
would feed and look after me. Then there was Auntie Rose, who
was a matriarch of our family for a long time, and her husband
Uncle Les. Auntie Anne was strong and well-spoken. Her husband,
Uncle Joe, was a beautiful, long-serving elected leader of our people.
You knew where you stood with them. As kids, we all grew up in
each other's home like siblings, and we did everything together. We
were all brothers and sisters, and that's why I call them my brother-
cousins and sister-cousins.

We picked on each other, and we lived through that vicious
cycle of violence where the oppressed become oppressors, but we
still stood up for one another and looked out for each other. It was
as if we lived in two worlds—one on reserve where we bullied each
other, and another off reserve where we took care of one another and
had each other's back. We'd take the bus into Vancouver together
as a big group of kids, maybe ten of us, so that we could protect each
other. I was always the youngest of the crew, so I was just a little
tagalong, but my brothers and my cousins took care of me and

made sure I was okay. I remember one time a cop wanted to fight us, and my cousin and I said to him, "What the hell is your problem? We are just little kids!" But that kind of thing was sort of normal. We'd get back at the cops by doing things like throwing snowballs at them. I remember once the cops were running after us and I couldn't keep up. My cousins waited for me and then just grabbed me and pulled me along. Whenever we needed to get away from the cops, we'd run into the forest. We knew those trails well because we played in there all the time, so we knew that once we were in there, the cops would never be able to catch us.

At school, my cousins wouldn't put up with being picked on or treated poorly because they looked different or had less than others, or because they had bad shoes or old clothes. If kids were acting racist toward us, my cousins would fight back and make sure it never happened again. We would even confront our teachers if they disrespected us. One of my cousins was very outspoken about the injustices of how our people had been treated, and he used to tell the teachers that they were being prejudiced or racist. In grade two, a couple of my cousins and I told the teachers that we didn't want to learn French because we should be learning our own language. We learned to use our voices to stick up for ourselves. We didn't necessarily know the proper way to communicate our frustration, but we understood that what was happening was wrong and we needed to protect ourselves, and that's how we did it. Even as little kids, we had to defend ourselves in order to survive. There was something deep inside us that told us we had to stand up for ourselves. My cousins taught me that.

We also had to protect ourselves on the reserve because we couldn't always rely on the cops to do that for us. So, if there was abuse going on, we had to take care of it on our own. If there was a dealer selling heavy drugs on the rez, we took care of it. I remember once in high school, a car full of seven guys came to the rez wanting to beat me up. We'd had some run-ins with these same guys in the past. It had started one night when they randomly attacked me and a group of my friends while we were on our way to the bus station. After that, word spread that we were planning on getting them back. So, this one night, they came onto the rez and started smashing mailboxes, yelling, "We want Rueben George." Justin was with me, and we ducked into the bush to hide from them. Then I heard one of my cousins say, "Rueben, are you there? Let's go deal with them." Two of my cousins came out with a bat and a machete, so now it was four on seven. The main guy from their group wanted to fight me, so my cousins told me that they would hold the rest of them off while I taught him a lesson. They told me to make sure that he never came back to Tsleil-Waututh. Sure enough, we never had any trouble from those guys again.

If my older cousins felt like we were being disrespected, they'd set up a roadblock and say, "Sorry, but no one is coming through today." They'd get a bunch of old tires, lay them across the road, and say, "If you disrespect us, then you're not coming through our land." Sometimes when the cops showed up on the reserve, my cousins would come out ready to fight and drive them away too. Back in the 1950s, my dad's generation did the same. I heard a story of the cops coming up to the rez one time when my dad was young; a bunch of my uncles started pelting the cops with empty wine bottles they'd grabbed from the bottle depot. Another time, a group of guys showed up wanting to beat up some Indians, and one of my uncles threw a Molotov cocktail at their car. They drove away with their car still on fire. One of the uncles saw them the next day driving around in their burned-out car.

I think those lessons of smeṅálh that were instilled in us by our Elders at a young age taught us to stand up for ourselves when people weren't respecting us. My cousins did that. They let people know that when you mess with one Tsleil-Waututh, you mess with them all, and the same goes for the Squamish and Musqueam. By following the teachings of smenálh and standing up for ourselves, our community started developing the character of who we were. We may not have expressed that in good ways all the time, and violence might not have been the right way of going about it, but it was an important step because we had to fight to hold on to our identity as Tsleil-Waututh. So, for the George family, it was rough, but it was beautiful. For my extended family, it was rough, but it was beautiful. For the Tsleil-Waututh people, it was rough, but it was beautiful.

We faced prejudices from teachers, from police, and from others outside our community, but there were good people outside our community as well. There were some really good people. I still have friends with whom I went to school from grade two all the way through to the end of high school. We partied a lot and had loads of fun, and everyone sort of treated each other as equals. Sometimes it felt like I lived two lives—my First Nations life on the reserve and my life at school. But my really good non-Native friends would come hang out with me and my family on the rez. They got to know my cousins, my brothers, and my sister. They were good to me, and their parents were good to me too. I played on a football team, and I used to get rides to practice with one of my friends and his mom. At one point, my friend was injured and couldn't play anymore, but his mom kept driving me to practice several times a week. They were always good like that.

We jokingly called ourselves "The Mutants," and we got into lots of funny trouble. Sometimes we would come back to my friends' homes early in the morning after a party, and we'd wake everyone up because we were making food and laughing. But surprisingly their parents wouldn't get too mad at us—sometimes they even laughed with us and thought we were funny. We all had cars by the time we were sixteen or seventeen years old, and we were really adventurous. Someone would suggest that we go somewhere or do something, and we'd all just go and do it. We'd go camping, kayaking, sailing, or hiking. We also played a lot of sports, especially soccer and football. In a way, they were innocent to all the things that had happened to me. As far as I know, they didn't know what I had gone through. Maybe they knew I was poor, but I don't think they knew about the trauma I experienced. Either way, they treated me the same, and in these moments I was able to be just another kid with them. Those friends, the Mutants, taught me a lot. They taught me to live in both worlds from an early age, and I probably wouldn't have graduated high school if they hadn't pushed me to get my work done. It was a happy time, and I really appreciate that group of guys. Because of them, I wasn't always alone—I had a good group of brothers, and I'm still friends with them today, though some of them whom I loved dearly aren't here anymore.

It was the same with the teachers in elementary and high school: there were some who were really good to me, who believed in me and really pushed me. I had trouble reading in elementary school. It wasn't that I couldn't read; it was a matter of self-esteem. I remember this one time, the recess bell went off, but my teacher, Mr. Bull, said, "We're staying put until we've finished reading this passage!" I loved recess, so I put my hand up and said, "I'll read it!" I think everyone in the class must have been thinking, Oh no, we'll be here forever if Rueben reads it! But I read the whole passage really fast because I wanted to get out of there and go for recess really badly. Mr. Bull threw down his book and started jumping up and down in delight, exclaiming, "I knew it! I knew it! I knew you could do this!" He was so happy that he was laughing with joy, and he ran over to give me a big hug, and then he let us all go for recess. So, it wasn't always doom and gloom growing up; there were some really good things going on too.

I'm so proud of residential school survivors. The colonizers tried to break their spirits, but they retained enough of our culture to plant the seeds for my generation and all future generations. Despite all the abuse that went on, those seeds grew. They grew strong, and that's what we are today as a nation. I'm a strong, proud Tsleil-Waututh. I'm a strong, proud First Nations man. My nephews and nieces and children are strong First Nations people. My mom is a beautiful, strong Elder. My brothers are beautiful fathers. My sister is such a strong, beautiful person—the glue that has held us all together throughout the years. I visit my brother Nathan every week, and we have fun, happy visits together. We make each other laugh. We are all growing together. We are all healing together—my mom, my children, my siblings, my cousins, my aunties, my uncles, my nephews, and my nieces. We're healing together as a community, as a family, and as a nation. My family has done Sweat Lodge ceremony together for thirty years now, and we do our Coast Salish ceremonies together too. We are growing economically. We are relearning our culture, our language, and all those things that were taken away from our people. That's smenálh.

My uncle Bob George was once asked what love is, and he said, "Come sit down with my family, and we will show you love." We love one another, and we share our love with others. Our Sweat Lodge ceremony is open to all, and sometimes it's overwhelming to see how many people come to receive that love that my Uncle Bob was talking about. But we share that love because we want everyone to feel loved and we want everyone to heal. We want everyone to grow, together. That's nəc̓əmat. We are saying, "That's enough!" and putting an end to the intergenerational harm and violence of colonization. It stops here. And that's the story I want to tell you.

CHAPTER 2

Words to My Grandpa

My grandpa Chief Dan George died when I was eleven years old. When I was young, Grandpa took care of me during the day when nobody else was around. I had six cousins who were all a year or two older than me, and when they all started kindergarten, I didn't have anyone to play with during the day, so I'd go hang out with Grandpa. We became very close. By that time, he had already become really famous as the first Indigenous actor from North America to be nominated for an Academy Award. But to me, he was Grandpa, and he was my babysitter. We would hang out all the time, and he was always really good to me. Every morning while everyone else was at school, I would walk over to my auntie's house where he lived and we'd have breakfast together. He would make me tea with cold potatoes from the previous night's dinner and sċeẏxʷ, which is wind-dried salmon. I was young enough that I sometimes drank the tea from a baby bottle, so I must have been only three years old. We'd go for walks together. The adults in my family would say, "Somebody has to go on a walk with Grandpa," and my siblings and cousins would all say, "Rueben has to do it!" because I was the youngest. So, it was always me, but I didn't mind. I loved hanging out with Grandpa.

Grandpa started his acting career and became well known at a time of huge social, cultural, and political upheaval across North America. It was the time of the hippies, the Black Panthers, the American Indian Movement, and revolutionary uprisings around the world. There was a strong appetite for pushing boundaries and creating social and political change, and that was when my grandpa came along and started to break the stereotypes of how Native American people were portrayed in Hollywood. When he was offered roles in movies, my family would read through the scripts together and discuss how they portrayed Native people, and that's how they would decide whether or not Grandpa should accept a role. In the roles he played, he tried to put his own spin on what it means to be an Indigenous person. He faced a lot of racism and verbal attacks. My mom told me that when he was in California for the Academy Awards ceremony, a taxi driver asked him, "How can you get an award for being an Indian Chief playing an Indian Chief?" My grandpa said, "Well, it actually happens all the time. It's very common for White men to get awards for playing White men!"

There's another story that my aunties and uncles tell about the filming of *Little Big Man*. Grandpa played the role of Old Lodge Skins, and in a famous scene, Dustin Hoffman's character rides up on horseback to a Cheyenne camp and learns that many people had died in an attack by the U.S. cavalry. When they filmed this scene, my grandpa began to say his lines and he just started crying. The director yelled, "Cut! What's wrong, Chief?" My grandpa said, "I remember this happening to my own family. My aunties, my uncles, my cousins." Grandpa lived through a time when many of our people were dying. They still had access to the harmony of Spirit and the medicines that helped them heal from the horrible things that were happening, but the impacts of disease and the genocide of our people were overwhelming. Our people couldn't remedy the harm quickly enough, and my grandpa lived through that.

When Grandpa died, the media were really invasive with our family. They set up all around our house with cameras trained right on our front door so we'd be filmed or photographed as soon as we stepped outside. Media were calling us from all over the world. It was a nightmare, because grief is such a private thing and the media were making it into a public circus.

Grandpa had a hard life before he became famous. His experience in residential school was brutal. He lived through many hardships, and at times in his life, he turned to alcohol to drown the hurt of all the painful things he witnessed and lived through. My grandma left him at one point, and he had to quit drinking to get her back. But he sure turned out to be a wonderful grandfather to me, and he became a voice for our nation and our people. Despite all the abuse that he lived through, and the pain of colonization, he managed to love all people equally. He was able to hold on to the teachings of our culture and spirituality. They couldn't assimilate him. They couldn't beat those teachings out of him. They couldn't punish those teachings out of him. They couldn't starve those teachings out of him. They couldn't imprison those teachings out of him. He held on to enough of the teachings to live through all of that and still find the strength to stand up for Indigenous Peoples across Canada, to stand up for Mother Earth, to stand up for our lands, our waters, and our air. He held on to enough of the teachings to show us a better way.

His peers were all like that too. They were beautiful, powerful, and spiritually gifted ceremonial leaders. They were amazing healers, people of miracles, who maintained our cultural and our spiritual knowledge and our traditional Coast Salish ceremonies, despite all they went through. They remembered the fundamentals of humanity and passed on these lessons to us. We've lost many of those super-holy teachers who made beautiful miracles in ceremony. There aren't many left.

We now have a new generation coming up that understands these lessons at an even younger age than my generation did. A lot of people of my generation, including myself, didn't begin their spiritual way of life until they were already adults. But many of the Indigenous youth of my children's generation were raised with spiritual teachings right from the moment they were born, and their gifts come out much earlier in their lives. I see this in my family and our community, and I've also seen this in my travels around the world. I see people wanting more for their children than what this ugly society teaches us to accept as normal. When people search, what they find is a connection with Spirit. To be connected to their own spirit as a human being is to be connected to the ancestors, to the Creator, and in turn to everything. They raise their kids this way, and the next generation becomes even more spiritually powerful. Seeing this happen gives me a lot of hope.

One thing I remember about my grandpa is that no matter how famous he was, and no matter whose company he was in, when he entered a room, he was always himself—he was always just Grandpa. That's what all my aunts and uncles and my mom say about him, and I saw it myself. He never let fame change who he was or what was important to him. He said, "People used to hate me because of the way I look, but now that I'm famous they love me for the way that I look." What other people thought of him didn't matter because he was proud to be who he was. He was proud to be Tsleil-Waututh, and he embodied smenálh.

One time he was in an airport in Dallas when a man in a suit approached him and said, "Chief Dan George, the only good Indian is still a dead Indian." My grandpa didn't get angry or upset; he just stared directly into the man's eyes without flinching. Eventually the man got so angry that he turned red and stormed away. Later my mom asked my grandpa why he didn't say anything to the man, and Grandpa told her, "If I had reacted, it would have shown that his words affect me." The reason the man got so upset was because he wanted his words to hurt my grandpa, but Grandpa showed the man that his words had no power. That's smeńálh. I always wanted to be like that too. If someone doesn't accept me for who I am, I'm not going to let it bother me and I'm not going to change who I am. I'm Tsleil-Waututh, and I'm not going to change that just because some people don't like First Nations or feel a certain way about me.

My grandpa taught our family to love who we are and to be proud of our culture and spirituality. That's probably one of the most important things he taught me because, at times in my life, I was ashamed to be First Nations. The intergenerational injustices and abuses of colonialism, the legacy of residential schools, and the lack of opportunities, which others had, wreaked havoc and embedded shame in me about being First Nations. Even though when I was younger I couldn't be proud of who I was, due to all the dysfunction, today I think of those lessons from my grandpa, and I try to carry myself well. I refuse to change who I am just because someone else won't accept me. That's what smeńálh means to me.

Sometimes I have to pray for strength. In a moment when I was feeling deflated about our fight against the Trans Mountain Pipeline, I reached for my grandpa's book, *My Heart Soars*. I opened it up, and right there staring back at me was a poem he wrote called "Words to a Grandchild." He wrote it in 1974, right around the time when he would have been babysitting me. Here I was, his grandson, reading his words forty-five years later in a moment when I desperately needed inspiration to continue to fight. They spoke powerfully to me. The poem talks about our future and how things are going to change, and how we have to stay true to who we are. Those were his words to a grandchild, and I am his grandchild. It was such a beautiful thing to be delivered this message of perseverance directly from my grandpa right when I most needed it. It was an affirmation of all that we are fighting for.

"Words to a Grandchild"
by Chief Dan George (1974)

Perhaps there will be a day
you will want to sit by my side
asking for counsel.
I hope I will be there
but you see
I am growing old.
There is no promise
that life will
live up to our hopes
especially to the hopes of the aged.
So I write of what I know
and some day our hearts
will meet in these words
—if you let it happen.

In the midst of a land
without silence
you have to make a place for yourself.
Those who have worn out
their shoes many times
know where to step.
It is not their shoes
you can wear
only their footsteps
you may follow
—if you let it happen.

You come from a shy race.
Ours are the silent ways.
We have always done all things
in a gentle manner,
so much as the brook
that avoids the solid rock
in its search for the sea
and meets the deer in passing.
You too must follow the path
of your own race.
It is steady and deep,
reliable and lasting.
It is you
—if you let it happen.

You are a person of little,
but it is better to have little
of what is good,
than to possess much
of what is not good.
This your heart will know
—if you let it happen.

Heed the days
when the rain flows freely,
in their greyness
lies the seed of much thought.
The sky hangs low
and paints new colours
on the earth.
After the rain
the grass will shed its moisture,

the fog will lift from the trees,
a new light will brighten the sky
and play in the drops
that hang on all things.
Your heart will beat out
a new gladness
—if you let it happen.

Each day brings an hour of magic.
Listen to it!
Things will whisper their secrets.
You will know
what fills the herbs with goodness,
makes days change into nights,
turns the stars
and brings the change of seasons.
When you have come to know
some of nature's wise ways
beware of your complacency
for you cannot be wiser than nature.
You can only be as wise
as any man will ever hope to be
—if you let it happen.

Our ways are good
but only in our world.
If you like the flame
on the white man's wick
learn of his ways,
so you can bear his company,
yet when you enter his world,
you will walk like a stranger.

For some time
bewilderment will,
like an ugly spirit
torment you.
Then rest on the holy earth
and wait for the good spirit.
He will return with new ways
as his gift to you
—if you let it happen.

Use the heritage of silence
to observe others.
If greed has replaced the goodness
in a man's eyes
see yourself in him
so you will learn to understand
and preserve yourself.
Do not despise the weak,
it is compassion
that will make you strong.
Does not the rice
drop into your basket
whilst your breath
carries away the chaff?
There is good in everything
—if you let it happen.

When the storms close in
and the eyes cannot find the horizon
you may lose much.
Stay with your love for life
for it is the very blood running through your veins.

As you pass through the years
you will find much calmness
in your heart.
It is the gift of age,
and the colors of the fall
will be deep and rich
—if you let it happen.

As I see beyond the days of now
I see a vision:
I see the faces of my people,
your sons' sons,
your daughters' daughters,
laughter fills the air
that is no longer yellow and heavy,
the machines have died,
quietness and beauty
have returned to the land.
The gentle ways of our race
have again put us
in the days of the old.
It is good to live!
It is good to die!
—This will happen.

"Words to a Grandchild" from *The Best of Chief Dan George*, copyright 2004 by Hancock House Publishers Ltd., ISBN 978-088839-544-3, used with permissions www.hancockhouse.com

I remember Grandpa saying that we are the last human beings who believe in this land and who believe that Spirit is alive in everything. He would say the most beautiful and profound things, like how millions of people wanted to hear him speak yet all he ever wanted was for the grass to hear him again. Grandpa taught these ways to my uncle Len, to my mom, and to my aunties and uncles, who in turn taught these lessons to my generation. I've incorporated these teachings in my own healing. I've also incorporated them into the work that I have done throughout my life—in the counselling work that I do, in the environmental work I do, and in business. I pass these teachings on to my kids. They already understand that there's a better way, and they see that we're reclaiming it.

In 1967, the year of Canada's centennial, Grandpa gave his famous speech, "A Lament for Confederation." He said:

> Like the Thunderbird of old, I shall rise again out of the sea; I shall grab the instruments of the white man's success—his education, his skills—and with these new tools I shall build my race into the proudest segment of your society. Before I follow the great chiefs who have gone before us, Oh Canada, I shall see these things come to pass.

> I shall see our young braves and our chiefs sitting in the houses of law and government, ruling and being ruled by the knowledge and freedoms of our great land. So shall we shatter the barriers of our isolation. So shall the next hundred years be the greatest in the proud history of our tribes and nations.

When I hear these words spoken by my grandpa, I think about how, prior to colonization, we lived such a rich and abundant life while maintaining a reciprocal relationship to Spirit and to the lands and waters. That was the basis of our sovereignty. Today we conduct ceremony at least twice a week, sometimes every day in the winter, but back then, we lived in connection with Spirit at all times, all day long, each and every day. And, like the Thunderbird of old, we're taking all that back.

Sometimes I get tired, and I want to quit. Sometimes I feel like I can't do it anymore. But when I look at my grandpa's speeches calling for equality and justice, it makes me remember all the people whom he fought for who didn't make it. Too many of our family members didn't make it, but my grandpa never stopped trying to help our people. He fought tirelessly to uplift our people until the day he died. He was ready and willing to take care of anything that needed to be addressed, to help anyone who needed it. He was gracious and hard-working. Even as an Elder, he was still travelling far and wide, working hard to uplift our community. He always persevered. I think of him, and I pray to him often.

One time when I was in ceremony at Sun Dance, two eagles flew overhead and I looked up and I thought, There's my dad and my grandpa. Then I walked over to my mom, and she said, "Did you see your dad and your grandpa up there?" My grandpa is there, and he's smiling. He gives me the strength I need so that when I'm tired, I get up. When I'm sick, I get up. When I think I can't win or can't do it anymore, I get up. I get up! He got up, and I will get up because there are those who can't. My dad couldn't get up. All my family members who died from drugs and alcohol, who died from colonization, they couldn't get up. So, I will. I will get up and I will take a stand. I'll get up and I'll do something about it. I'll get up and I'll make it better. I'll never stop fighting. And now my son says to me, "We will not be the generation that stops fighting." My son says that! He fights, and my daughter does too. They don't even know the meaning of "give up." Never stop, never give up. That's my grandpa.

SOBERING UP

As I said before, many of the adults in our community drank. One of the first people to sober up was my mom's brother, Chief Leonard George, who was always sitting us kids down and telling us that we could have a better life. His words stuck. Uncle Len was a bit of a miracle baby. Grandma and Grandpa thought that they couldn't have any more kids, but then much to their surprise, he was born. Because he was so much younger than the rest of our family, everyone showered him with love. Then he was sent to residential school, where he had an especially hard time. He arrived a little late in the school year because he had been sick and was placed in a dorm room with older boys. He got the beats from them as well as from the nuns and priests. He went from being the focus of all the family's love and affection, treated as a miracle baby, to not knowing anyone and being abused. My mom told me the story of how she saw him arrive at the residential school with his big eyes wide open, just trying to find somebody who loved him. She finally locked eyes with him, and they looked at each other with so much love from across the room. She felt so sad for him that she almost started crying. Then a nun came out of nowhere and slapped her on the side of her head so hard that her ear started ringing. The nun told her to quit googly-eyeing the boys. There she was getting beaten for trying to make a loving connection with her baby brother. Uncle Len got it so bad in residential school that decades later when it came time to receive the peanuts of a settlement that the government was offering survivors for all the mental, physical, emotional, and spiritual abuse they had suffered, he was shaking so much that he could barely hold the pen and sign his name to receive the payment.

I admired Uncle Len so much because despite all the hardship he faced, he did the healing work. He was the type of leader who wanted to set an example. He was so persistent at teaching us about smeńálh, telling us that we could have a better life if we made better choices instead of falling in that dark hole of drug and alcohol addiction. He would say things like, "I love you so much, and it hurts me to see you drinking because I know so many people who have died or gotten ill from alcohol, and I wouldn't want to see you suffering in that way." Auntie Anne would say similar things. I remember she once said, "Rueben's such a handsome young man, but he's not as handsome when he's drunk and swearing."

Once when I was a teenager, I threw this huge party at my mom's house, and maybe six or seven hundred people showed up. People came from as far away as the neighbouring city of Surrey. There were so many people there that I had to start telling people they couldn't come in. Total strangers were saying to me, "Rueben invited us," and I told them, "I'm Rueben, and I don't know who the hell you are!" Uncle Len came by to try to shut the party down, and I was being such an ass to him. After the party, he said to me, "Rueben, look at the power you have at bringing people together. You have a party, and hundreds of people show up. You have this ability to organize these big, beautiful gatherings. Our people are suffering. Can you imagine what you could do with those powers if you used them to do good for our people? If you and I did that together, just imagine how much change we could create!" Holy crap, did that ever stick with me.

Uncle Len encouraged us to incorporate our culture into everything we did. Like my mom and all my aunts and uncles, he pushed us to be our best. He had so much drive and initiative, and he worked hard doing a lot of different types of jobs over the course of his lifetime. He helped raise money to get the Vancouver Aboriginal Friendship Centre built, and he was also very involved in First Nations housing initiatives in the city. Uncle Len would find rundown apartment buildings that could be bought cheaply right down at Main and Hastings in the Downtown Eastside, where a lot of people need housing. He would get materials donated from local hardware stores, and he would find skilled construction workers who had fallen on hard times and were living on the street. He'd give those guys the materials and get them to fix up these old buildings to be used for Native housing. He told a funny story once about how he was showing a group of potential funders some of the Native housing initiatives he'd been working on, when this guy who lived in one of the homes came outside, a bit tipsy in his underwear, and started yelling across the street, "Leonard! Thank you, Leonard! Thank you, man!"

Like my grandpa, Uncle Len was an actor, and he also served as Chief of our nation. He worked tirelessly to help our people. When I was around twenty, I listened to him make a deal with someone to get our nation some traditional canoes. Uncle Len had paid this guy to build us two canoes on a handshake deal. The guy called up and said, "Your canoe is ready." Uncle Len said, "Canoe? We paid for two canoes." The guy told my uncle, "Oh, well, you're only getting one now." I heard Uncle Len say to the guy, "Well, I guess it was stupid of me to trust you by making a handshake deal. Now you've got me by the balls, and you can do what you want, but know that it's your reputation on the line. We're not a rich nation by any means, and you're being greedy by taking money off my people, but that's on you." A couple days later we got our two canoes. I was still young and in school then, but the way he dealt with that really stood out for me.

I think what Uncle Len taught me was that if you have the drive and if you have the capacity, then there's always a way to find an answer to a problem or to create something. That's something I've carried forward in my life. I have no background in environmentalism or in business. I'm not a great writer, or good at math, or anything like that. But when I believe in something or when I need to know something, I'm driven to figure it out, and I can usually do pretty well at it. I noticed that many of my spiritual uncles—Len,

Lee Brown, Phil Lane Jr., and JC Lucas—had a spiritual room in their homes dedicated to ceremony where they kept their spiritual artifacts, such as their pipes, eagle fans, drums, rattles, and medicines. I think they would sit in these rooms and pray to find a way for their people. If there was a problem in the community, Uncle Len would go to his spiritual room and pray on that problem until he found an answer. If there was a squabble between families within the nation, he would pray on finding a way to fix that problem. If he was going to give a speech and wanted to reach lots of people, he would pray to find the words to touch the hearts of the people to whom he was speaking. If he was going to make a big business deal for our community, he would pray to make that deal work. I call it finding a way. We find a way in accordance with our teachings to help us make things better. Uncle Len's spiritual room was a finding-a-way room. I believe he would sit in that room and pray to the ancestors to help him find a vision for the Tsleil-Waututh Nation, and then he would seek insights on how to implement that vision. He would pray for the right time, the right place, and the right situation for things to happen. Then he would work hard to achieve his vision because you can't just pray for something and then sit back and expect it to happen. You have to work for it.

When my brother Damian was young, Uncle Len gave him some tobacco and asked him to run ceremony and pray for the community every week, and Damian did that. He was doing ceremony long before I started, and I know that he was praying for me to be there with him. One time, I ended up in the hospital

Chief Leonard George. Image courtesy of *North Shore News*.

because I took so many drugs that I passed out and nearly killed myself. I didn't want to live any longer, and I hurt myself so bad that I almost didn't make it through the night. I spent a day or two in the hospital and then came home and slept for two days straight. When I finally woke up, my head was still spinning from all the drugs, and I walked over to see my brother Damian. I sat on the stairs in front of his house, and he came out to speak with me. He said, "I'm glad you came to see me, brother. I heard what happened and I've been praying for you. I prayed that you would come to speak with me, and you did, but in my prayer Uncle Len was here with us." Right then, Uncle Len came walking out from a trail in the bushes! I thought, Oh shit, the prayers are working!

They told me how much they loved me and how much it would hurt our family if I were to die. They told me how much it hurts them when they see me hurting myself. They talked about my worth and how I'm a beautiful human being. They said that when I'm sober, I'm one of the nicest people to be around. They talked about how I needed healing, counselling, and therapy. They said I needed culture and spirituality. They talked to me for a very long time about smenálh and about carrying myself well. It had such a profound impact. I had just tried to hurt myself, and here they were sharing such difficult, profound, beautiful teachings with me. Something shifted in me in that moment, and it was a deep-seated shift. I told them, "You know what? I'm not gonna quit drinking because you tell me to. Because if I did that, I'd be quitting for the wrong reasons. But you're right—I do have a problem, and I do need healing. And I'll quit soon."

I'd already been trying to heal in ceremony before Damian and Uncle Len talked to me that day, but it was then that I really started to dedicate myself to that path. A couple of months later, after I'd been doing a lot of praying, I went out drinking with my friends. I popped open a bottle of beer and went to take a sip, but just before the bottle touched my lips, I started dry heaving. I knew instantly what was happening: the words of my brother and my uncle had touched me so profoundly that my spirit was now rejecting the drug and alcohol spirit. That's the power of smeńálh. Those heartwarming words of smeńálh my brother Damian and my uncle Len shared with me that day, and all those times that my aunties and my uncles and my cousins had talked to me about smeńálh, and all those teachings I received in ceremony from Uncle Bob, all of that culminated in this one moment. It all connected in my soul and spirit to send me in the right direction.

A similar thing happened to me with cigarettes. After I quit drinking, I kept smoking until my son was born. My wife at the time, Debbie, was leading a high-profile campaign to promote tobacco use for traditional purposes only. One day the campaign was holding a photoshoot for some promotional materials, and their model didn't show up so Debbie stood in. Her picture ended up on all these campaign flyers and brochures that were spread all over our home. I would see her picture on all these materials encouraging people to quit smoking, and I started to feel that if I had another cigarette, I'd get sick the same way I did with alcohol. My spirit was rejecting it because Debbie was working so hard to help people quit.

When your spirit grows, it requires the mental and physical and emotional parts of you to grow in tandem so that they can all remain in balance, and you begin to reject the things in your life that you don't need. It could be drugs or alcohol, but it could also be an abusive relationship or a bad habit. With the help of my family and community, my spiritual growth started to push out of my life all the things that weren't aligned with smeńálh, with the spiritual teachings of the Sweat Lodge, the Sun Dance, our Coast Salish ceremonies, or the Coast Salish teachings of the canoe. Each contributed to my spiritual growth.

Sobering up was the beginning of some big changes in my life. It was hard, but I know that I'm here and doing better today because people prayed for me, and I still think of them praying for me. I know that my aunties and uncles and family were all praying for me. All their prayers called me into ceremony. People dedicated themselves to praying for me and believing in me, just like I believe Uncle Len used to do in his finding-a-way room. Sweat Lodge is a little dome where we find a way. When we go to Sun Dance, we go to find that way. We go to our mountains to find that way. Sometimes we'll meditate and pray; we'll let our spirit work on those things. Once we believe something mentally, emotionally, spiritually, and physically, our spirit wills it. And that's what the spirit of all those people praying did to me—it willed me to be better, to move forward, and to quit drinking. When I went to take that sip of beer and started dry heaving, my spirit pushed it out of me and I never drank or did drugs again because it wasn't part of my being anymore. So, I'll always be grateful to everyone who helped me in ceremony. I honour them often, and I'm thankful to them for saving my life.

CEREMONY

In Sweat Lodge, we're taught that everything has a spirit, including drugs and alcohol. The drug and alcohol spirits are so powerful that they can take your life away, as they almost did to me. They can take your home. They can take your freedom. They can take the place of the spirit of your family or of someone you love. They are powerful spirits that can place their grasp on you and take control of your life. In some of our ceremonies, we offer a little bit of alcohol to appease the alcohol spirit and ask that it leave our people alone. My uncle said that one surefire way of dealing with addiction is Native spirituality, and I've seen that to be the case in our community. The return of ceremony led to a lot of healing and big changes among our people, and we're doing a lot better now because of it. Five years after our ceremonies were reintroduced, eighty percent of our people quit drinking. I was part of that eighty percent.

I started therapy at the age of twenty-one, and I did it on and off for two years, but it didn't really help too much. The objective of a lot of Western practices of psychiatry, psychology, counselling, and therapy is to teach us how to be functional in a dysfunctional society. I think that's why it didn't work too well for me. I remember feeling that way in later years while learning psychology at school. Around the time I started therapy, my brother Damian kept asking me to come to Sweat Lodge with him. I kept telling him that I wasn't interested, but I did wonder what they were doing in there. There were a couple of years when I would look down at the Sweat Lodge along the inlet and wonder what the heck that old man Frank Supernault was doing down there. Wintertime, it would be freezing cold, and he'd be down there making a fire. Springtime, it would be raining out, and he'd be down there making a fire. Summertime, it would be scorching hot out, and he'd still be down there making a fire. Finally, when I was twenty-three, my curiosity got the best of me, and I went down there and gave it a shot. That's when I started praying with my brother Damian, Frank, and all the other beautiful people at that Sweat Lodge, and it fed my spirit in a really good way. They saved my life.

I remember crawling into the pitch-black of the Sweat Lodge for the first time. The Elders were pouring water on the lava rocks that were glowing red at the centre of the dome. It got really hot, and I remember thinking, Okay, I can take this. They started praying and saying things, and eventually they told me it was my turn. I asked them what to do, and they told me to pray. I asked, "How do I pray?" and they told me to ask for good things in my life and good things for my family. I said, "Who am I asking?" and they told me to ask the ancestors. They suggested that I begin by introducing myself to the ancestors by saying, "Hello, my name is Rueben George, and

I'm your grandchild." I thought, Okay, I can do that, but as soon as I opened my mouth to speak, I started bawling. It was the first time I had a real heartfelt cry since my grandpa had died ten years earlier. I prayed so hard, and I cried through the rest of that ceremony. When it finished, I crawled out on my hands and knees, completely exhausted. Two men were standing outside the Sweat Lodge, one of whom passed a couple of years ago and the other is still one of my close teachers. They helped me up and reached out to hug me. That was the first time I had really allowed somebody to hug me since my grandpa had passed away. The spirit of that ceremony had touched me, and I was finally able to push aside all the sexual abuse, the physical abuse, the mental abuse, the emotional abuse, and the spiritual abuse I had suffered as a child. I was able to let somebody hug me for the first time in a long time.

After that first experience at Sweat Lodge, I started doing Sweats at least once per week, sometimes twice in a day, for the next year. I slowly started to reverse all the negative things that had happened to me, peeling them back layer by layer. The unfortunate reality of living in an Indigenous community with tons of hurt and pain is that traumatic things happen all the time. I've had many aunties, uncles, and cousins die, some in natural ways but some in really horrible ways. Because I grew up with some but not all of the fundamentals of humanity—without all of the physical, spiritual, and emotional conditions that every human needs as a baby, toddler, child, and teenager—I turned into that violent person who didn't think he was going to live and who liked to hurt himself and others. I turned into that person who couldn't love or be affectionate and who couldn't hold or care for anybody. A person who couldn't allow himself to cry or to express emotion in a good way. A person who expressed his hurt and pain as rage and who woke up some mornings wanting to fight. I passed on a lot of that pain to others through my violence toward men and my disrespect toward women.

Even during ceremony, I was disrespectful at first. I also hurt my kids, and it still pains me to think about that.

I was disconnected from my own spirit, and I had to work really hard to reverse all of that by filling myself with the spiritual and emotional support that I didn't always get when I was younger. In the darkest periods of my life, I experienced anxiety every single day. I experienced depression and had suicidal thoughts, and I medicated myself with drugs and alcohol every day for years. When I quit and started to sober up, I learned to have a connection to Spirit—the spirit of the fire of Sweat Lodge, the spirit of the smudge and the Coast Salish ceremonies. The spirit of all the ceremonies that kept me alive and helped me get unstuck from all the hurt, pain, and dysfunction. I had to sit in circle with my Elders and face the people I had hurt and say, "I'm sorry. We can heal together." I had a lot to forgive, and I had to ask for a lot of forgiveness. I had to learn to love myself and to accept love from my friends and family. I'm no longer the abusive person I used to be, but I'm still learning, and I will continue to learn.

The first couple of years I was making fire for Sweat Lodge, I was still drinking. At one point, I was told not to come around because in some Sweat Lodges you're required to be four days sober before you enter, and I just wasn't able to do that. Elder Frank came to my house one day to ask me why I wasn't coming anymore, and I told him that I wasn't sober. He told me that if I needed ceremony, I should come. I said, "I can't right now—I have booze breath." He said, "Do you need ceremony?" and I told him I did. He said, "Well, then come to Sweat Lodge."

I ended up going to a men's treatment centre. I knew I had been getting something out of ceremony, but I didn't understand why or what it meant to be a Sweat Lodge fireman. At the treatment centre, we focused all day, every day on healing. It was hard work, but each day we would look forward to our visits from Lee Brown, who would mesmerize all the brothers in the program with his teachings. Lee has a PhD in educational studies, and he's also a spiritual leader. Throughout the six weeks of treatment, he talked to us about how everyone has a gift, and how finding your gift feeds your spirit. He said that your gift is your passion, so when you work with your gift, you are working with your passion. He said it's called a gift because it's something you're talented at and something you can give back to your community. There are multiple types of gifts. For instance, in our ceremonial community, some people are really good at making regalia. Some are really good with songs—they will hear a song once and always remember it. Others know how to build things at Sun Dance or at our Coast Salish ceremonies, and that's their gift. Others are great speakers, or perhaps really good at their jobs outside the ceremonial community and able to contribute back financially. These are all gifts. Uncle Lee said that some people don't find their gift until the day they die, which is really tragic. But in our ceremonial community, we encourage people to find their gift and bring it back to our circle. This way, teachings are shared and spread widely throughout our community. It helps us all become healthier and makes the community grow stronger.

One of Uncle Lee's gifts is receiving messages from the ancestors. On the last day of treatment, after six weeks of receiving these beautiful teachings, he told our group, "I have three messages, and two of them are for Rueben." He asked if I wanted the good news or bad news first, and I said, "Give me the bad news, I guess." Uncle Lee said the bad news was that if I ever drank alcohol again, I would die. He said it might be that I get sick and die a slow death, or it might be that I have a few drinks one night and get in a terrible accident. But one way or another, the ancestors wanted me to know that if I drank alcohol again, I would die. Then Uncle Lee gave me the second message. He told me that my gift is my breath. He said that when I'm older, people would come from all over the world to hear me share my knowledge and wisdom. I thought to myself that this was kind of ridiculous. I was just trying to sober up and not die because I had been killing myself with drinking. I didn't care about anyone; I didn't care about life; I didn't even think I was going to live to the age of twenty-five. I certainly didn't think anyone would ever want to listen to what I had to say. Uncle Lee said that he was hesitant to give me this message because I still had a lot of learning to do, and he didn't want me to get a big head. He told me I had to stay humble so I could continue to learn the teachings. And that's the moment I decided to be a ceremonial fireman for fourteen years to make sure that I listened and learned before taking on any kind of leadership role. I thought if it's true that I was going to have any sort of responsibility for helping people, I better help myself first.

I served as a fireman for multiple teachers and learned many lessons along the way. Making the fire is a spiritual process, and through that process we prepare ourselves spiritually for the Sweat Lodge ceremony. As I made a fire, I'd think about all that the trees had witnessed and all the wisdom they carried. I'd think about how we were putting a blessing on the rocks in the Sweat Lodge by smudging them with such a beautiful tree, and I'd thank the tree for helping us heal. It's the fireman or firewoman's responsibility to take care of people, so you have to have a good heart and a good mind as you make the fire. People need the fire to be nice and hot so they can have their medicine. By providing that, the fireman or firewoman is taking care of people. I would also smudge the ground inside the Sweat Lodge and smudge each person as they entered. Uncle Lee taught me that to make a fire, you build a little home out of kindling—either a little teepee or a little longhouse—and you place the paper in the middle of the home. That little home is where your spirit sits. When you light the paper, it represents the spirit inside your home, which is your body. I'd think of all these teachings as I was preparing the fire, and they were lessons that helped me become a better person.

I loved that life and I worked hard at it. Sometimes I'd chop the wood with a lot of aggression because I was dealing with my hurt and pain. The teachers never said anything because they knew I was releasing, but some people would tell me I was going a little crazy on the logs. They'd say, "What kind of energy are you putting into the rocks?" But I'd just ignore them and keep on chopping because it was a release for me. It didn't matter if it was raining, freezing cold, or if there was a foot of snow on the ground—I'd work so hard that my body would stay warm. By the time I started to get cold, it would be time to light the fire and it would warm me right back up. Frank Supernault once said to me, "Come hell or high water, you're gonna make the fire," and he was right—no matter the conditions, I'd get it done. I remember one time I arrived at a Sweat, and there was nothing but a chainsaw and a tree. I picked up the chainsaw, cut that tree, bucked up all the logs, and had the fire going in forty-five minutes. Sometimes the tree we harvested was a hundred yards back in the woods, so I'd have to cut it into six-foot lengths and pack those out one at a time. I'd pack out just what was needed to make the rocks hot because it was hard work dragging those logs out from the bush. For a while, I thought making fires was my gift because I sure loved it. I did it about once a week for fourteen years, and it taught me tools I needed for healing. Those fourteen years were part of the process that I had to go through to learn more about my gift. And I'm still learning.

The Sweat Lodge is a little dome, and being in it is like being in the womb of our mother, which is the safest place we've ever been in our entire lives. During those nine months spent in our mother's womb, we were taken care of and provided with everything we needed physically, spiritually, mentally, and emotionally. During that time, we were essentially perfect, and that is how we're born. The idea of Sweat Lodge is to create a ceremonial space that brings us back to the time we were in our mother's womb, when we had everything we needed. It helps us hold on to that perfection and move forward with it in accordance with our spiritual law and the fundamentals of humanity. The Sweat Lodge is hot and cramped, just as it is inside the womb of our mother, but it's also a big beautiful safe space that allows us to be vulnerable. It's the womb of Mother Earth. When we enter the Sweat Lodge, we feel that safety of being in the womb of the mother, and once we're comfortable, our spirit expands to the size of that space. You can take a deep breath and release whatever it is you're holding on to. When I run ceremonies, I can feel people release. I can hear that hurt and pain leaving them, like a beautiful song. If we hear somebody crying, for instance, we know that they are releasing something. And when we feel somebody else releasing, it can help us release what we're holding on to ourselves. It's like a chain reaction of empathy that we all experience together in ceremony.

Mother Earth is constantly regenerating herself. I think of a salmonberry bush. In the winter, the salmonberry branches are so brittle that you might think they're dead. They are so fragile that if you even brush against them, they might break. But come spring, they grow flexible and rubbery again, full of life. I also think of the magnolia tree in front of my house, which looks so naked in the winter; when the spring comes, the foliage grows so thick and green that you can't even see the sun when you're standing beneath it. Then the flowers blossom, and it looks so beautiful. In the depths of winter, you might be forgiven for thinking that a plant is dead, but Mother Earth brings it back to life each spring. That's part of the circle of life and death. You could imagine a catastrophic event like a meteor hitting the Earth, kicking up a massive cloud of dust that blocks the sun and wipes out much of life on the planet. But given enough time—and Mother Earth has nothing but time—life

would gradually return. The Earth is constantly regenerating, reju-
venating, and reviving itself. In the spirit of nəc̓əmat, the interconnectedness of all things, every living being in this world is going to
heal and regenerate over time.

The purpose of the Sweat ceremony is to connect to nəc̓əmat
and ask the spirit of Mother Earth for regeneration. We drink water
to replenish, and we eat food to replenish, but we also need spiritual
replenishment. Through ceremony, we regenerate ourselves by healing our hurt, our pain, and our trauma. That energy of rejuvenation
reminds us that we are loving, caring, compassionate, respectful, and
humble human beings. That's why we need our ceremonies back.
That's why we need to approach ceremony not just as a thing we do
for a couple of hours each week, but as something we incorporate
into everything we do. That's why we have to practise ceremony as
a way of life, as our ancestors did.

In Sweat Lodge, we use wood from trees that are rooted deep
into the ground, which suck up nutrients from far below the surface
of the earth and which also reach way up into the heavens to catch
energy from the sun. When we burn wood from these trees, we are
releasing that energy from the sun, and we use that energy to heat
lava rocks. Lava comes from the centre of the Earth. Our spirit is in
the centre of our being, so essentially lava comes from the spirit of
Mother Earth. In pushing lava from the centre of her being, Mother
Earth is sharing the gift of her regenerative healing powers with us.
Those red-hot lava rocks, the spirit of Mother Earth, in the womb
of the Sweat Lodge help us heal. Then we pour water on those hot
rocks and steam rises up from them, giving birth to a new spirit that
fills the entire space. We can physically feel that heat and steam
encompassing our entire bodies, filling the ceremonial space along
with the sage or medicines that we use to smudge. It gets so hot in
the Sweat Lodge that you want to leave, and at any time you can
leave by yelling, "All my relations, let me out!" But if you stay and

persevere through the discomfort, and if you pray really hard, eventually you find peace with the heat. We become immersed in that spirit, and we implore it for help with our prayers. Those prayers and our songs introduce the air element. My grandpa and my mom would always say that every word we use has a spirit. When we speak or sing, we are using our breath, which comes together with the air spirit to create words or songs that carry their own spirit. That spirit extends as far as your voice can be heard. In this way, our songs create a connection between ourselves and the spiritual realm.

We also call on the songs of the Spirit that people need. Everything has a rhythm, and if you start to understand that, then you can start to understand what that rhythm sounds like. The key is to connect with and relate to it, and to let the rhythm speak to you. My grandpa and Uncle Bob sat in ceremony and prayed about nature, and a nature song came to them that we still sing today. Some of my friends know four or five hundred songs. There are songs about grass, songs about thunder, songs about lightning, songs about wolves and whales, mountains and trees, and water. There are numerous thank-you songs. There's a thank you for answering our prayers song, a thank you for this meal song, and a thank you for my family song. I've been praying with some of the singers in my ceremony for so long that when I ask them for a song, they know exactly which song is the right one for that moment. For instance, if we are praying on the lava rock and connecting to what it represents, its rhythm might come out in a song. And perhaps somebody in the ceremony needs the medicine of that grandfather lava rock song to help them deal with their own grandfather, father, or father figures. Or maybe that grandfather song helps someone to be a better father or a better grandfather. Songs come to us because the ancestors release them, and the spirit of the air holds on to them. Sometimes people will sing a song and say that it came to them, but my singers will recognize it from somebody else's territory. Maybe that song did come to them in ceremony, and maybe they are meant to use it in that moment, but that doesn't mean it belongs to them.

When we sing and pray in Sweat Lodge, our spirits expand and overlap with one another. We call in our ancestors, our grandparents, our great-grandparents, and our grandparents' grandparents, those who know us best, and we ask them to take our messages to the places where they're needed, perhaps to the Creator or to someone who needs healing. We ask them to listen to us and to all that we are in that moment. We beg them to take care of our hurt and pain, and to help us be better human beings. We try to explain things to them, and we reason with them; we even implore them to help us. When we do, our prayers create a spirit with the water and the medicine from our ceremony, and it fills the entire lodge. So, you have the medicines of the songs, the rattle, the drums, the smudge, the heat of the rocks, all coming together in the circular rhythm of ceremony to create the spirit of love, which helps us release our hurt and pain. They all come together to help us nurture the freedom of love and to evoke healing. Love is the most powerful teaching. Somebody in the Sweat may be going through a hard time, dealing with hurt or pain or trauma, but by invoking the spirit of these medicines, our spirits come together and we can push that pain out gently with love. At the end of the ceremony, when we open the door to the Sweat Lodge, you can see the steam leaving and taking our prayers with it, releasing the spirit out into the world and on to the spiritual realm.

As we bring each of four elements—fire, earth, water, and air—into Sweat Lodge, we are in ceremony at every stage. When we collect the lava rocks, we put down a little tobacco because we are in ceremony, and we say a prayer asking if we can use them. When we construct the lodge, we place sixteen willow branches in the ground and bend them to make perfect half-circles; then we tie all of those branches together to create the dome. My mom always says a prayer and places a pinch of tobacco in the hole before we put the willow branches in the ground, so that's a ceremony. When we harvest the medicines, we are in ceremony. When we chop the wood, we are in ceremony. When we build the fire, we are in ceremony. When we bring the lava rocks into the lodge, we thank each one and give them a blessing by placing a little bit of medicine on each. My mom always boils a bit of sage in the water that we use for Sweat Lodge. The entire process is spiritual, and in fact it's a spiritual process that began a very long time ago when the lava came out from the centre of the Earth. Every step has meaning, and all these things have to happen before we can bring the rocks inside the lodge, and before we put the medicine down and start to pray.

Each of the elements of ceremony brings their own wisdom with them. The trees that we use for firewood bring all the wisdom they have gathered from all they have witnessed since they first started growing from a little seed, rooting down into the earth and reaching up to the sun with their first leaves, like little hands trying to catch the sun's energy. Then you have the sage, the sweetgrass, and the tobacco, and all the medicines that carry their own specific teachings, which also become incorporated into ceremony. When we start to understand the teachings of each of those elements, we learn that they each have a spirit, and that everything has life and spirit within it. When you're in the Sweat Lodge, you can feel the spirit of the water and the rocks and the steam and all the medicines. They are all there to protect us, and that's why we need to protect them. That's our law. Through our ceremonies, we come to understand our law, and we build a spiritual connection to it.

Trauma is also a spirit. It's a pain spirit from a time when we were hurt that stays with us and continues to affect us. It's like an open wound that still hurts because it has not fully healed. When a traumatic event happens to someone, their senses are often fully engaged, and the things that they see or smell or hear in that moment can become imprinted on them. Maybe a song is playing, you are eating something, or a certain smell is in the air, and you come to associate that sensation with the traumatic event. When you later hear, taste, or smell whatever it is that you associate with the trauma, it can be triggering and can take you back to the traumatizing moment. In ceremony, the reverse happens: we come to associate certain senses with beautiful feelings. When you enter into ceremony, you smell sage or tobacco. You feel the heat of the rocks on your skin and the coolness of the earth you're sitting on. You hear the songs of the ancestors. All your senses become engaged and aware in the presence of ceremony. The next time you feel triggered by those things you associate with a traumatic event, you might light some sage or sing a song, and doing so will evoke the positive association that you have with ceremony. It can help to bring you back to a good place and reverse the traumatic associations. It might bring you back to your first Sweat Lodge when you left feeling so good, feeling that spirit still alive in you.

When I was younger, instead of looking at my pain and dealing with it, I drank and did drugs. It was as if I was taking painkillers to numb the pain of an open wound rather than treating the wound itself and allowing it to scar over. This just continued the negative spirit of the hurt and pain. My wounds didn't heal and scar over properly until I started going to ceremony. Now when my hurt and pain surface, I pray, and that helps bring me back to the place of nəč̓əmat. If I just look at my abalone shell or my feather or my medicines, I start to feel better even before I use them to smudge. My pain is a bit like the scar on my hand from chopping wood—it's still there, and it's a part of who I am, but it's no longer an open wound, and it doesn't hamper me. It doesn't hurt me; it doesn't slow me down. It has healed.

But I have to remain diligent because to this day I still carry a lot of hurt and pain from all of the abuse and intergenerational trauma I've experienced. I experienced severe abuse for a big part of my life, so it's no wonder that it still creeps up on me at times and expresses itself as fear, anxiety, and depression. I pray every day, and my first prayer is always for my kids. I have to stay focused because sometimes I feel like the drug and alcohol spirit might still be there, stalking me and waiting for a moment of vulnerability to ruin my life. I think of that place where my dad died, in the ugly stink bathroom at the bottom of the stairwell on the corner of Main and Hastings, and how I might have been one bad decision away from being there myself. We are born spiritually perfect, but once we experience trauma in our lives, we begin to spiral away from that state of perfection. Ceremony helps us reverse that spiral by dealing with our traumas in healthy ways, and it helps us to start spiralling in a better direction. Through ceremony, we can create a relationship with Spirit: it will love us back, feed us with good energy, and help push us forward. That powerful spirit of the sage, cedar, sweetgrass, or whatever medicines you use can replace the ugly spirit of drug or alcohol addiction. And if we do ceremony every day, it makes the path to fulfilling our prayers and our visions easier.

There was a time in my life after I had ended a relationship with a girlfriend I cared for deeply when my heart was broken. When two people come together and share a love for one another, their two spirits create a new spirit—the spirit of love. When you break up with somebody, that shared spirit between you begins to die. That's why it hurts so much—because something inside of you is dying. When I broke up with this girlfriend whom I loved, the spirit of that relationship was no longer there to feed my spirit with love anymore, and I missed that dearly. But after a couple of weeks, I realized that if my girlfriend had filled my soul by loving me, and if she was no longer there to do that, then I could fill my soul by loving myself. I started smudging for forty minutes each day, and I prayed really hard to express the sadness I was feeling. I tried to feel the sadness as deeply as I could and to hold on to that feeling for as long as I could every day. At certain points in my life, I mostly heard only negative affirmations about myself. Either directly or in subtler ways, I was constantly told things like, "You're stupid," "You're ugly," "You're weak," or "You're incapable." When I realized this, I started offering myself positive affirmations to replace those negative ones. I started telling myself, "Rueben is good. Rueben is strong. Rueben is smart. Rueben is capable. Rueben is happy." These were things that I didn't believe about myself, but after doing this for a period of time, the sadness eventually went away. One morning, I woke up and looked at myself in the mirror, and I gave myself butterflies. I had replaced the sadness with love. I was in love with myself, with my own being, with my mind, my body, and my soul. I loved myself the same way my girlfriend had loved me, and I was able to feed my spirit with that love. That's nəċəmat.

It was the same when I quit drinking. Rather than using alcohol to evade the pain I was feeling, I used ceremony to lean into the pain and gradually replace it with love. Once I had opened up the doors of healing and was able to love myself, I was also able to love my kids, my mom, and my family more. The more I dealt with all the issues in my life, the more I was able to love myself and love others. I started to notice that when I walked into the forest, I could feel the spirit of the trees again. I could go into the water and feel the spirit of the water. I could feel the spirit of the salmon and the salmonberry bush. I could open my eyes to the beauty of all that we are connected to as one spirit. That's nəċəmat.

When people learn about the suffering, pain, and abuse that Indigenous people have experienced in Canada, or when they see Native people on the streets in the Downtown Eastside of Vancouver, they often pity us and think that we need their help. But it's not just Indigenous people who need to heal from colonization; the colonizers need healing too. I pity the colonizers. On one side of the world, people are dying from material impoverishment, but on the other side of the world, people are dying from spiritual impoverishment. When I go downtown to the business district of Vancouver, I can see people's lack of connection with spirit, their lack of connection with their ancestors, and even their lack of connection with the spirit within themselves. When my kids were little, they called it Zombie Town, because nobody says hello, and nobody makes eye contact. There is no life in people's eyes. Their spirit has left them. Compare that to the Downtown Eastside, where people may be living on the streets and suffering from poverty, addiction, or mental illness, but people make eye contact and acknowledge each other way more than anywhere else in Vancouver. On the Downtown Eastside, people are suffering, but at least they look out for one another. They check in with each other, and they care for one another. They are a community.

For a lot of Indigenous people, Native spirituality is like riding a bike. Even if we've been disconnected from it for a while, it's still pretty familiar to us, and we can pick it back up quickly. For instance, when I first started Sweat Lodge, it wasn't as though I was coming in entirely green. From a young age, I was taught about our reciprocal relationship with the water. Even before ceremony had been reintroduced to the community, my Elders taught me lessons, such as how we always return shells or bones back to the water and say thanks after we eat from the river or the inlet. We may not have been praying in our ceremonies or in Sweat Lodge, but we still had those teachings. So, when I first went to Sweat Lodge, I realized that the teachings were a lot like the things that my grandpa had said, or that my mom and my aunties and uncles had taught me. They were always giving us teachings and imparting knowledge. Residential schools and the cultural genocide that was inflicted upon us blocked some of those teachings, but the teachings were still there, and when we started to listen again, they spoke to something that was deeply familiar to us.

But many settlers have been disconnected for so many generations that it's much harder for them to pick back up that connection
to Spirit. In some ways, society is better equipped to identify and fix
the types of problems that I've faced, such as alcoholism, addiction,
and trauma, even though society deals with those problems in problematic ways, by teaching people to cope in a dysfunctional society.
Colonial society is far less equipped to help people who are disconnected from their own spirit. It is not set up to help people who are
trying to be the same as everyone else, or who are pursuing money
over and above genuine connection with other human beings.
Instead we call that normal, and we even call that success. From a
very young age, we're taught to aspire to be part of the global one
percent that owns half the world's wealth. This lack of spirit is wide-
spread in our society, and when we're spiritually impoverished, we
make decisions that are harmful to ourselves, to society, and to the
Earth. Just look at the consequences in the world we live in today,
and imagine how different it would be if people were connected to
the spirit inside themselves and to the spirit that they share with all
other beings. Wouldn't it be amazing if we were all raised without
prejudice and hate? Imagine if we were raised to know that everything has Spirit and that we are connected to Spirit. Imagine if we
collectively enhanced our physical, mental, and spiritual growth in
ways that helped us connect to one another and everything around
us. Why wouldn't we want to strive for that?

It took the colonizing countries of Europe a couple of thousand
years to establish the racial and gender hierarchies that are part
and parcel of the colonial systems we live in today. In the process
of doing so, they killed tens of thousands of women, calling them
witches and breaking down matriarchal systems. They broke down
their own spiritual connections to nəċəmat. For how many generations have colonizers normalized their own trauma and lack of

spirit? Pushing aside and normalizing the disconnection from spirit is a form of trauma itself.

I have one friend who came to our ceremony and told me, "I don't know why I'm struggling. I've had a privileged life. My parents were always well off, and I'm a lawyer. I'm successful and doing well for myself. So, why do I struggle? Why can't I feel that goodness and freedom that you feel?" I told him to look at the medicine wheel. The medicine wheel teaches us that we have physical, mental, spiritual, and emotional aspects of our being. I asked him which one of those he was missing in his life.

He thought about it for a moment and said, "I'm missing Spirit." I asked him how long he had been missing Spirit, and he said, "My whole life." I said, "Is that all?" He didn't understand my question at first, so I said, "What about your parents—did they have a connection to Spirit?" He told me that they didn't either. I asked about his grandparents, and he said, "I don't think they were connected to Spirit either."

I said, "Holy smokes, bro! That's a long time to be disconnected from Spirit. That's at least three generations of spiritual neglect and spiritual trauma. It must be hard to work through that because your family hasn't been connected to Spirit for a long time. You say you've had a privileged life, and in some ways you have, but if you think about how long you've been disconnected from Spirit, whose life can we truly say is the privileged life?" The people who struggle the most in ceremony are people like my friend. I tell them to dig deep into their family history and find out how far back they would have to go to find that connection, because if they go back far enough, they will find that they have spiritual roots too. Every human being does. And if they can't go back far enough to find that connection from their ancestors, then we work to uncover that connection in other ways.

Sometimes when people have been living without Spirit for a long time, they resist it. They tell themselves they're happy as they are and that they don't need to care about their reciprocal relationship with the earth, the water, or the air. They don't bother trying to make things better; they just keep on living the way they have been in this dysfunctional society. That's also a form of trauma—it's a fight-or-flight response. But I think every human being in the world has loved someone. Maybe they love their kids or their parents or someone else, but that love can act as a starting point to reconnect with Spirit. Love itself is a reciprocal relationship of spirit with another. You can start to find the connection to Spirit by celebrating and exploring that feeling of love, and from there you might learn to feel that same love for the land, the water, the plants, the salmon, the air, and everything.

It took a lot of hard work for my lawyer friend to find that connection again, but eventually he did. In ceremony we call that work, because it really does take a lot of effort to release and shed all the hurt and the pain. In the capitalist world we live in, everyone is looking for easy answers, but there are no easy answers when it comes to healing our traumas and connecting with Spirit. You can't just show up at ceremony once and think you'll walk away fully healed and enlightened. It's a journey and a process of growth, and everybody grows in different ways. Creeks and streams all want to find their way to the ocean, but their pathways there are unique. Some water, like the Fraser River, rushes very powerfully and arrives at the ocean quickly. Other water meanders and takes longer, barely making it at all. Likewise, there's no singular path to spiritual growth.

The teachings of any religion or culture aren't inherently or fundamentally bad. Problems occur when religious beliefs are manipulated for destructive purposes and interpreted by people in ways that serve their own selfish interests. It's the same with the laws and constitutions of governments like Canada and the United States, which use the law to harm certain people for the benefit of others, or to advantage powerful corporations that are profiting from destructive activities. I think about how the Constitution of the United States was modelled on the Iroquois Confederacy, which was intended for goodness and to protect people, but those laws are often manipulated to benefit powerful interests. They were when we went to court against the Trans Mountain Pipeline expansion. People pick and choose bits and pieces of the law or of religious beliefs and use them to their own advantage. They even persecute people who are different than themselves, believing that what they're doing is the right thing, in the name of religious beliefs. They use religious and spiritual teachings to mess up the world.

My grandpa used to say that if you believe in a spiritual path, and if you follow that path in a good way, we can sit down and have a good soulful prayer together because the fundamentals of humanity are the same no matter what your religion may be. My grandpa did that, my uncle Len did that, and now I've done that in this battle against the pipeline. Grandpa said that when we share a moment like that with another, we're giving birth to a new spirit that we share with them.

That's one of the reasons we are taught not to turn away anyone who needs ceremony and who wants to come pray with us. We invite everyone in, and people join us from all walks of life. Despite all the abuse that my mom has experienced from the colonial system, despite all that, she welcomes everyone into our community and says, "Call me Ta'ah," which means Grandma. She has conjured up the forgiveness to open her arms to everyone, no matter who they are, and she says, "Come to my ceremony and call me Grandma. I'll take care of you. I'll help you heal." That's what my entire family says. Even as people who have suffered from the legacies and ongoing violence of colonization, we open our door and help people as best we can. We have helped thousands of people.

We try to show them a better way. No matter who you are, we'll do that for you when you come to us with sincerity. Some who come may not even care about the Tsleil-Waututh people or the homelands where these teachings come from. But maybe they'll learn by sitting with us in ceremony for a little while. Maybe they'll start to feel that connection to Spirit and that genuine love that they deserve. Maybe they will find the freedom to be themselves. Maybe, by experiencing that, they'll gain a better understanding of what we, as Indigenous Peoples, have been through.

Sometimes I go into ceremony, and I cry. Sometimes I go in there and release anger. Sometimes I go in there, and I laugh. Sometimes I meditate. I get in tune with who I am, with my spirit, with my ancestors, and I work on those relationships. But when I sit in Sweat Lodge and run ceremony, I think that's when I'm the best person I can be. When I'm in that space, I can deal with any hurt and pain that arises. Ceremony brings us back to a time when we were a little baby, born with no prejudice, no anger, no hate, and no judgment, and I want my life to emulate that moment. I want to be as I am in ceremony all the time, carrying myself in a good way. I want to practise ceremony as a way of life, not only for a couple of hours a week. And I want that for everyone else too. I want to practise ceremony as a way of life with my community, living in a state of nəc̓əmat, as our ancestors did. I was taught that if we allow ourselves to put our dysfunctions aside and have a really good ceremony, eventually that will happen.

One time I came out of the Sweat Lodge feeling almost dizzy with a sense that I was close to reaching a higher state of spiritual consciousness. I sat under a big pine tree and looked up at its branches hanging over me. It was a dark night, but I could still see the brightness of the spirit of this tree—it looked so radiant and beautiful. I could feel the tree's presence, and it gave me butterflies, as if I was standing beside someone I love. It gave me the healing I needed to deal with my sorrow, my hurt, and my pain. That's the feeling we get from ceremony. That feeling of connection with the tree is the feeling of oneness that is nəċəmat, and that's what we strive for. It's a type of spiritual love that's far more powerful than any love you've ever felt before. When we learn the lessons of the smudge, of the rocks, of the trees, of the songs, of all the elements that carry a spirit into Sweat Lodge, that's when we begin to see clearly and understand nəċəmat. Ceremony teaches us to be connected to that oneness of where we all come from, the oneness of the Creator. That's how we begin to see that everything has spirit, and that every-thing is therefore interconnected—that we are all related. These teachings come to me and help me understand nəċəmat in different ways. Some of these teachings aren't lessons that someone sat down and taught me—they came through ceremony, and they make sense. Then we take these teachings and apply them to the things we love.

If I start to understand the lessons of lava rock, for example, when we heat it up and bring it into ceremony, I can ask how to take its lessons and apply them in my life. By doing so, I begin to incor-porate myself into nəċəmat. I synchronize the rhythm that I carry within me with the rhythm of nəċəmat. Unfortunately, my rhythm was disrupted by colonization, residential schools, segregation, relo-cation, and all the things that I've already talked about. My rhythm was knocked out of sync. Just as the circle of life is a pattern, I have a pattern within me, but it was obstructed and violated. My pattern became destructive and led to abusive relationships and self-harm. When a difficult thing happens in our lives, such as a loved one pass-ing away, we tend to deal with it based on the patterns with which we are raised. So, if our pattern and our rhythm are destructive due to the intergenerational pain that we inherited, we tend to deal with that pain in destructive ways.

We go to ceremony to heal and change those patterns. When I go to Sweat Lodge, or when I smudge, I'm working to change the pattern of my own rhythm, my own circle of life, and I am learning how to apply this toward my kids and all the people in my life who I love, to all my relations. I tell people who come to ceremony that they might cry and feel a lot of sadness, but they're actually releasing something. Crying can be like a beautiful song that makes us feel better. No matter where people are in their process, if they surrender to the goodness of ceremony, they will feel the connection of Spirit, and they will feel better afterward. And if they're feeling that connection with Spirit, all clear-eyed and beautiful, then it's their responsibility to share that feeling by being loving, kind, and caring to those around them. If you allow Spirit to touch you in a beautiful way, your love for all the special people in your life will also be better.

So, I was looking up at that pine tree on that evening after Sweat Lodge, feeling its gentleness, its strength, and its energy. I was noticing how its branches reached up to the sky to catch the energy of the sun, and I was thinking about how its roots were anchored into the ground of our ancestors. I envisioned how the tree soaks up the water and nutrients from the earth, and how it takes in carbon dioxide and turns it into oxygen. I saw that the tree, just like humans, uses all four elements—fire, earth, water, and air. The reciprocal relationship of Spirit that I shared with this tree was revealing itself to me, and I was taking in all these lessons from it. I started to understand that I also need to catch the energy of the sun, the earth, the water, and the sky to feel the spirit within me. I have a spirit that must heal and be nourished and grow. My connection with this tree was teaching me to overcome my hurt and sadness. It was teaching me to stand tall and straight with my roots firmly anchored in the ground of my ancestors, and to see what I need to feed myself. It was a really beautiful experience, and that's how ceremony helps us take baby steps on the road to healing from the violence and traumas of colonization. That's how ceremony helps us pull ourselves out of the despair of that hurt and pain. And that's how we are winning.

Frank Supernault said the best way to thank him is by continuing these teachings, and that's why I run ceremony every week. That's why I've helped to create a ceremonial family, a Sun Dance family, and our Coast Salish ceremonial family. That's why we dedicate ourselves to creating change. I want to help feed people's spirits, so that their spirits start to reject those things they don't need in their life. No drugs or alcohol can make me feel as good as I do after a Sweat Lodge. No drugs or alcohol can make me feel as good as I do after ceremony in the mountains. No drugs or alcohol can make me feel as good as I do when I finish a Sun Dance. My spirit is fed in those moments. I think of my dad and others who passed away without feeling what I feel in ceremony, or connecting with Spirit in that way. They were robbed of the opportunity to feel that love of themselves and their own spirit connecting to the Creator and their ancestors, who are our angels. They were robbed of the experience of feeling that oneness of nəċəmat, and the freedom of receiving that love from the ancestors and the Creator. My dad didn't have that opportunity, nor did so many other people whom I loved, because the colonial system broke them down, and they died because of it.

That's why we run ceremony—to continue that dedication my grandpa had to feeding people's spirits so much that their spirits will them to make their lives better and to protect our lands, waters, and people. That's what my grandpa did; that's what my uncle Len did; that's what my mom did; that's what my brother Damian did; and now that's what my kids are doing. My kids tell me that I may help other people, but I have to remember to apply those same teachings to myself—that's my kids teaching me! We grow together, and we help each other.

So, we welcome you. We open our ceremonies to everybody. No matter who you are, or where you're from, we will welcome you. Despite all the hurt and pain that my mom has been through, despite what the colonial system did to my mom in residential school, and despite the racism that she still experiences today, she will turn to you and say, "Call me Ta'ah—I love you equally." Despite what my grandpa went through, and what my aunties and uncles went through, they had nothing but love in their hearts. That's the Tsleil-Waututh way. We know what it's like to be oppressed and to be hurt, to be walked on and abused, to experience injustice—we know that all too well. But that intergenerational pain has fostered compassion. The Tsleil-Waututh will pick people up. Yes, we've had bullies, and yes, there's been abuse in our community. Yes, horrible things have happened. But far more beautiful things have happened than all the bad things.

The colonial system nearly wiped out the Tsleil-Waututh people, first with disease and then by creating the residential schools designed to crush our spirits. But we rose up. Today the greed spirit still dominates the world, and the colonial system still exists. But we grew through all the adversity we have faced. Through our connection with Spirit, we now say, "No more. I will treat you like a human being. I'll treat you as you deserve to be treated." We lost so many people too young due to colonial suppression. My mom lost two husbands, yet she still turns around and says, "I will love you all." My aunties say, "I will love you all." My uncle Len said, "I will love you all." My grandpa said, "I will love you all." We know hurt and pain, but that hurt and pain, which was once an open wound, is now healing and that spirit of trauma has been transformed into a spirit of love and compassion. It turned into something that allows us to understand the pain of others. That's a feeling of freedom. And if we can alleviate some of that and show others a better way of life, then we will do that too. There's always room to heal, and as I say in my ceremonies, there's nothing wrong with making good people better.

What's happening now is that we're gathering strength to heal the wounds of colonization by using medicines to make our lives better as a community. We're picking ourselves up and brushing ourselves off. We're dealing with our hurt and pain by feeding ourselves with the fundamentals of love, respect, honour, dignity, pride, compassion, and we're applying these fundamentals to our mental, spiritual, emotional states of being. This is how it all comes together. My brothers and sisters and I are taking our teachings of smeńálh back into ceremony, and we're taking the teachings of nə́čəmat out into the world. We're incorporating these teachings of smeńálh and nə́čəmat into everything we do. We're growing together as a family.

Right across Turtle Island, I see beautiful brothers and sisters who are educated, cultural, and spiritual people. They've had a hard life, but they're doing something about it, and they're doing it together. They're teaching the next generations a better way to move forward and to surpass them. They're making a difference.

And we're coming together. We're collaborating with one another. We're taking lessons from our ceremonies; we're making them our way of life; and we're giving back to our people. Like the Thunderbird of old, we're taking back the tools of our ancestors, tools that are so easy to work with because they're the teachings of humanity and Spirit. We're remembering all

Rueben George. Image courtesy of Ben West.

the horrible things that happened to us in the past and standing up to the ways that colonization remains in effect today. We're fixing things to make them better for the future. And it's working. There's a whole generation of powerful Indigenous warriors coming up, like my son, who told me, "I'm the first generation that hasn't been taught that our cultural and spiritual ways are the way of the Devil, and that we will go to hell if we practise them."

CHAPTER 3

The Last of the Human Beings

In 1994, Leonard Crow Dog Sr. visited our Tsleil-Waututh Sweat Lodge and led us in a pipe ceremony. I was twenty-four years old at the time, and I had no idea who Leonard Crow Dog was, but he reminded me of my grandpa, so I sat beside him at the ceremony. We started chatting, and he asked me all about the salmon and the water and the land and our people. After the ceremony, he pointed to me and said, "This young man is going to come to the Lakota lands to Sun Dance with me." I said, "Okay, I could do that, I guess." I didn't really think much of it at the time.

The following year, I sobered up and went to the treatment centre where my uncle Lee Brown was working as a spiritual teacher. I asked Lee lots of questions about Sun Dance, until he finally told me, "Rueben, if you really want to know about Sun Dance, just go to one and you'll learn what it's all about." I had no job, no money, and no car, but three weeks later I found myself at a Sun Dance in Arizona.

At that first Sun Dance, I really wanted to dance but the Chiefs didn't want me to, so I had to accept that. I returned home and soon after met a bunch of people who were on their way to Crow Dog's Sun Dance out in Lakota territory. They invited me to join along, so I set off with them driving across the country. Once we arrived, Crow Dog greeted us and said, "I'm glad you've come to dance." I asked one of the other guys if I could dance with him, and Crow Dog said, "I already told you that you would dance with me, remember?" It was only then that I remembered Crow Dog had told me that when he visited our community. It all fell together so beautifully, and I danced for the first time.

Leonard Crow Dog was an iconic Indigenous spiritual leader. He had the gift to make miracles happen. I witnessed him heal people and make miracles happen right in front of me. I saw him pick up a red-hot lava rock and place it back down without it leaving even the faintest mark on his hand. Even when I saw these things with my own eyes, I'd catch myself questioning if what I'd seen was real. I'd ask myself how it happened, and I'd try to come up with an explanation instead of accepting what had happened. But asking *how* is not part of being. You don't have to question what you are a part of.

In those moments of doubt, I was reverting to the teachings passed down intergenerationally from the ugly residential schools, which told us that if you believe in Spirit, then you go to hell. That's where my blockages still lie at times. A key lesson of Indigenous spirituality is that you don't have to *try* to be spiritual; you have to learn to accept that you already are. I didn't have to try to be a part of the miracle that my spiritual leader Crow Dog was showing me because I *am* a part of it. It's being, not trying. It's existence. It's happening. It's experiencing the oneness of Spirit and the higher state of spiritual consciousness. It's like nəčəmat—one heart, one mind, one prayer. Crow Dog taught me that. He'd say that the only thing that separates me from doing what he did was my own belief. Crow Dog really wanted to help me by sharing his teachings with me, and he never gave up on me. He once told me he had heard that a lot of ceremonial leaders were using drugs and alcohol, and he said, "You are good, son, and you will stay that way. If I find out that you have not been good, you will hear from me." Boy, did I ever remember that.

Sun Dance is a physically exhausting ceremony during which we strive to reach a higher state of spiritual consciousness by dancing for four days while refraining from eating or drinking water. Sun Dance was banned by the colonial governments of Canada and the United States in the late nineteenth and early twentieth centuries, but the tradition was carried on in secrecy during that time. About five or six thousand people attended Crow Dog's Sun Dance each summer, and of those about five or six hundred were dancers. It's a very trying ceremony that tests one's spiritual endurance and teaches us not to quit. Sun Dance gives you the strength to persevere and makes you feel like you can endure any struggle and win. But it gets really hard. It's like the canoe race in a way. You want to quit, and you're so tired, but you dig deep and summon the energy needed to continue.

That first year, I started feeling dizzy and had a headache by the third day. I'd never had a headache before in my life, so I got quite concerned and I broke my fast, which knocked me out of the trance and prayer. My brother told me that the reason for my headache was because I was passing between the physical and spiritual realms. He said I was having a physical memory of being born, which is why my head felt like it was being squished. He told me that if I pushed past that feeling, I would enter a spiritual state. The following year I did push through, and that's exactly what happened. But even to this day, when I'm at Sun Dance, I sometimes think, What the heck am I doing? One time I asked an Elder, "Uncle, do you ever get that feeling where you wonder why you are doing this?" He told me, "Every single time!" Sometimes I tell myself that I don't want to do it that day, or for the next four days, but then I pray and do it anyway. Because I don't give up in ceremony, I learn not to give up in all the other struggles I encounter in life.

The Chiefs, aunties, brothers, and sisters in our Sun Dance family really took me under their wing. They took time to teach me. I had some wonderful teachers in my Sun Dance family, like Chief Oscar and Elena Moreno, Carter Camp and his sister Casey Camp-Horinek, Chief Crow Dog and the whole Crow Dog family, Chief Tomas, Auntie Sharon, Robert Nahanee, the Pompana family, Frank Supernault, Phil Lane Jr., Gene Iron Shell, JC Lucas, Darrell and Theresa Fenton-Bob, Lee Brown, Joe David, Sam George, Richard Baker Hoya, and many more. I've been very fortunate to have such beautiful spiritual mentors, and I've done my best to apply their teachings in my life. After my fifth year of dancing with Crow Dog, he came to me and said that he was going to make me a Sun Dance Chief, but I didn't want to be a Chief because I was really committed to my role as a ceremonial fireman. I told Crow Dog that there were lots of other good people he could choose to be a Chief. I said, "Johnny can do it!" But Crow Dog insisted that it would be me. I objected again, but he said, "Son, sometimes it's not me who's telling you these things," and then he turned and walked away. There were many Lakota Chiefs gathered, as well as others from across North America, and one of the Elders came to me and said, "What the heck do you think you are doing saying no to him like that?" Another one of my spiritual uncles, Oscar Moreno, told me, "You better go talk to Uncle Crow Dog and accept that chieftainship." But I was still committed to my role of making fires, which I had been doing for years. My brother Tracy Nordio once told me that the slower you go with this way of life, the faster you'll grow, and I thought he was right. That's why I wasn't in a hurry to become a Chief.

It wasn't until five years later, after I was ten years sober and had been dancing for a decade, that I told Crow Dog I was ready to be a Chief. But even then, I told him that I also wanted to remain a fireman until I finished the fourteen-year commitment I had made to myself. One of my brothers told me that once you're a fireman, you're always a fireman, and even now that I'm a Chief, I still think of myself as a fireman. At the same time, I listened to my uncle who told me that I had to take my chieftainship. Crow Dog put his hands on my head and started praying. Once he finished praying, he said, "Okay, you are a Chief now." I asked him when my training would begin, and he said, "Your training began the moment we met." I walked out into the ceremony and lined up with the other Chiefs. One of them said, "Hey, you're finally a Chief!" They had already been calling me Chief for years, and when I asked them why they called me that, they said, "Because Uncle Crow Dog said you were!"

In Sun Dance ceremony, we strive to reach a higher state of spiritual consciousness that allows us to access the Creator, the oneness of everything. But first you have to understand that you have a spirit inside yourself, because you can't open up a doorway to the Creator if you haven't even opened a doorway to your own spirit. We also need to understand the spirit of our ancestors. That's who we pray to—our angels. A first step is to learn smudge.

People from many different Indigenous cultures practise smudge in different ways, but every ceremony brings together four elements: fire, earth, water, and air. When we smudge, we use a bundle of medicine—this might be sage, sweetgrass, tobacco, or cedar—which represents the earth element. We place the medicine in an abalone shell, which represents water because it comes from the sea. Then we light that medicine, which introduces fire, and finally we fan the fire using an eagle feather, which brings in the air element. In some Native American cultures, an eagle feather is used because the eagle flies closest to the Creator and it's a beautiful messenger. When you bring these elements together with intention, it gives birth to a new spirit, which is the smoke that we use to smudge. That smoke is a spirit, and you can pray to that spirit for love and goodness, for heal-ing, or for clearing energy. When you pray to the spirit of the smoke, you want to allow yourself to go where the smoke takes you. You allow yourself to be connected to it, and for it to be part of you.

All the religious and spiritual traditions that I have seen use the elements of fire, earth, water, and air in their ceremonies in some way. These are also the elements that we need for life. In the absence of any one of these elements, life can't exist; it's a stroke of luck that we have them all here on Earth. The four elements also relate to the four directions—north, south, east, and west—and each direction has its own teachings. They are also the four seasons of the year and the four stages of life: infant, youth, adult, and Elder. They are the four aspects of our being: physical, spiritual, mental, and emotional. In ceremony, the four elements come together to give birth to healing. When people smudge, they clear their eyes to help them see. They clear their mouth to help them say good things. They clear their ears to listen well, and they clear their mind to think positively and heal any negative thoughts. They clear their heart and their spirit. They brush away any hurt, pain, or negativity. That's what a smudge is: it's a ceremony to clear energy and open things up.

If you're inside when you smudge, the smoke from your smudge will fill that space, which makes that room holy and also clears a space for your spirit to expand to the size of the room. When the spirits of everyone in that space expand in this way, their spirits overlap with one another. The smudge creates a space in which each heartbeat ripples, like a pebble thrown into a pond, pushing out any energy that's not needed, giving us the healing we need. And when we do that collectively, together in a ceremonial room pray-ing to push things out, helping each other with our spirits overlap-ping, it's as if multiple pebbles are thrown into that pond, pushing out different energies, whether they be the trauma of colonization, the pain of alcoholism, or some other wound.

Smudge is important, and so is pipe ceremony. In pipe ceremony, we're taught that the bowl of the pipe represents the female, and the stem of the pipe represents the male. The female and the male spirits exist within each and every one of us, so we have to celebrate them both. When the tobacco is lit, a new spirit is born, and as we draw from the pipe, we take that spirit inside ourselves and it becomes part of us. As we inhale the smoke, we are part of the process of two spirits coming together, and we pray for all the things we need in our life, such as love, honour, respect, dignity, and pride. As we exhale the smoke, we release our prayers with that spirit out into the world. JC Lucas gave me my first pipe when I was twenty-six years old. I made fire for him for a couple of years, and he gifted me with beautiful, gentle, and powerful teachings. Not long after I received that pipe, a woman told me, "Now that you have a pipe, you have to walk like a priest." I remember thinking, I don't want to walk like a priest because that's not who I am! I just want to walk like myself, guided by my teachings. I thought that if I had to walk like a priest, then I wouldn't be able to walk like myself, and I might diminish part of my unique gift by doing that. But smudge and pipe ceremonies are two important steps to take before participating in Sun Dance.

A lot of the spiritual mentors in my life have been men, and I think that's partly because I didn't have a father growing up. Both my father and my stepfather died from overdoses, and my mom never dated again after that because it had been too devastating for her to have both of her husbands die in that way. So, I was kind of adopted by my spiritual fathers. Some of them like Lee Brown, Phil Lane Jr., JC Lucas, Crow Dog, Sam George, Robert Nahanee, and Frank Supernault, knew me when I was young and messed up.

They are all so proud of who I have become today. Other teachers came along later, like Joe David, Richard Baker Hoya, Calvin Pompana, and Darrell Bob. These are all beautiful men who have been so loving and caring to me. It makes me emotional thinking about how they were always there for me and about all that they taught me. I came to them with some pretty horrible problems, terrible things that were done to me or that I had done, yet they always accepted and loved me unconditionally.

Now that I'm a mentor to others, I try to do the same. I accept people who come to me for help without judgment. I run my ceremony every Sunday, and I work hard for those who need it. I give back because of all the gifts that I received from others. My life is dedicated to helping my Indigenous brothers and sisters across North and South America because I've been lucky enough to experience that connection of Spirit, and it has helped me. My life is dedicated to fighting for Indigenous rights and for the Earth, just as my grandpa did until the day he died. I'm lucky to have received the gifts of Sun Dance and the other ceremonies that I've been a part of.

LIVING IN CEREMONY

My grandpa used to say that we are the last of the human beings, but thankfully I've found others on my travels. They are the Indigenous Peoples of the world. I've travelled to Brazil, Central America, Mexico, throughout the U.S., Australia, and Southeast Asia, and everywhere I've been, I've always found people who have experienced feeling connected to Spirit. Whenever we meet with someone on our travels, we always sit and do ceremony first because that's where we draw our strength from. Their ceremonies may be different from ours, but they're all connected to the same thing. They all incorporate fire, earth, water, and air. They connect to the fundamentals of love, honour, respect, dignity, pride, compassion, truth, knowledge, wisdom, and all those good things. Having that connection to nəčəmat is something you can't fake. A Mayan Elder from Guatemala once came up to me and asked, "Grandson, do you know why we love each other?" I said, "Yes, Grandma, I do." Then she said, "The stars are a reflection of heaven, and I see the stars in your eyes, like you see them in mine, because we have both experienced heaven, which is the higher state of spiritual consciousness that we access through ceremony." That's what Sun Dance and other ceremonies teach us. And that's the driving force behind all the work that we do.

I was in the Amazon with my spiritual father Phil Lane Jr., and we attended a ceremony with over a thousand Indigenous dancers all dressed in their full regalia, painted black and red, wearing huge headdresses and beautiful anklets and bracelets. They were lined up with their families to form a massive circle in a space about the size of two soccer fields. As Phil and I approached the circle, the Chief who was running the ceremony pointed to us and invited us to get our own regalia and join the ceremony. Afterward, a large family of fifty people who were all giggling walked up behind us. I could tell something was going on, but I wasn't sure what. Suddenly they hollered and ran toward us, grabbed us by the arms, and basically said, "You're ours now." They started singing and stomping in sequence; it sounded like thunder. Next thing I knew, I looked back and there were a thousand Amazonian people dancing behind us, with us in the lead. We danced in a big circle for what must have been four hours, and then we danced right into the feast hall. They all had the most beautiful eyes.

One thing I've noticed when I've travelled and met with Indigenous Peoples in other parts of the world is that they often don't have protocols the way we do. We need to have ceremonial protocols because we have people joining us from all walks of life, including people who have never been a part of any kind of ceremony before but have been called to join us. We use protocols to teach people how to conduct themselves and what it is that we're working toward. But in some places, they don't need protocols because they are living on the land in such a way that they're already in a reciprocal relationship with Spirit; they're living ceremony all day every day. I've also seen this with some of my relatives from nations like the Nisga'a and the Haida, who are living their spiritual practice by being on the land, working with the land, protecting and loving the land. As I harvested devil's club with my brother Mansell Griffin from the Nisga'a Nation, he told me stories about how they harvest the plant, how they use the needles on the stalk, and how to use the bark for medicines. Those stories were a form of ceremony and connection, and he was living it.

I witnessed that deep connection to Spirit when we were meeting with some Chiefs in Panama. Their village was deep in the jungle, and I had to take a water taxi for several hours to get there. As I was waiting for the others, I noticed this guy walk into the jungle with a machete. Two and a half hours later, I saw him return, dragging a tree with him to be used for firewood. I could see the roots dangling from the bottom of the trunk, so I knew that he had walked until he found a tree that had already fallen over on its own. He didn't chop down a living tree that was closer. I thought about the loving connection this man must have had: to be surrounded by what seemed like millions of trees, and he walked through the jungle until he found one already dead, so he didn't have to kill a living tree.

Our relations in Peru tell me that in order to understand the medicinal properties of plants, they exclusively eat one plant until that plant speaks to them. They told me that it could take a couple of hours, or it could take a week. They do this with every single plant, one at a time, and there are thousands of plants in the Amazon jungle. Some might be good for your liver, and some for your heart, and they learn this by using the plant until it speaks through them.

Only once they've mastered every plant can they then learn the mother and the father medicines of the jungle. It was like this with our people too. Many of the world's medications derive from Indigenous plant medicines from the Americas. When people ask me how the ancestors learned these medicines, I tell them that the plants spoke to the ancestors, and the ancestors listened.

I imagine how beautiful it must have been for our Tsleil-Waututh ancestors to live in such a spiritual and ceremonial state twenty-four hours a day throughout their entire lives. Our ancestors were profoundly connected to everything around them. My mom told me about how much pain her grandparents felt when they witnessed the destruction of the forests and the desecration of the water. When they witnessed living beings treated as resources ripe for extraction, they said it felt like having your hair grabbed and torn right out of your scalp. That's also how it felt for those people I met in Panama who wouldn't even cut down a tree for firewood despite being surrounded by lush forests in every direction. My grandpa came from that perspective too. He once told me that when you harm something, you are taking away its spirit, so you have to walk gently and respectfully on the land. That's the place where we come from.

I've had Elders tell me that the feeling they have in ceremony is what life used to feel like every day. They're in the twilight of their lives, and when they reflect on their lives, they don't say, "I wish I had made a million dollars," "I wish I had travelled the world," "I wish I had been more successful," or "I wish I had done this or that." What the Elders say is "I wish it could be like it was before, when we were connected to everything around us and every day felt like being in ceremony." That's all they wish for. That's nəc̓əmat.

Traditionally we lived in longhouses together with multiple generations of our entire extended family—our parents, grandparents, aunties, uncles, siblings, all under one big roof. We spent so much time together and we would have known each other so well that we could have communicated without many words. Perhaps a certain look would communicate a message, almost like telepathy. The Elders would have been in the presence of the children all day, teaching them the fundamentals of respect, generosity, and how to be a better human being. We would have applied these teachings to everything we did. It was how we took care of each other, how we took care of the lands and waters, and how we governed ourselves. We had abundant food. We had art, song, and leisure time, and we lived in ceremony. When we say that we are stewards of our land since time out of mind, this is how we were. We were nəčəmat with everything. One heart with everything. That's what it was like prior to colonization. That's where we come from, and that's where we're returning. There are four levels of spiritual consciousness, and the most holy people that we know today are only at the top of the first level. These are beautiful spiritual leaders, including some of my teachers and mentors. But we come from a place and time when every clan around the world had someone who could make miracles happen and heal their people. That's also what we're heading back to. There is no limit to our capacity for spiritual growth, and I think that deep down every human being wants that connection.

We are born into this world with nothing, and we leave the world with nothing. As I've mentioned, we don't believe in hell or the Devil; we believe that we're born spiritually perfect, and our ceremonies help us return to that beautiful place of spiritual perfection, which is nəčəmat. When one of our relations passes away, the spiritual relationship we share with them continues. I've had some dear friends pass away, like my friend Lacy. It took me a long time and multiple ceremonies to be able to pray to her because I missed her so much. In the Sun Dance I run for the Pompana family, we do a wiping-away-the-tears ceremony for those who recently passed to the other side. If we're feeling sadness when people pass, then we're holding on to them, and we have to let them go. Only once we've let them go can we address them as an ancestor and ask them to help us with our prayers.

MY CHILDREN

When I was twenty-six, I met this beautiful woman from Tulalip Tribes in Washington State named Debbie. She was super intelligent, very cultural, and really ambitious. When we met, she had already finished her first degree and was just a couple of months shy of completing her master's. I'd been sober for a year and was doing well, but there were parts of my old lifestyle that I was still struggling to change, and my relationship to women was one of them. I'd been to treatment three times and had started learning all these beautiful cultural teachings. I had also started college. I was on the right path, trying to heal, but it was a transition; I was still a little rough around the edges. I didn't feel very good about myself, and I suffered from anxiety. I could drink away the anxiety, at least temporarily, but once I quit drinking, the anxiety was still there and I didn't have the tools I needed to deal with it yet.

On one of my first dates with Debbie, we went to a fortune teller. Some of the things the fortune teller told us were actually quite amazing. For instance, she told me, "There's a wolf in you," and our clan is the Wolf Clan, the children of Takaya. She also said that in three weeks I was going to receive something very ceremonial; I received a ceremonial pipe three weeks later. Then she looked at Debbie and me and said, "Wow, you two are going to be in each other's lives for a very long time. You are going to have a boy and a girl." Debbie looked at the lady and said, "Do I have to?" And, of course, that's exactly what happened.

When I first held my son, Cedar, and my daughter, Kayah, I could see how much they loved me, and it made me cry. I was amazed that such little, tiny human beings could love so unconditionally. They introduced a whole new love to my life, far more powerful and profound than anything I'd ever experienced before. I still feel that way when I see them today. But when I first became a father, I felt undeserving of that love because I'd been such an ugly and negative person. I had done so many horrible things to people, beating up men and mistreating women, that I didn't think I was worthy of their love. I remember holding my son as his eyes peered up at me and thinking how incredible it was that he was alive. At that moment, I thought to myself, I'm going to change. I never really had a dad in my life, and I was determined to be there for my kids. The only problem was that I didn't know squat about babies. I didn't even know how to hold a baby, let alone raise a baby! I thought I was too big to hold a tiny baby; I was scared that I would drop them. But Debbie and I read books about how to be parents, and I loved everything about being a dad—holding my kids, loving them, and feeding them. I would sit them on my chest and sing traditional Coast Salish songs as they fell asleep. It was a phenomenal gift to have them in my life.

Debbie and I separated when the kids were nine and seven years old, but those early years were happy times for us as a young family. We lived on Commercial Drive in East Vancouver, and we didn't have much money but we were very happy. People really loved us. We'd be out shopping on Commercial Drive and people would insist on paying for us because we didn't have enough money, but we wouldn't take handouts. I'd say, "We don't need it. We're fine." And we were fine; we could pay for everything we needed. I remember walking up Commercial Drive one time and a guy asked us if we had any change. I gave him our last two dollars. Debbie couldn't believe I did that. But they were happy times.

We moved to Washington State, and I took care of the kids for the first couple of years while Debbie was working on her career. She's become very successful, and among many other achievements, she worked on the reauthorization of the Violence Against Women

Act. She's a very powerful speaker and a strong advocate for our people, as well as an excellent mom. While I was looking after our young kids during those early years, I tried my best to raise them in accordance with our cultural and spiritual teachings. I was raised with spiritual restrictions placed upon my beliefs, and we wanted to raise our kids without any such restrictions. They weren't raised to believe that Native spirituality is the Devil's work, or that you'd suffer eternally if you didn't believe in God. They weren't raised with the doubt about our spiritual connection that was fostered by residential schools. We taught them to have no doubt about the potential of what they can achieve and to have no limit to their ability to make miracles happen, just as our Tsleil-Waututh ancestors did when their spiritual connection to the land and waters allowed the medicines to speak to them.

At no point can you come to ceremony and think that you're done and have nothing else to work on. We can always go deeper with our connection to one another. We can always go deeper with our connection to our ancestors, to the Creator, and to the oneness of Spirit. We can always continue to grow and explore the vast amount of freedom that our spirit has in connection with all beings. When we run ceremony, it's our responsibility to teach people to surpass us. If we're not doing this, we're failing. I'm happy to say that people in my ceremonial community have surpassed me and are now teaching me. They've learned their gifts, and they're sharing them with us. We taught them that the capacity for spiritual growth is infinite—that we always have room to grow no matter where we're at.

I was always taught—in our Sweat Lodge, in Sun Dance, and in all our ceremonial homes—that we do not succeed in our role as teachers and leaders unless we teach others to reach a higher state of spiritual consciousness than we have. The same applies to parenting. I remember telling my kids that they were going to be bigger and more powerful than their mom and me. They would say, "No

way, we can't possibly be as strong and as capable as you two are!"
But they already are: they're fearless in pursuing what they want to
achieve and how they want to be. By the time they were teens, they
were as culturally and spiritually aware as I was in my early forties.
As a teenager, Kayah told me that she didn't want any more gifts
for birthdays or holidays; instead she wanted to offer warm clothes,
blankets, and toiletries to people who were living on the street and
in need. Cedar said the same thing. That's the way they think. When
they see someone on the street, they don't think, there's a homeless
person; they think, there's a person who was pushed down by a
colonial system that hurt and abused them and their family. They
know this because they have felt this pain themselves: colonialism
hurt our whole family, including them. Now that they're in their
twenties, I see them stepping up as leaders and making a difference.
Cedar once saved up about $10,000 and could have used that
money to go travelling or to go on holiday, but instead he spent it on
the work he was doing to protect our lands and waters from the Trans
Mountain Pipeline. This is just one example of his giving heart and
his willingness to do anything to stand up for what he believes in.
They both stand in solidarity with other Indigenous communities
protecting their lands, waters, and people all over the globe.

When Cedar and Kayah first started travelling internationally
on their own, they were still teenagers, and they wanted to go to
places where Indigenous people get killed for doing the type of
work that they do. I told them they couldn't. I was so afraid for
them that I'd phone the event organizers and I'd say, "You better
pick up my kids at the airport, and make sure someone is with
them at all times!" But they were fearless. They incorporate our
culture, our spirituality, and our law into everything they do, and
they are one hundred percent committed to protecting what we
love. In their short lifetimes, my son has already spoken at the United
Nations five times, and my daughter has spoken there four times.

Rueben George and daughter Kayah George.   Cedar George-Parker at a climate strike.

They get nervous, and I tell them to be the voice for the people who couldn't speak, like many of our ancestors who have passed. I still see them as I did when they were first born, looking up at me with their beautiful brown eyes, even though my son is taller than me now and they are surpassing me spiritually. They go far beyond where I'm at, and then they come back and teach me new things about how to grow and be a good person. They teach me and show me a better way. Sometimes I forget the teachings that I taught them, but they turn those teachings back on me and tell me that I have to try harder, that I have to be better, that I have to grow, too, that these are my teachings and I have to apply them to myself. I'm excited to see what is to come for my kids in the future and all they're going to accomplish. They're amazing young people, and despite all they've been through, they're both so strong and talented at what they do. I'm proud of them and I love them dearly.

But I wasn't always a great parent. I failed my kids in a lot of ways, and the intergenerational harm of colonization was a big reason for that. They've experienced other traumas too. Twenty-two kids in their Tulalip-Marysville community died in one year, including five in a high school shooting. They knew every one of those kids. That was devastating and traumatizing, and they worked hard to heal from that, and now we're healing together. They want Spirit to be incorporated into everything they do. Cedar will call up the Elders in our community and sit with them, asking them questions about our culture and our people. And I'll never forget holding the university invitation letters that Kayah received and admiring how smart she is. She said, "Dad, you know what's going to dictate the path of my future, right?" I said, "Yes, I'm holding it—it's the letters from all these universities." She said, "No, Dad, it's our culture and spirituality that will guide my path." I cried because I was so proud of the person she'd become.

At home, our conversations are often about our Tsleil-Waututh culture and spirituality. The house is often full of smudge. Now that my kids are older, they sometimes run the Sweat Lodge in my place. They both come to Sun Dance with me too. Kayah started to Sun Dance at age twelve. Her first year, I told her to try it for two days only, because dancing with no food or water for sixteen hours a day under the scorching summer sun of South Dakota is a really difficult thing to do. The following year, she came back and completed the entire four days. At one point, she was lying on the ground and said to me, "Dad, I'm crying but I don't have any more tears because there's no water left in my body. I can't do it. I can't get up. Give me a reason to get up." I said, "Your grandma Addy." Then she stood up and started dancing again, for her grandma Addy who had cancer. That made me cry. On the last day of Sun Dance that year, Crow Dog Jr. came to me and said, "After today your daughter will be a Sun Dancer." He was impressed, and so was I. She's such a strong, powerful woman.

We grew together as a family. When my kids were babies, my mom came to Sweat Lodge and made an oath with my son and daughter. I remember my mom wrapped the kids in towels and passed them to me through the Sweat Lodge doors. Holding my little babies, I imagined that the Sweat Lodge must have been a really familiar place for them because it emulates the womb. As I closed the door to the lodge, I thought how powerful it was to have three generations of Georges praying together, sitting in ceremony, and saying, "No more! No more hurt. We're going to break the cycle of trauma. We are going to move forward and heal together." Three generations of Tsleil-Waututh saying that we would do our best to raise my son and daughter together as a family, to instill the teachings of smeńálh and of our culture and spirituality. By sitting in ceremony together, we were saying that we would raise them with no boundaries on their spiritual capabilities and that we would give them the tools they need for healing, because hurt and pain still happens. Today my grandnieces and grandnephews join us, too, which makes it four generations.

The colonial system that created the residential schools remains with us today. My own cousin served thirty years in prison for breaking and entering, whereas the man who shot Colten Boushie was acquitted. Our children are still being taken away from our families and placed in the child welfare system. We still face these problems of systemic racism. But my kids are far better equipped to deal with these problems today than we were at their age because we started giving them the tools they would need from the moment they were born. When my children were born, we buried their placenta and planted a cedar tree on top so that no matter where they travelled in the world, their roots would always be here in Coast Salish territory. My mom gives my kids the same teachings of smeńálh that I received. She teaches them to carry themselves in a good way, and we do it together as a family just as we do in the canoe and just as we do in our ceremonies.

We do many ceremonies together as a family. In the Sweat Lodge, we ask for the energy that rejuvenates Mother Earth to rejuvenate us back to that place where we had no prejudice, no anger, no hate, and no judgment. We ask for that energy to keep our eyes clear. And my kids are good that way. My nephews and nieces are good that way. Cedar and Kayah may often be the voice for the Tsleil-Waututh Nation, but I'll tell you any of my nephews or nieces could do that—they can all speak eloquently, and they all have. Coming from the dysfunction that I grew up with, it's been incredible to see this next generation carry themselves so well, stepping up culturally and spiritually to protect what we love. As the George family and as a nation, we've been healing together and it's been really impressive.

We're not perfect by any means, and I'm not saying we are. There were some traumatic things that were passed down. I failed as a dad in a lot of ways, but my kids healed with me. They both sat me down with their pipes and created a safe ceremonial space to address me and the ways I have failed them. They spoke to me about what I did wrong and how that caused them hurt, pain, and anxiety. And I listened. It was hard to hear that I had failed in these ways, but it was important for my kids to say what they needed to say so we could work to heal those wounds. They've done this multiple times, whenever things came up that they needed to talk about with me. We talk so that we can heal and move forward, just as my mom did with me. My mom told me she knew she had hurt me, and she invited me to say whatever I needed to say to help me let it go. I did the same with my kids. I understood that it was the colonial system and residential schools that caused the hurt and pain that my mom, my grandpa, and my brothers experienced. My kids understand this too. That's how smart they are: they can see that there's intergenerational pain affecting our family and that we have to heal for at least as long as it's been affecting us. Again, it was hard to hear how I had diminished their beautiful light, but I'm grateful that they had the teachings and spiritual tools they needed to sit me down and tell

Left to right: Cedar George-Parker, Kayah George, and Rueben George.

Kayah George. Image courtesy of Morgan Hoyt / *The Everett Clipper.*

Ta'ah Amy George and Cedar George-Parker.

me what they needed to say. They hold me accountable, and I'm really proud of them for that. They're so loving, caring, and respectful. Together we're saying, "No more! The intergenerational pain stops here. Let's move forward together as a family." And it's working.

GIVING THANKS

Two of my cousins and my sister all married into the Chehalis Nation, so we have close family ties there. My sister Cecily is such a shining example of how to be a good person who lives with righteousness. Despite everything we went through, she has a big heart and is always smiling. She could be giving you heck and she'd still be smiling at you, speaking so compellingly that you'd probably be nodding in agreement—before realizing that you just got in trouble! Cecily is a powerful matriarch of our family, the glue that holds us together. She's always been like that. Growing up in an ugly house of violence, where my brothers and I were exchanging blows, she would jump between us and break up the fights even though she was much smaller than us. Despite all the problems we went through as children, Cecily remained kind and beautiful. She had the strength of being born into smeńálh.

Since she was young, my sister was a canoe race champion, and she continues to embody the lessons of the canoe today. She lifts up everyone around her and makes everyone feel special and that we're all in the canoe together. She's a canoe champion, and she's a champion for our family. There's no spirit that can break her, and she married someone who is just like her in that way. Chad Paul also has a big, beautiful heart. He's younger than us, but he's one of our spiritual mentors and a strong leader. The two of them have taught us a lot about our Coast Salish way of life. They know intimate details about all the plants and animals, like how migration patterns are affected by changes in weather, or the slight variations in the colour of salmon that come from different rivers. I once heard someone ask Chad how to identify different species of salmon, and he said, "By looking at them." For Chad, this was so obvious that it was like asking someone how they know what a house is when they see one. But he went on to point out all the little differences between the species that other people might not ever notice.

Cecily and Chad are always out on the land hunting and fishing, providing our family with traditional foods. They are constantly giving me elk, deer, moose, and salmon. It's amazing that people can live through hell and still be so generous and giving. They eat a lot of fish and crab and seasonal fruit. They live a beautiful way of life, and it motivates me to do the same. It's because of them that about ninety percent of the meat I eat is wild. I didn't grow up with the luxury of eating a traditional diet, but I'm only one generation removed from that, and my kids have made the decision to eat that way too. It makes you feel happy just being around Cecily and Chad because they are always smiling and always giving. Their love and generosity is boundless, and they do so much for our people.

I've travelled throughout the world, and the Coast Salish territories are still among the most astonishingly beautiful places I've ever seen. It's like paradise. Today we went swimming and fishing with Cecily and Chad in crystal-clear pools at the bottom of a canyon. The waters were so clean that you could drink them. A cathedral of trees towered atop cliffs that enclosed us on both sides. As we were walking along a river at the bottom of the canyon, we noticed this delicate little purple flower, perhaps no more than a centimetre in diameter, growing all on its own on the side of a sheer cliff. The cliff face was bare rock, almost completely vertical—you'd never think that any soil could settle there, let alone that it could provide habitat for such a beautiful little flower. It's a real miracle to think that a seed must have landed there at some point, set roots into the smallest hairline crack, grown, and blossomed at the very moment we were there to see it. What are the odds of that? But there it was, so peaceful and serene. It was a gift. There aren't a lot of visitors who come to that spot, so we would have been the only ones to appreciate its beauty; it was so striking that it drew us in to acknowledge its being. I think of the lessons of perseverance and strength that that little flower teaches us, surviving against all odds with minimal soil or sunlight at the bottom of a rocky canyon alongside such a fast-flowing river. It persevered and blossomed into something that was strikingly beautiful.

Equipped with our snorkels and flippers, we got into the cold glacial water and swam in these large cascading pools among hundreds of little minnows, some larger trout, and probably a hundred spring salmon. When you're in the water, you see all the life around you under the surface, and the beauty of the valley and the trees above. The salmon couldn't quite figure out who I was or what I was doing there, but they didn't seem spooked by me either. They may have thought I was a big fish. I had my speargun with me and I wanted to take home a salmon to feed my family. I felt a rush of adrenaline as I pointed my gun toward the fish and pulled the trigger, but I kept missing. I took at least ten shots and missed every time. I wasn't even close. Then I remembered a story I was told about my grandpa long ago.

When my grandfather was young, he was out hunting with his dad, George Sla-holt. They came across a deer that was facing them straight on, about thirty yards away. My grandfather raised his rifle and prepared to shoot, but his father said, "Wait! Lower your gun, son. That's not how we do it." My great-grandfather explained that we must always take a moment to pray for an animal before we take its life because the animal has a spirit. It's our relative, and it is going to sacrifice its life for us. He explained that when we pray, we must thank the animal for giving its life to feed our family. We must express our appreciation for the sacrifice it's making, and we must explain how we will use its hide to make drums or buckskin for clothes, its hooves for ceremony, and its bones for tools—how we will use everything. So, my grandpa closed his eyes and started praying. He told the deer that he was sorry that he was about to take its life, but that he needed to feed his family. He told the deer that it was his brother. He expressed gratitude and told the deer that he would use everything it gave him in a good way. He prayed in all the ways that his father had taught him. When Grandpa opened his eyes, the deer was less than five metres away and its side was completely exposed to my grandpa, giving him an easy shot. My grandfather spoke to the deer in his prayer, and the deer sacrificed itself to my grandfather. That's the reciprocal relationship and connection of nəċəmat. Those are our teachings.

I remembered that story while I was in the water, frustrated that I kept missing the salmon with my speargun. After many failed attempts, I popped up from the water and Cecily asked me if I had prayed, and I realized that in all the excitement of the moment, I had forgotten to. I stopped and took a moment to give a little prayer of thanks, acknowledging the sacrifice that the salmon made by giving their lives to feed our people. Shortly after that, I felt something in the water graze my ankle. I turned back thinking it was my daughter, but nothing was there. Perhaps it had been a piece of wood or something floating by. But then I felt something touch my hip. I turned around, and again nothing was there. The rapids were getting a little bit faster as I moved further upriver, and my visibility was less clear. Then something hit my shoulder. I turned, and this time, to my astonishment, I saw a big, beautiful spring salmon staring right at me, just a foot away. I swear that we had this moment where we were both sort of stared, mesmerized, at each other. I looked at the salmon and smiled, and I thought, Wow, prayers really work! As we locked eyes, I said thank you, and then it turned its side right in front of me and offered its life to feed my family. The long metal spear from my speargun is attached to a thick fishing line, and when I shot it, the big salmon started swimming away while attached to the line, and it was pulling me further into the rapids. I had to kick really hard to get back up to the surface, but when I did, I yelled out to my family and my friends, "I got one!" Everyone was really excited for me; at that point I'd probably been in the water for about forty-five minutes with nothing to show for my efforts. I came to shore and pulled the salmon out of the water. It was so big and strong that it had bent the spear. But I was just so happy.

That's the power of our prayer. At the very least, that salmon needed to be communicated with in prayer; it needed to be asked if we could take it home to feed our family, as my ancestors have done for many thousands of years. The majestic salmon are so important to the life of the Coast Salish people, just as the buffalo were to the plains people. They're such an integral part of our culture and we love, respect, and honour them. We take care of the salmon, and they take care of us. Eating salmon is one thing, but being in that water with the salmon, being connected to the salmon and to where it comes from, is a really beautiful thing. I thought about how these thousands of salmon swam all the way from the middle of the Pacific Ocean, then hundreds of kilometres upriver to this very spot. I reflected on all the things that need to come together as nəc̓əmat to feed that salmon, and to feed that delicate purple flower we had seen growing from the cliff.

It's a big contrast with going to the grocery store. I once saw a transport truck at the side of the highway that had tipped over while delivering chickens to be slaughtered. The crates of chickens from the truck had burst open and the chickens had fallen out, but instead of running away to freedom, they were standing there beside their broken crates at the side of the highway. Their whole existence had been in those crates, and they didn't know anything else. Their chance at freedom was right there before them, and they didn't even know what to do with it. Their spirits had been too badly broken.

And people are eating those broken-spirited beings. That's very different from eating wild salmon, deer, or elk. After you are in the water with the salmon, the experience of eating the salmon turns into something more—it turns into a ceremony and a giving thanks. But that's not the society we live in, and I can't help but think that a lot of human beings are just like those chickens. Are those chickens much different from all the people going to work at the same time, finishing work at the same time, going to sleep at the same time, living in the same routine day after day, year after year? If you put people in a forest, would they notice that beautiful purple flower? Would they feel the crystal-clear river cleansing their spirit? Or are they like those chickens at the side of the highway, whose freedom was mere steps away and they didn't know what to do with it?

At the end of the day, I laid back floating in the water and allowed the current to carry me downriver. As I drifted along, I looked up at the cliffs and the sky, and I noticed the moss hanging off the rocky ledges, and the giant trees growing atop bluffs that rose a hundred feet above us at some points. And as I floated along, I finished my prayer by giving thanks. I gave thanks to the salmon for giving its life. I gave thanks to the ancestors for passing on their teachings. I gave thanks for the beauty of all that we protect, and for our law that obliges us to protect it.

We returned to the city with our spirits fed and with this precious gift of a fifteen-pound salmon to feed our families and loved ones, just as my ancestors have been fed for thousands of years. Our hearts and our spirits were nourished from everything we'd done. Nourished from spending time with my wonderful sister, her husband, and my niece. Nourished from swimming in that clean cold water. Nourished from being with the salmon, and nourished from being with each other. Just like in smudge, when the elements of fire, earth, water, and air all come together and give birth to a new spirit, the elements came together as we bathed in those waters. Our spirits

Rueben George's favourite place to go swimming.

were cleansed and connected with the spirit of that place. That's nəćəmat. That daze that we felt as we headed home, almost like we were spiritually drunk, was the feeling of our spirits being full. That's nəćəmat. Tomorrow I will bring the guts and bones of the salmon to the ocean to give them back, as my mom taught me to.

COLONIAL SOCIETY AND COLONIAL ECOLOGIES

It's not just Indigenous Peoples who are being held down by the colonial system: Black and Brown communities and poor White people are suppressed too. When I lived in Tulalip, the closest grocery store was a Walmart that had opened on tribal lands in the late 1990s. I would run in there to grab whatever quick groceries we needed, and over the years, I came to recognize this one White woman who worked there as a cashier. Recently, while visiting Tulalip, I stopped in at that Walmart for the first time in years and I saw her again. She was straightening the Walmart uniform shirt of a young man, and I heard her say to him, "Have a good day at work, son." He was the second generation of his family to work at Walmart.

We believe that everyone has a gift and boundless creative and spiritual potential. However, the colonial order squashes people's dreams by placing limits on what they can aspire to do in their lives. Starting in elementary school, it's drilled into kids' heads that if they are really smart, then the greatest thing they can dream of becoming is a doctor or a lawyer. This limits what people believe they're capable of. We believe that each of us has a unique gift, but in colonial society, even the children of the elite aren't permitted to pursue their gifts because they're placed in an education system that systematically strips away their independence and creativity by teaching them to do what they're told. The children arrive at school at the same time, they eat at the same time, and they take recess at the same time. They all play the same games, which are all based on competition. They're told that if they don't look the same as everyone else, then they're some kind of a weirdo. All these different children each try to be the same. Even the children's families all strive to be the same, modelling themselves on idealized images they see in the media. The end result is that kids start acting like robots. They've been told their whole lives what to do, how to think, what they are capable of, and what their careers should be. They grow up to perpetuate the colonial system because they think nothing else is possible. For First Nations kids, all the horrible things that happened to our people in residential schools are placed on top of this, and that's how you end up with three or four generations of families living on the streets in Vancouver's Downtown Eastside.

In colonial society, we're given these cookie-cutter expectations and constantly told that we have to look a certain way, act a certain way, be a certain size, or else we're considered a loser. But in our culture and teachings, we're taught to celebrate and honour the uniqueness of each person. We see our differences as gifts, and we support each other in tapping into the boundless potential of those gifts in ways that better our community collectively. We help each other get in touch with our individuality and grow into better human beings. For instance, my brother Damian is what the Lakota and Dakota would call a heyoka, which is a gift. You never know what a heyoka is going to do or say. A lot of times they're funny without meaning to be, and when they want to be funny, they're really funny, but you just never know what they're going to do or say. One time Damian came to sit beside me at ceremony and I told him, "Don't sit beside me. You're loud and you'll make me laugh, and you'll get us both in trouble!" I told him I was going to sit somewhere else, but he said, "I'll still talk to you even if you sit over there." Sure enough, I started laughing, and an annoyed Elder at the front of the ceremony said, "Who's laughing back there?" But when they looked back and saw that it was Damian and me, they said, "Oh, it's those rascals!" and they couldn't help but start laughing with us. Thunder and lightning spirits have this ability to ease the tension in serious situations, like at funerals or memorials, and it's accepted by most of our family that that's their gift.

Maybe being heyoka helped my brother in his life. He and another one of my cousins never really drank or did drugs in a community where nearly everybody else did. They were strong that way. They saw that it wasn't good for them, for our family, or for our community. I always thought it was incredible that he chose sobriety despite living in a community with so much drinking and drug use, but maybe his heyoka spirit helped him do the opposite of what everybody else was doing. By choosing that, he led us all to a better life. He became one of our spiritual leaders at a very young age. As a young man, only a couple of years older than me, he taught me a lot, and I was always grateful for that. He used his fierce, strong, and funny heyoka spirit to persevere, heal, and become the beautiful man that he is today.

The spiritual aura of a heyoka is really powerful and can be ten times larger than that of other people, which also makes them super sensitive while they are growing up and still learning to be heyoka. One of my best friends, Curtis, is also a heyoka. When he first started coming to ceremony with us, he would roll on the ground in anguish. He couldn't take it, and I'd be sitting there thinking, what the heck is up with this guy? He'd been sober for around a decade already, but he couldn't seem to handle the Sweat. Then we realized that other people's prayers move through him because he's heyoka. If people's hurt and pain is not being released, it will go straight to him. He feels their sadness, anger, or trauma directly. He learned how to release all those feelings so that he no longer experienced the anguish. We started to work together to make use of his gifts. I would hand him the water bucket and medicines, and he would splash water on the rocks to make the Sweat Lodge really hot and help people release the hurt and pain they were holding. So now when there's a feeling that people are holding back in ceremony, or when we feel like the energy needs to shift, I'll pass Curtis the bucket. We just look at each other and know what to do. He pours water on the rocks and prays, and he manages to reverse the energy in ways that help people release. Heyoka spirits have an ability to flip the energy in a room because they're opposites, and that's what Curtis would do in ceremony.

My son, Cedar, is also a heyoka, and sometimes funerals are too intense for him to attend. He's on pins and needles because he can feel everyone's sadness and he takes it all on, so sometimes he chooses not to put himself in that space. He has been like that since he was a small child. One day we were driving, and a deer jumped out from the side of the road and flew over the hood of the car in front of us. Just before colliding with that car, the deer tensed its whole body in fear, bracing for the impact, and Cedar did the exact same thing in that moment. He straightened out his whole body and froze just like the deer. I think the spirit of that animal swept over our car and Cedar felt it. He was only three or four years old at the time, and he started crying, "Why did it have to die?" He could feel the energy of that deer in a way the rest of us could not, and I knew right then that he was heyoka. Following that incident, I had a talk with him about being heyoka and he seemed to understand. As parents, we've always encouraged him to find and embrace that spirit and all the gifts that come with it. Today, whenever somebody is upset or has some bad news, he can feel their pain and tries to help them. When I'm hurting, I can't hide it from him, and he will drop everything to be by my side and make sure I know I'm not alone. He's always there for me when I need him, whether it be for help with ceremony, work, or family matters.

Not long ago, everyone in our societies was celebrated for their gifts. Some excelled at working with traditional medicines, and others at farming or hunting. Some were incredible artists, and others were leaders of the community. Everyone was different, and they were all supported and celebrated for the gifts that they carried. After developing those gifts, people would use them to give back to their community, just as we ask people today to share the love and the goodness that they walk away with in ceremony. We are coming back to that now, but colonial society strips that creativity and difference away from people rather than honouring it. Sometimes when I see someone who's supporting a harmful cause or who doesn't believe in their ability to enhance their community and make the world a better place for future generations, I wonder what their gift is. I wonder what creative potential they have that they haven't been encouraged to explore and develop. It makes me feel sad. It's sad that we normalize a dysfunctional situation and tell ourselves that there is nothing we can do about it. We adapt, we accept, and we ignore the problems that are right in front of our faces in order to survive. It's like someone who's been incarcerated for so long and become so institutionalized that they can no longer function outside prison. In a certain way, we're all institutionalized, locked up in closed minds and closed hearts, choosing to look away from the violence, pain, and abuse around us. There are disasters happening all over the world every day. Australia is burning. Indonesia is flooding. Lots of people are talking about these problems, but very few are actually standing up to take the actions needed to do something about it. Instead we stare at our smartphones, numbing ourselves from the pain. Studies show that people perceive time as passing by faster because they aren't present in the moment. They are forgoing the opportunity to have a beautiful relationship with one another and all living things.

When our spiritual connection is severed, we don't make decisions that are right for the Earth; we don't make decisions that are right for our relationships with the four elements; and we don't make decisions that are right for our relationships with other human beings. We ignore the destruction, the warfare, the homelessness, the hunger, and the addiction because we don't recognize that everything and everyone has a spirit that must be honoured and cherished. We are so far away from that person in Panama who didn't want to chop down a living tree for firewood, who couldn't bear the thought of harming it unnecessarily.

During the time that we've been suppressed, colonial governments developed laws that allow them to destroy the Earth and the things that we love. In my short lifetime, the world's wildlife populations have declined by nearly seventy percent. The oil companies are draining fossil fuels from the ground for profit, and they're aided and abetted by governments that offer them subsidies and create laws to allow them to do that. People are told it's all about jobs, but other countries create jobs by investing in renewable energy. What it's really about is rich people getting richer. The colonial governments create laws to buttress a broken economic system that marginalizes not only First Nations but also that lady and her son working at Walmart. The system crushes people's dreams of sharing their gifts in ways that could better their communities and help them accomplish beautiful things, all in the name of making money.

As much as the environment has changed in the last fifty years, these changes are only going to accelerate in the years and decades ahead. My son and daughter took six months to travel the world because it won't be the same in five or ten years from now. It's been predicted that global fish stocks will completely collapse by 2050. Our future generations may not know what it is to taste fish. How messed up is that? The colonial system will put a price tag on anything, even its own future generations. Our law is based in our reciprocal relationships with the lands and waters, which are being ruined before our eyes. It's like holding a loved one and watching them slowly die in your arms.

Not long ago, prior to the colonization of our lands and people, every stream on the north shore of Vancouver had abundant trout and salmon in it. Even when I was a kid, you would see thousands of little salmon and trout fry swimming down every stream and creek in the spring. I loved them because they were so tiny that they made even the smallest stream look like an epic rushing river. I remember seeing schools of what looked like hundreds of thousands, if not millions, of silver minnows in the ocean. We could never catch them, but they looked really cool. I haven't seen that since I was a kid. Back then, the waters were so clear and clean that you could drink from any creek, stream, or river. They weren't full of the toxic pollutants that they are today. The shores of the inlet were lined with rocks covered in barnacles, and once you walked about fifteen yards out, you could feel the cool muddy sand under your feet. Another twenty yards out was where the long eelgrass would grow. We noticed that the eelgrass grew further and further from shore with every passing year. It started receding really quickly.

The last time I saw any eelgrass out there at all was around 1995, just before my kids were born. Today when you walk out there, the floor beneath your feet feels mucky and oily; it doesn't feel the way it used to.

When I was in my early twenties, we were told that we couldn't go swimming in certain places anymore because the waters were too dirty. Growing up, I'd see many of our people out by the water on a hot summer's evening as the sun was going down, playing and swimming, or lying out on the rocks. We were raised to be out there on the water. Today you don't see kids out there. We used the waters for ceremonial bathing between Sweat Lodge rounds, and we've been told not to do that because the fecal coliform levels are too high. I still bathe in the ocean, but I have to bring a bucket of clean water with me so I can rinse my ears, eyes, nose, and mouth immediately after I get out.

It makes me sad to think that the seaweed that was abundant on our beaches when I was a child is now gone. The fish that were the basis of our food system for many thousands of years are slowly dying off. Humpback whales are washing ashore all along the West Coast. I remember being out on the shore of the inlet in the mid-'90s, making a fire for my uncle Len's Sweat Lodge, looking out past Whey-ah-wichen toward the Second Narrows Bridge, and we could see fish jumping out of the water for miles into the distance. You don't see that too often anymore. One day, somebody from our community opened a clam and it was filled with this ugly, sludgy-looking muck; we knew something was badly wrong. Not long after that, we were told that we could no longer eat the clams or shellfish from the inlet because they were full of biotoxins. That was a massive blow to our food sovereignty and culture: eighty-five percent of our traditional diet came from those waters. I didn't want to eat the Dungeness crab anymore either because it tasted different. We never had to worry about where the salmon was or how much we could catch each year because it was so abundant. One time when we were kids, my brother jumped off this really high cliff that we called Cooks, which was probably ninety or a hundred feet high, and he landed right on top of a salmon. He completely knocked it out, and so he grabbed it and we took it home to eat for dinner. That's how abundant the salmon were back then. These days there are so few salmon that we have to count them in all the rivers to ensure that their populations are strong enough for us to fish. We still see lots of deer, racoon, skunk, and bear around our territory, and that's a good thing, but one reason we're seeing them more often is because they're coming out of the woods hungry and in search of food.

In addition to the oil refinery and the Westridge Marine Terminal that sit on the shores of the Burrard Inlet, we have radioactive uranium shipped through our waters. There were significant oil spills in the inlet in 1973 and 2007. There's also a chlorine plant on our shores that produces and transports tens of thousands of tons of chlorine each year. Chlorine is a highly toxic chemical, so that's a major danger, especially considering that we're located along a major seismic fault line. Then there are the giant piles of bright-yellow sulphur on our shores, piled as high as a five- or six-storey building. That stuff is produced as a by-product of the fossil fuel industries and brought here to be stored on our territories, right at the edge of the inlet. The cement plants on the inlet are probably the worst contributors to local air pollution and carbon emissions—although the coal port ships millions of tons through the inlet each year to international markets where it is combusted, wreaking havoc on everything, so it depends on how you measure that. In addition to all of this, massive volumes of grains are shipped through the inlet, and there are two cargo container terminals that ship and receive commodities from all over the world. Between 1970 and 2010, the total volume of cargo handled by the Port of Vancouver grew more than fourfold, and much of that cargo came right through our waters. Underwater noise pollution from international shipping has had detrimental effects on local orcas, which are endangered and rarely enter the Burrard Inlet anymore. All of this has been driven by colonization and the removal of our people from our lands and waters.

I once watched an old documentary about my grandpa that had footage from the 1970s of him sitting on a beach I've been to many times in my life. In that film, my grandpa says that because of pollution and industrial encroachment on our territory, "Our children cannot enjoy the days that I used to enjoy." He says that living on the land the way he did as a child is "just memories for me." He had the foresight back then to see that his children and grandchildren would not experience the world the way he experienced it. He could see that everything was dying. My grandpa was hurt when he saw this destruction because he knew that everything has a spirit. He was hurt when they polluted the water because he knew that the water has a spirit. He was hurt when he saw a tree being cut down because he knew that tree had a spirit. How would his parents and grandparents feel if they saw what the world has turned into today? I can't imagine how hurt and disgusted the ancestors would be if they were alive today and knew that wildlife populations have been reduced by nearly seventy percent in my short lifetime. I can't imagine how sad they would be to see that the abundance of salmon—at one time in every creek, stream, and river on our territory—is gone, or that our people can't eat out of the inlet anymore. I can't imagine my grandparents or great-grandparents witnessing the glaciers melting or the hurricanes and floods happening where they shouldn't be. I can't imagine the hurt and pain they would feel to see the world burning. Being so connected to Spirit as they were, how would they feel if they knew that, despite all the destruction that's already been caused, people continue to make choices that harm other people and harm the Earth? They would ask, "How can you no longer be one with everything and experience nəȼəmat?" And it's not only our ancestors who would be devastated to see the damage caused by the colonial system; all the ancestors across Canada would feel that pain. People say that all these fires and floods are the new normal, but they're not. It's going to get worse, and we need to do something about it now. Yet the government tells us that the only way for us to help ourselves is to buy into the same colonial system that caused this devastation in the first place.

It all makes me think of something a Buddhist monk said to me once. I asked him what Buddhists believe in, and he told me he believed that everything wants to be happy. A little tiny mouse will live its life just trying to be happy. It will eat food, have babies, and do things that make it happy. It will seek to live where food is abundant and where it does not have to fear predators. So, we might ask why our society is structured in a way that reduces our happiness and diminishes our reciprocal relationship with Spirit. I think of all those fish, and the barnacles, and the eelgrass, and the inlet itself, just trying to be happy. But instead their homes are polluted, their lives are disrupted, their health is compromised; they are starving, getting sick, and dying. We believe that everything has a spirit: the seaweed, the clams, the Dungeness crabs, the salmon, and the inlet itself. They have all been so good to us, and we always made sure that we gave back, like when my mom would tell us to bring the fishbones back to the water to keep the cycle going. Everything has a spirit, and we are connected to that spirit, so when things go missing, I sort of see it as part of the spirit of that place going missing.

It's not just the spirit of the environment that is missing—I see it in our human communities as well. I remember when we met with Justin Trudeau's Cabinet, there was a moment when I looked across the table at some of his ministers and I thought, I'm so sorry that you are messed up. I'm so sorry that you won't have an opportunity to let Spirit touch your heart. I'm so sorry that you don't understand nəċəmat. I'm so sorry that you are such pitiful human beings. They are so colonized that they think we're crazy for wanting something different. But why wouldn't we all want to experience the feeling of loving our children more, loving our parents, our siblings, our partner, and the Earth more? Why wouldn't we want to experience that profound love for the water, and the trees, and the forests, and the lands, and the mountains, and the clouds, and the sunsets? Or that loving connection to a beautiful plant with its green stem and leaves, reaching out to catch the sun and blossoming into a magnificent colourful flower, sharing sweet smells for the world to enjoy? There is such immense beauty in the world, and only when we start to see that a spirit exists in everything can we begin to see the extent of that beauty. Our own spirits are crying out for us to open up to that connection. People are yearning to be fed by that connection someway, somehow. Their spirits are hungry to be part of nəċəmat, and we're going to show them how. It all hurts, and it bothers me, but at the same time we can harness that pain and use it as motivation to make things better.

Indigenous Peoples are like the canaries in the coal mine. When the canaries start dying, it's a sign that everything else has started dying too. We are not the only ones who are being hurt. And that's what I told Trudeau's Cabinet. The Canadian state and its extractive industries have harmed our people for so long, but the truth is that they've been harming themselves this whole time as well. In accordance with the teachings of smeńálh, it's my job to help them see that. So, I told Trudeau's ministers that if they were too stuck in their own greed to make responsible choices for their own future generations, then we were going to do it for them. My people say no because the Earth is dying and we need to do something about it not only for the future generations of Tsleil-Waututh but also for the future generations of everyone.

Just as every living being seeks happiness, they also try to protect what they love, and that's what we do as Tsleil-Waututh. The inlet may be dirty, it may be polluted, but it's still our mother and we will protect and heal it. It's part of our law to take care of everything on Mother Earth, and that includes even taking care of Trudeau, his Cabinet, and their future generations. We have to make those choices for them because they're so addicted and dependent on fossil fuels that they're incapable of making the right decisions for themselves. They think we're stopping progress and trying to seek revenge by harming them. But I told them we're trying to save them from themselves. Because if they win, everybody loses. If we win, everybody wins. And we're winning.

I pray for this nation of Canadians to wake up, because it's not too late. If the Tsleil-Waututh Nation can clean the waters of the biggest port in Canada well enough to eat clams from our inlet for the first time in forty years, if we can restore the salmon count and reintroduce elk into our territory, then just imagine what we could do collectively. There's not much time left. Fires are getting worse each year throughout British Columbia and the world. In the winter of 2021, floods cut off overland access from Vancouver to the rest of the country. If it hasn't affected you yet, it's coming. Don't be a chicken that escaped from its crate and then staring at freedom didn't know what to do with it. We know what to do, and the key is tapping into who you were before you were colonized by this shitty system that we live in. We have hope for everybody to no longer be a prisoner of colonial thinking. We want happiness for everybody, like that little mouse. We want people to experience the freedom of nəćəmat—a reciprocal relationship to Spirit, to the ancestors, to the Creator, to the lands, to the water, and to all beings. We have hope for everyone to create change. If our nation can do that, then Canada can too.

CHAPTER 4

Warrior Up!

Our fight against the Trans Mountain Pipeline expansion began in 2010. Rex Weyler, one of the co-founders of Greenpeace, got a phone call asking if he knew why there were so many oil tankers out in the Burrard Inlet. Rex looked into it and learned about Kinder Morgan's plans to twin the existing Trans Mountain Pipeline. This project would triple the volume of crude bitumen and other fossil fuel products that the pipeline moves daily from the tar sands in Alberta to tidewater on the shores of our inlet. It would also lead to a nearly sevenfold increase in oil tanker traffic through the fragile marine ecosystems of the inlet and the Salish Sea. An oil spill in these waters, or anywhere along the path of this pipeline, would have long-lasting and devastating ecological consequences.

Rex wanted to put a stop to this project, but as a long-time environmental activist, he was smart enough to realize that he would need First Nations support to do so. He called up his friend Ben West and asked him if he knew any Native folks who could help him. Ben said, "No, but let's go find some!" The two of them started driving around the rez looking for some First Nations people to partner with. That didn't work out so well for them though; I think they were too nervous to actually talk to anyone, so they sort of drove really slowly and creepily around the rez, staring out their car windows at people. But Rex and Ben had another friend who told them that she knew a guy who was really well connected with Indigenous communities across North America. That guy was Phil Lane Jr.

Phil Lane Jr. is one of my spiritual fathers and a spiritual brother to my uncle Len. When I was a kid, I would often see them together. Phil's father was well known internationally for taking the Dakota spiritual message around the world, and one of his uncles was Vine Deloria Jr., the renowned author and visionary who spent his life defending Indigenous rights and speaking out against colonialism. Phil is my adopted father. I call him Papa. He has shared a lot with me. We've travelled together to conferences in France, Brazil, and Panama, and we've met with spiritual leaders from all over the world. We've always made a good team working together. Not too many people know how many degrees Phil has, or that he was an associate professor for many years. He's a real intellectual, but to me and many others, he has always been more of a spiritual person and a very caring mentor, a lot like my grandfather was. Rex and Ben were put in touch with Phil, and Papa Phil told them, "I know the perfect guy for this—my son Rueben."

Papa Phil asked me to attend a meeting in a big house up in the British Properties, which is one of the wealthiest neighbourhoods in Greater Vancouver, if not all of Canada. I didn't quite know what I was getting myself into, who I was going to meet with, or what we were going to talk about, but as a steward of our lands and waters, it seemed natural that we should be at a meeting like this since it was directly concerned with our unceded territories. I was with my buddy Curtis Ahenakew, and before we stepped into that meeting, we said a little prayer to remind ourselves not to change anything about who we were, no matter who we were meeting with, because you never

Rueben George with Papa Phil Lane Jr. Image courtesy of Nancy Bleck.

know what people in the British Properties might think about us. We prayed that we would always speak our truth wherever we were.

There were about twenty key environmental leaders and organizers gathered at the house, and they all turned out to be good people. Many of them later became our friends and key allies. We went around in a circle, everyone taking a turn to speak. They spoke about Kinder Morgan's plans to expand the pipeline and explained how it would lead to a sharp rise in oil tankers navigating through the inlet, each carrying hundreds of thousands of barrels of this toxic substance. They talked about the lasting impacts of the *Exxon Valdez* oil spill and the potential consequences if such a spill were to happen here. They discussed the environmental impacts of ports, and how increased tanker traffic would impact the inlet's ecology. Curtis and I listened to everyone in the circle before we spoke. I sensed a bit of nervousness in the room because it seemed like people felt that this movement should be Indigenous-led, and they were eager to work with us, but they didn't know what we were thinking.

Once everyone else had spoken, Curtis said, "This is wrong, and I will die putting a stop to this if I have to." I looked at him and thought, Cripes! I guess we'll have to stop this then, because I don't want Curtis to die! Then it was my turn to speak, and I explained a little more about why we would do this by talking about our nation's history and our connection to the lands and waters. After we spoke, I sensed a lot of relief from people, knowing that we would stand with them.

I left that meeting feeling like something very significant that would require a lot of my time and attention moving forward had just happened. I also thought about how these waters feed us and have fed our ancestors since time immemorial. I thought about how our First Mother has given us so much and how I had to do something to protect her. I thought about all the other polluting industries already on the inlet—the oil refineries, the giant sulphur piles, the shipping of coal, and the uranium. I thought about all the rivers and streams in our territory that had been abundant with trout and salmon when I was a kid, and how my kids didn't get to experience that. I thought about all these things, and I knew that my life was about to change. I had to do something.

There were also Elders from the Squamish, Tsleil-Waututh, and Lakota nations at that meeting, and they told the group, "We will help you, and we will let you help us, but first we want to show you why we want to do this. We want to show you Indigenous law, and that law comes from our culture and spirituality. So, if you want to work with us, you'll first have to come to ceremony for a while to learn a little bit of our law. Only once you've done that will we work with you." We wanted them to come to ceremony for six months before we did any business, so they would understand our spiritual connection to the lands and waters that we were working to protect. They were very receptive to this invitation, so a bunch of these environmental leaders all started coming to Sweat Lodge with our community to learn from me and my spiritual teachers, Robert Nahanee and Papa Phil Lane Jr.

In ceremony and Sweat Lodge, we taught them why we were choosing to take a stand to defend the inlet. As I've discussed before, in the Sweat Lodge we use each of the four elements: fire, earth, water, and air. We wanted our environmentalist allies to learn that you can fall in love with these elements through ceremony, and once you do, you will feel compelled to protect them from the greed that destroys them. We showed them how every part of the Sweat Lodge is ceremony—gathering the rocks, chopping the wood, making the fire, singing the songs. We wanted to show them that all those ceremonies add up to the oneness to which we belong, and how it doesn't make sense to hurt something that we're a part of. When we experience the oneness of Spirit, the higher state of spiritual consciousness, our spirit starts to require it; we want to feel that goodness all the time. That's what we showed them, and only after a few months of sitting in ceremony together did we sit down and talk about how we could work together to stop the Trans Mountain Pipeline expansion. Rex Weyler later said that sitting together in ceremony like that not only helped to foster a reciprocal relationship with the lands and waters but also built a reciprocal relationship amongst each of us. It brought us all closer and helped to create a beautiful movement and a community of resistance.

Pretty early on in this battle, I sought advice from some Elders whom I Sun Danced with at Leonard Crow Dog's, down in South Dakota. Some of the Elders there had been involved in the American Indian Movement and were at the Wounded Knee Occupation at Pine Ridge in the 1970s—people like Russell Means, Carter Camp, and of course Crow Dog himself. As seasoned warriors, they were among the first people I turned to for guidance on how to approach this fight against Kinder Morgan and the pipeline. I went to see Carter Camp and said, "Uncle, I'm going to be fighting this pipeline, and I need some advice. There are many powerful people against us. How can we win?" Carter sat down with me and shared some important teachings. He talked with me about the importance of Indigenous law, which he said is grounded in our culture and our spirituality. He told me that I was already living our law through ceremony. He talked to me about fire, earth, water, and air, and how we must protect the sacred. He told me, "You're a warrior, and warriors stand up for their lands and waters and people. This is our sacred responsibility."

To be a warrior is to take up the sacred obligation to protect that which we love and that which we are a part of. It's an obligation to protect the sacred. An obligation, grounded in Indigenous law and learned through ceremony, to protect our reciprocal relationship with fire, earth, water, and air. Our ceremonies teach us that the four elements all carry spirit. They feed us, they love us, and they help us heal from our wounds. When I leave ceremony, I feel refreshed. I feel free of all the hurt and trauma that I've experienced from colonization and systemic racism. When we're called to be a warrior, it's a bit like that feeling we have after ceremony because we have to put aside our deep wounds and focus on protecting what we love. The Tsleil-Waututh are water people. Our First Mother is the water, and we have a relationship with the water that dates back to the beginning of time. We go to the water as a community for cleansing, and we love it. I would do anything to protect my kids and my family, and we feel the same about our water. That's what I thought about when Carter told me to be a warrior, to protect what we love, and to protect who we are.

The other crucial guidance that Carter offered me was that we needed to make sure we had the support of our community from the outset. This advice was especially pertinent because we had not officially secured the support of the Tsleil-Waututh Nation, so we were still on a bit of shaky ground in this regard. Very early on, with only a day's notice, I was asked to speak about the pipeline at a Vancouver city council meeting. Admittedly, I didn't know too much about what I was talking about at the time, but I did it anyway. After the meeting, the mayor of Vancouver, Gregor Robertson, asked me, "Is Tsleil-Waututh really going to do this? Are you going to take this on?" and I had to tell him that I was there representing myself, not the nation. The next day some staff members from the Tsleil-Waututh Nation approached me and said, "Hey, why did you do that? You don't represent the nation, and you have to be careful when you're speaking in public like that." I did have to be careful because I was working as the director of community development for the Tsleil-Waututh Nation at the time, and at that early stage, not everyone from the community was convinced that having this oil infrastructure on our territory was such a big problem. Even some of my own family members and cousins were saying that it wasn't worth fighting because we couldn't stop this project from happening even if we tried.

There were a lot of powerful people lined up against us and not much working in our favour. Kinder Morgan was a company worth tens of billions of dollars, backed by the Government of Canada and the Province of Alberta, both of which were intent on doing anything in their power to push the project through. Christy Clark, who was the premier of B.C. at the time, seemed content to let it happen without putting up a fight. The National Energy Board, which was the federal government's energy regulator, had a reputation for rubber-stamping everything that came across their desks. We were up against some very powerful interests, and it felt like everywhere we turned we encountered people who told us it was impossible to win. It was all pretty discouraging.

The Chief and Council of the Tsleil-Waututh Nation started hearing things about the proposed pipeline expansion as well, and we began to discuss our options. We heard that the company was offering other nations tens of millions of dollars to sign mutual benefit agreements, so a decision had to be made to negotiate a deal or to fight. Ian Anderson, the CEO of Trans Mountain, started phoning almost daily wanting to talk with the nation, but we refused to talk because we didn't want his calls to be misrepresented as "consultation" with our nation. Around that time, my mom and my niece Rachel George hosted a town hall meeting at Tsleil-Waututh with various speakers and scientists whom they invited to address our community. This got people talking about the pipeline, and it was an important starting point in the process of informing our community about the issues.

My brother-cousin Justin was Chief of the Nation at that time, but before the Chief and Council could take a firm stance on the issue, they required input from the community, so in 2012 they held a community referendum on the question of whether the nation would formally oppose the pipeline. Prior to the vote, the whole community gathered to discuss the issue. At that referendum meeting, we presented both the pros and the cons of the pipeline expansion. Melina Laboucan-Massimo from the Lubicon Cree Nation joined the meeting to present the case against the pipeline. She stood before our community and spoke about all the horrible deaths and destruction happening to her homelands and to her people as a result of tar sands extraction on their territory in northern Alberta. After Melina spoke, we talked about how other First Nations had been negotiating agreements with Kinder Morgan, and how such an agreement could potentially pay out millions of dollars. The choice we had was between spending the little bit of money that our nation had at its disposal to fight this project, or negotiating a monetary settlement that could potentially feed millions of dollars back into our community.

After we presented these two options, one of our Elders stood up. He picked up his little baby granddaughter and said, "This is why I'm saying no! This is our future. I will fight for my grand-daughter and for the future generations of Tsleil-Waututh!" Another Elder stood up and said, "If our relations over there in the tar sands are dying, that's reason enough for us to say no!" One by one, people stood up to speak out against the pipeline expansion. Even young kids from our community stood up and spoke. I felt so proud as I listened to each member of our community speak about what it means to be Tsleil-Waututh, about our connection to the water, and about how we have to stand up to protect our First Mother. It didn't matter that we were up against a very wealthy company and the Canadian state. What mattered was that we stood together as Tsleil-Waututh, as the stewards of our lands, just like our ancestors. I felt such pride to be Tsleil-Waututh in that moment and to see our community rise up together as nəčəmat.

If we'd taken a monetary settlement from Kinder Morgan, it could have helped some of my family and community members who really needed it. That money could have gone toward housing or toward helping the Elders and the youth. I've been approached by some wealthy people connected to the oil industry who have asked me, "What's Tsleil-Waututh's price? How much do we need to give you to get you to go along with us? Name your price. Just give us your number and we'll make you happy. We'll give you so much money that even your grandkids will be taken care of for life." And I said to them, "You know, I've been respectful to you in the past, but if you ever come to me again asking me to put a price on our land, water, and culture, then that respect will end. Don't you ever ask me that again." And they never did ask me again. But they were perplexed. They couldn't understand why we wouldn't take their millions of dollars. They didn't understand why we wouldn't want to negotiate for this thing that society worships. But I'm also perplexed. Why would they want to sacrifice their connection to Spirit, to the water, to all the essential things that we need to live, just for money? I'm sad that they're missing the connection that we have. We are the Tsleil-Waututh Nation. We are the People of the Inlet. As our community said so eloquently, that water is our mother, and the fossil fuel industries are causing damage to our mother in violation of our law.

One thing that a mother does is feed you. As I've said, prior to colonization, eighty-five percent of our traditional diet came from these waters. Our lands and waters were so abundant that you didn't have to go anywhere to hunt or fish. Our ancestors ate deer, elk, all the different species of salmon, trout, oysters, crabs, octopus, whale, and seal. Our villages were between the shores of the inlet and the mountains, so the migratory path of the deer, elk, and other animals went right through the places we lived. The techniques we used to manage our food systems were second to none. Our ancestors had expansive gardens and orchards filled with many different vegetables and fruits. We had several types of potatoes and many different types of berries, strawberries, apples, pears, and cherries. We had clean, clear, and fresh water. We lived very rich and abundant lives. Before the arrival of European infectious diseases, there were around fifteen thousand Tsleil-Waututh people living along the shores of the Burrard Inlet, and our people were healthy. We had relatively few of the medical problems that we have today, and those that we did have were treated with traditional medicines and plants that grew right here. We had many village sites to ensure that we would never deplete our resources in any one place. We didn't take more than what we needed, and we took care of what we had. We had a reciprocal relationship with the spirit of these lands and waters.

Being Tsleil-Waututh, we grew up out there on the water, and it was beautiful. When I was a kid growing up in the 1970s, there was still salmon in every river and trout in every stream. We used to say that when the tide was out, the table was set. And it was true: there was an abundance of delicious foods, and when the tide was out it felt like the whole community would be harvesting together. There might have been fifty people from our nation out in the inlet at any one time, and back then we were only a couple hundred people. We would harvest various types of clams. There were so many Dungeness crabs that everyone got as many as they could eat. My cousins taught me how the rock crab eats the Dungeness crab and about the different kinds of cod, sole, and flounder. They taught me which birds nest out there in the inlet, like the ospreys, and all the different ducks and gulls. We used to cook right out on the beach as well. We'd make a fire, fill a pot with salt water from the inlet to cook our crab in, and then eat it right there. That's how we lived. It was a beautiful paradise.

I grew up really poor, so it was a wonderful feeling to go down to the inlet knowing that we would come back with a delicious meal. In the summer, when the log booms were parked in front of Maplewood Mudflats, we'd paddle out there to fish. At night, it sparkled with reflected moonlight, and the bubbles lit up like stars as you moved your paddle through the water. Sometimes the water glimmered with bioluminescence, and other times the northern lights danced across the sky overhead. It was pure magic. Sometimes there would be dozens of us out there fishing on the log booms at once. We'd catch a whole bunch of fun things, like mud sharks, sole, flounder, eel, cod, and bullheads. The mud sharks would travel in packs, and when they came through, you'd pull up your lines so they didn't get tangled up. There was an abundance of food in the forests as well. We ate huckleberries, blueberries, strawberries, and the young shoots of the salmonberries and blackberries when they first popped out of the ground in the spring. They were all so tasty. I'm only one generation removed from my traditional diet, but just imagine how abundant it would have been for our ancestors.

Growing up Tsleil-Waututh was like an adventure. At low tide you could walk out about three hundred yards, or maybe further, to the lighthouse and see all sorts of beautiful marine life. You could see big tidepools filled with cod and other big fish, or you might see an eel in there. When the tide was out, the Dungeness crab would burrow themselves under the mud to avoid being burned by the sun, so we would look for the outline of their shells and pick them right up. You had to be careful when you were far out because the tide could come in really fast, and you didn't want to get stuck out there. When the tide came in, you could still see the bottom of the inlet even if you were a hundred yards out because the water was only about eight to ten feet deep. The water was so clear that I would go out with my snorkel and a potato sack filled with leftover bits of fish. Sometimes we would go out with a boat, and you could attach the potato sack to the anchor and drop it right to the bottom. Then we would chill out in the beautiful sunshine, getting nice and warm; after about a half hour, we would look down and see Dungeness crab trying to get at the bits of fish in that sack. We would dive down and grab the crab. It was so much fun fishing that way.

We were raised out there on the water. My uncle Art, who was a bit of a beachcomber, built this beautiful dock by tying together a bunch of driftwood logs that he had collected. It was a little rickety, but it didn't matter. We used to run out and play tag on it, which was fun because the dock would start to sink if you didn't step quickly enough from one log to the next. If you fell in, you'd get cold and wet, and you'd have to go home, but we'd dare each other to do things like that. As teenagers, my cousins and I would go every-where in our little boat. We'd go all the way out to Wreck Beach, or up Indian River to catch some salmon. I loved it. It was hard at times, but it was good at times as well.

The fun part about growing up in Tsleil-Waututh was that we were outside all the time. In the summer, we'd go down to the rivers and swim every day. We were very adventurous. My cousins and I would explore the watershed by following every little creek and river as far up into the mountains as we could. I remember following McCartney Creek starting from the inlet, through a tunnel that passed under Mount Seymour Parkway, and out the other side. We'd trudge through the water the whole way up, and the stream would open up into these little pools along the way. Most of the Tsleil-Waututh reserve was still forested back then, and the forests were like a sanctuary. We spent a lot of time climbing trees. We'd climb the vine maples and get as high up in them as we could before the branches would start to bend down, and then we'd jump from the bending branches over to the next tree. In the winter, we'd pour water down the side of a hill to get the ground nice and icy and then slide down on scraps of plywood. We called it Indian luge. Sometimes all the little kids would pile on one of the bigger kids and we'd go down in one big heap. We had a great time. And then there was the canoeing, which is still a big community activity at Tsleil-Waututh. Our canoe teams compete against other nations, and when the teams travel for competitions, the families and the Elders accompany them. We set up camp along the water with about fifty or sixty people from the community. Those events are very cleansing.

Uncle Bob, my grandpa, my mom, and all my aunties and uncles always taught us that we are Tsleil-Waututh. Even though it was hard, even though there was alcohol and drug addiction as a result of the intergenerational traumas of colonization, we still learned what it meant to be Tsleil-Waututh. They made sure that those fundamental teachings were with us. That was at a time when nearly all our people had already left the Church and our ceremonies hadn't come back yet, but our teachings were still there. My mom and aunties and uncles passed those teachings on, and even if we weren't praying or meditating on them, they were still spiritual teachings. We also sang a lot of songs, which was another way the Elders ensured that we held on to our teachings. We spent a lot of time out on the land and water, which fed our spirit. When we were out in the little bits of forest that we still had left, or out on the water harvesting the food that we had, we got a little taste of what it is to be Tsleil-Waututh. We knew that we were doing what our ancestors had always done, and that reminded us of who we were. Tsleil-Waututh means the people of that water right there, and our Elders made sure we knew that and lived it. Sometimes we'd all be out there on the water at once, and it was fun to feel connected as a community fed by the abundance of our First Mother.

Living on the land was our spiritual practice. Those trees were our cathedrals, and the inlet our holy waters. Diving down into the inlet made your spirit feel clean. Even though we weren't doing our traditional ceremonies back when I was growing up, when we swam in our waters they cleansed our spirit. When we walked through the forest, we would get brushed off by cedar branches, just as people use cedar to brush themselves off in smudge ceremony today. I was taught that when walking along a forest trail, you should stick to one side on your way up the trail and the other side when you come back down—that way you're not picking up the energy that the tree has already brushed off you. So, our First Mother was taking care of us and feeding our spirit even when we didn't have the spiritual practices that we do now in our Coast Salish ceremonies and Sweat Lodge. Our First Mother is giving all of that to us; the very least we can do is give back to her by being Tsleil-Waututh.

These were the teachings that came up during our referendum on the pipeline. Even though our community was sometimes dysfunctional as I was growing up, there were always these very beautiful, soulful times, and that's what everyone talked about during the referendum meeting. People told these stories about the importance of the inlet to our people and our culture. They said that they wanted their kids and grandkids to experience what every Tsleil-Waututh generation since our First Mother had experienced.

Once everyone finished speaking, my mom stood up and said, "Okay, everyone, it's time to vote. All of you get your butts out of your seat and warrior up!" One after another, people stood up and voted no to the Trans Mountain Pipeline expansion. We had one hundred percent consensus among the community members who were present, and that's really quite significant. If you took a sample of Canadian society, dangled millions of dollars in front of them, and told them that they could have that money if they let you build a pipeline through their home, how many do you think would accept the offer and how many would say no? Even if you took the most powerful and committed environmentalist and offered that money to hundreds of their family members and relatives, it's hard to imagine that every single one of them would turn down that money. But that's what the Tsleil-Waututh people did. Our law, nəčəmat, told us we had to. That's what we did because the water is our First Mother. That's what we did because the lands are like a family member to us, and we wouldn't ever sacrifice a family member for money. There's no price that you can put on the reciprocal relationship of love that we have with our lands and waters. That's who we are, and we wouldn't sacrifice who we are at any cost.

Sure, the money would have been nice, and it could have helped us a lot, but we do what we do because money can't help us more than clean water and clean air can. The elements of fire, earth, water, and air that we use in ceremony are the same exact things that these dysfunctional companies are ruining. Money can't help us as much as the Tsleil-Waututh lands and waters have been helping us for thousands of years, and that's the truth. We're protecting what we love because it is part of us, and we are part of it. We are the People of the Inlet, and that's why each and every one of us voted thumbs-down to the Trans Mountain Pipeline expansion.

After the vote was completed, one of the Elders stood up and said that we not only were going to defeat Kinder Morgan but also would defeat them using our own law. What she meant by this was that we would stop this by asserting our own law, rather than depending on the Canadian legal and political system. Our law is much older than Canadian law, and it takes precedence. She said that our job now was to explain to the company and the government, and to settler society at large, what our law is and why it tells us that we have to protect the inlet. I remember thinking, How the heck am I going to explain our law to Canadian society if they don't even understand that they carry spirit inside themselves? But that was the start. Being Tsleil-Waututh was the start. The path started right there, and it's been over a decade of my life so far.

EARLY DAYS OF ORGANIZING

During the first year and a half of the fight against Trans Mountain, I was still working full-time as director of community development for the Tsleil-Waututh Nation and doing all the pipeline-related organizing work on the side. And when I say I was working full-time, it wasn't a forty-hour workweek. In that role, community members who needed support would come see me at any time of day. Often people felt more comfortable dropping by my house after work hours than coming to my office, so I'd have people coming by to see me at all different times of the day and night. Our nation has a protocol agreement with the police and social workers that requires them to ask permission before engaging with people on our reserve, so sometimes I'd get calls or knocks at the door from the authorities late at night asking if they could speak with community members. On top of all that, I was still running ceremony, volunteering in the prisons, and sometimes working in the Downtown Eastside, so I was constantly on the go. I was living at my mom's at the time, and I remember arriving home one evening at about seven o'clock after a long day of work and just collapsing on the couch, completely exhausted. My mom came in and said, "Take your shoes off and get some rest, son." I looked at the clock and suddenly remembered that I had to go speak at an event in half an hour, so I got up and ran out the door again. It felt non-stop like that almost every day for the first four years. But no matter how busy I got, I always reminded myself that we could never rest because Kinder Morgan never rests, so I was putting quite a lot of pressure on myself. I would often come home exhausted at the end of the day and question if we could really do this.

It was frustrating that we had to fight so hard to try to stop this project because the project simply didn't make any sense, and alternatives to fossil fuels exist. There are solutions to the crises we face, and there are other technologies that could help us make the world a better place. We are standing there with righteousness saying that this isn't a good thing—that fossil fuels are killing people and everything else. But then you have the oil companies and the governments saying we need to do this to make more money. It's frustrating because no matter what reasonable evidence we presented to them, the company and government remained intent on building the pipeline. We showed them evidence that tar sands extraction is making people sick and killing them, and they said, "We're gonna do it anyway." We showed them that this project would lead to an increased risk of oil spills that would harm the environment, and they said, "We're gonna do it anyway." We told them about the ecological impact of increased shipping through the inlet, and they said, "We're gonna do it anyway." We talked about the consequences of increased carbon emissions, and they said, "We're gonna do it anyway." What would it take for them to say that the impacts are too costly?

The way I see it is that the spirit of money and the spirit of the person who has a lot of money come together to give birth to a greed spirit, and the greed spirit makes them do anything to get more money. It will make them lie, cheat, manipulate, and even kill to get more. And the greed spirit will convince them, as they do these terrible things, that they're doing the right thing. So, it's a fight because you have people with the greed spirit who are so misguided that they'll harm everything in their pursuit of money, and then you have us standing up to protect the things that we love. Their belief comes from greed. Our belief comes from our reciprocal relationship with the lands, the waters, and the people. That's why we have to fight.

One day, not long after the community referendum in 2012, the chief administrative officer of Tsleil-Waututh stepped into my office and said, "You were the one who started this fight against Kinder Morgan, so you are going to lead it. We've decided to move you to a new position where you will be working on this full-time." The nation had decided to start a new initiative called the Sacred Trust entirely devoted to stopping the pipeline expansion, and they had chosen me to manage it. I asked the chief administrative officer if I could think about it and get back to her, and she said I had about an hour to decide.

Dedicating myself to this struggle full-time was a big decision, and I was nervous about changing careers. At the time, I was running a treatment program that had been very successful at helping our people. I believed in the healing work I was doing, and I found helping people in that way to be very fulfilling. I also wanted to be an expert at whatever work I was doing, and I felt like I didn't know enough about environmental issues to lead the pipeline fight. This decision would affect my whole family and I wanted to speak to my kids about it, who were eleven and thirteen at the time. I was feeling a little emotional as I went to Cedar and Kayah and told them that we had a decision to make together as a family. I told them that if I accepted this new position, I might be making less money and I'd be even busier than I already was. Their response was, "Daddy, we can do it together, and we'll beat them!" So, I went back to the office and formally accepted the job.

In the beginning, the Sacred Trust consisted of me, my sister-cousin Carleen Thomas, my brother-cousin Gabe George, and Evan Stewart. Carleen is such a strong matriarch for our community and such a hard worker. She did so much beautiful work touring along the pipeline to different communities and speaking out against it on behalf of our nation. Gabe is a cultural and spiritual person. They both worked so hard, and neither one of them would admit it. I consulted a lot with Uncle Len and Papa Phil Lane Jr. Uncle Len would meet with me once a week. He was constantly meeting with municipal, provincial, federal, and international officials or business representatives about all kinds of issues, and he never stopped working, but he still wanted to meet with me once a week to discuss the pipeline. He always wanted me to come to his house for those meetings, and he wanted all the lawyers and staff to come there too. I think the reason for this was that his house looked out on to the inlet and he wanted us to always remember what motivated us to create change. We would sit and discuss how we could be more innovative, and we would come up with big ideas to help our community. He was always guided by strong morals and values, just like Grandpa had been.

My brother-cousin Justin, who was Chief of the Nation at the time of our referendum, said that we should do our own assessment of the pipeline proposal, and that's exactly what our Treaty, Lands, and Resources department did. They drew on thirty years of water-quality data that we'd been collecting, as well as maps, stories, and documentation of the traditional uses of our territory. Thankfully, some of our Elders had had the foresight to map and document much of this information a couple of decades earlier. They had documented our stories, knowledge, and teachings, and they had also mapped out many of the places where we were known to fish, hunt, swim, farm, and eat since time out of mind. The Elders remembered how we lived all along the inlet as Tsleil-Waututh. They even remembered when the big fancy shopping district along Robson Street in downtown Vancouver was a hunting trail.

It's amazing to see how well our Elders know our territory. In 2007, there was a big oil spill in the inlet from the Trans Mountain Pipeline, and the government spill response teams couldn't figure out where the oil was dispersing in the water, so they went to talk to one of our Elders. Our Elder considered where the oil was entering the inlet and he considered which way the tides were headed, and then he pointed to a map and said, "The oil is right there." He was right. Another time I was with some Elders who were eating salmon, and they said, "This tastes like Fraser River salmon," and again they were right. They could taste the difference between salmon from the more brackish waters at the mouth of the Fraser River and salmon from the upper valley that have gone through that transition to fresh water. All the nations say that their salmon taste the best, and the taste does differ slightly depending on where the salmon is from. The Elders can match the taste to a specific place. All this knowledge comes from our reciprocal relationship to the spirit of our mother, which is that water. Back when they were in their early twenties, Justin and Damian worked on documenting much of that Elder knowledge, and it's a really good thing they did because it became the basis of our pipeline assessment and our subsequent court challenges.

Sacred Trust also worked in close collaboration with the Tsleil-Waututh Nation's Treaty, Lands, and Resources department, which was led by my brother-cousin Ernie "Bones" George at that time. Ernie works tirelessly and gives so much to our community because he cares deeply, and he knows that he's responsible for resources that belong to our entire community. He works with excellent staff, like Erin Hanson and others, who went full throttle for months at a time. After the referendum, the Elder told us that we had to explain things using our own law, and I think that's exactly what the Treaty, Lands, and Resources department did by drawing on all our traditional knowledge. Our lawyers—Scott Smith, Paul Seaman, and Eugene Kung—also did this really well. Eugene was always there to prep me for big events. I bet there aren't too many lawyers in the world whom you can call late on a Sunday night to ask a question, but I knew I could always count on Eugene to pick up the phone.

A lot of the time, I may have been the public face of Tsleil-Waututh in our fight against Trans Mountain, but there were so many brilliant people working hard behind the scenes who were instrumental in our successes. We've had a really big team that put in a lot of overtime hours creating our pipeline assessment, economic study, spill analysis, clean analysis, all the GIS mapping of traditional uses of our territory, and, more recently, our air-quality analysis. Every Tsleil-Waututh Chief and Council that we've had over the past decade believed in the cause and fully supported what we were doing. Chief Justin George, Chief Maureen Thomas, and Chief Leah George-Wilson were dedicated leaders of our nation who took a strong stance against Trans Mountain. Time and time again, whether they were speaking with the media, meeting with the federal government, or participating in meetings and public hearings, they each said the most beautiful things as spokespeople for our nation. All these people I've named as well as the entire staff of the Tsleil-Waututh Nation and many others from our community put their blood, heart, and soul into this work because they believed in it, and they believed in that spirit of our ancestors that we are working to protect. We treat a lot of our non-Tsleil-Waututh staff as community members. People I worked with at Sacred Trust are brothers and sisters and friends.

I'm just so proud of everybody supporting us in this fight. Our Elders were always willing to help. My ceremonial communities were always willing to help. And my mom, of course. In the beginning, she travelled with me and would prep me for my speeches by telling me what Grandpa would do. I learned from Uncle Len how important our culture and our spirituality is to the work we do, and how it has always been the force that drives us. I would sit with Uncle Len, and he would pray on a vision for our battle against the pipeline. I learned from him how to come up with a vision by praying and meditating on it in Sweat Lodge.

An Elder received a message that we have to lift up our warriors in ceremony, and that was such a valuable lesson, because if we're working within our law, we have to implement it through our ceremonies. That's why our Coast Salish ceremonies put blessings on the work that we did. I gathered a lot of strength from those ceremonies. They blessed not only me and my colleagues at Sacred Trust, and our Chief and Council, but also our lawyers and all the staff who helped us. Our cultural teachings and spiritual tools were perhaps the most powerful things we used to stop the pipeline and stand up for the lands, waters, and people.

In our communities, we're supposed to teach people to surpass us, and that's what my role models and mentors are teaching me. They taught me to learn my spiritual gifts and bring them back to help make our circle stronger, make our community stronger, make our hope stronger, make our belief stronger, and make our passion stronger. Our work was exhausting at times, but the endurance we needed came from these good teachings, ceremonies, and the love of community and culture that we had around us.

I didn't have a girlfriend or a partner during those first couple of years; I was too busy to date, but I also needed to go through a process of learning to respect women, which I hadn't always done in the past. One of my friends decided that he would go for two years without any physical intimacy to give himself the time to unlearn his unhealthy patterns before starting a new relationship. At the time, I thought it was kind of weird that he would do that, but

Rueben George at the launch of the Tsleil-Waututh Nation's assessment of the Trans Mountain Pipeline. Image courtesy of Peter Mothe.

after I did that myself, I felt that I had to have a spiritual connection with somebody before I could be intimate with them.

My kids were pretty much the only thing I made time for outside work during those years, and they were incredibly supportive right from the start. One time I was with Kayah and Ben West, who was a very instrumental organizer in the work against Trans Mountain. Ben asked if I would speak at an event on a Saturday, and I told him that was my kids' time. Kayah said, "That's right, Daddy!" My mom helped look after them a lot during those years. Cedar would play a funny trick on my mom whenever she was looking after him. He would say, "Ta'ah, I don't feel very well," and my mom would say, "Oh no, what do you need, son?" Cedar would say, "I think I need some hamburgers," so she would take him out for burgers at a local chain restaurant to make him feel better. Kayah and I always set aside time for what we called daddy-daughter days, when we would spend the day talking or enjoying some food together. Sometimes I'd take the two of them to the big market on Granville Island and tell them that they could pick any food they wanted, and then we'd go home and cook it. They loved to try new things, and they'd pick anything from squid to frog legs, snail, or chicken feet. They also came with me to a lot of meetings and events because we wanted to spend more time together. Once I was up on stage speaking in front of a hall packed with a couple hundred people, and Cedar was standing at the very back of the centre aisle trying to make me laugh while everyone in the audience was looking up at me. He was about ten at the time, and he started doing this silly dance. Then he pulled his shirt up, stuck his finger in his belly button, brought his finger to his nose, and pretended to faint from the smell. I was looking at him lying down in the aisle, pretending to be passed out, and I had to try so hard not to burst out laughing while I was in the middle of giving my speech.

Once my kids got a little older, they were the ones up on stage speaking passionately and eloquently to the issues. They had understood and retained a lot of what they'd heard at all those meetings and events that I had to take them to while they were growing up. The first time they spoke was at a rally in Seattle, Washington. Their mom, Debbie, was asked to speak at that event, and she said that she'd only talk briefly because she wanted her kids to have a chance to speak. They were only thirteen and eleven at that time, and they both resisted. They said, "No way! We won't! Dad, please tell her no!" But sure enough, Debbie got up there and spoke for a little bit, and then told the audience, "I'd now like to introduce you to my son and daughter, Cedar and Kayah." They got up there and absolutely killed it. I used to tell them that they'd be natural media darlings because they're so young, hip, and articulate. Now they're speaking out at events and rallies all the time, including at the United Nations. One time I got a call from an event planner in San Francisco who needed some speakers. I said, "Okay, when do you

Cedar George-Parker and Ta'ah
Amy George. Image courtesy of
Nancy Bleck.

Cedar George-Parker and Kayah
George at the United Nations.
Image courtesy of Deborah Parker.

need me?" and they said, "Oh, we were actually wondering if your son and daughter would be available." I'm so proud of them.

WORKING WITH NGOS AND OUR NON-INDIGENOUS ALLIES

When we first started organizing, before we had support of the Tsleil-Waututh community, I was working with a lot of environmental activists from NGOs, hosting various rallies or town hall meetings throughout B.C.'s Lower Mainland. Our first town hall event was held in Burnaby and only a handful of people showed up. In those early days, nobody seemed to know or care very much about the pipeline. There weren't very many of us, but we persisted, holding small rallies and events, trying to educate anyone who would listen, and doing whatever we could to get the word out and bring attention to the issue. Just like healing, or like writing a book, accomplishing your goal can seem like an impossible task at the beginning, but you have to start somewhere and take one step at a time. In our hearts, we knew that we would eventually win people over to our side.

Gradually our persistence paid off. Our first really successful event was with Naomi Klein: she helped to bust it right open and put us on the map. From what I recall, we had to turn people away from that one. We honoured her, and she spoke beautifully. There were Indigenous speakers there, too, like Adam Beach and Ta'Kaiya Blaney, who was still very young back then. That was in 2011, and at that time Naomi was one of the few high-profile people to stand up and say that the only way to win this fight was by following the lead of First Nations. She was adamant in telling people that they had to get behind First Nations' leadership. Not long after that, I did an event with Bill McKibben. I really admire the work that he does. We ended up becoming good friends and we now call each other brothers. Whenever we do events together, we pray together first.

Once the little snowball started rolling, it gradually gained speed and got bigger and bigger. When people heard our vision and our

2011 event at the Rio Theatre, Vancouver. Image courtesy of Jerome Kashetsky.

Naomi Klein and Rueben George. Image courtesy of Ben West.

dream, and when they saw how diligently we were pursuing that vision, they stepped up and were ready to help us. People I had never met would send me information out of the blue, and sometimes it was really helpful. Even my doctor said, "We need you healthy so you can continue the work you are doing for us." We had support from smaller community groups such as BROKE (Burnaby Residents Opposing Kinder Morgan Expansion) and NOPE (North Shore No Pipeline Expansion). Wilderness Committee was involved from the very beginning, and eventually all the big environmental NGOs in Vancouver jumped on board with our cause, including Greenpeace, Sierra Club BC, Dogwood BC, and ForestEthics (which later became Stand.earth). A lot of them put First Nations front and centre at their events, probably because they realized that we all stood a better chance of winning by working together. But they were also on our territory, and we came in so loud and proud that of course they would want to follow our lead. There was some learning on both sides, for us and our NGO allies. For instance, at the start of our partnerships, a couple of the NGOs would get the different First Nations confused. When they put on events, they'd ask if someone from the local nations could come and give a welcoming, which was good, but we had to teach some of them to offer honorariums to our Elders. I told them that I don't care whether you give me anything, but when you invite an Elder, you have to pay for their transportation to the event. When an Elder gives a welcoming, it's a blessing on the work that's going to be done on our territory. We have our law here in Tsleil-Waututh and Coast Salish territories, and when we welcome people, part of that welcome is giving them permission to conduct their business here in accordance with our law and protocols. To give a welcoming is to call upon our ancestors who are a part of the land; that's why the welcoming must be done by someone from one of the local nations. So, I had to explain to some of the NGOs that the Elders are supporting them, and that they have a responsibility to reciprocate by supporting them. We had to do some educating around those sorts of protocols and understandings.

I learned from the NGOs too. When I started this work, I put a lot of pressure on myself to be an expert. I did a lot of reading up on the issues, but a lot of it was new to me, and at times I'd get down on myself. When I watched some of the long-time environmentalists speak—people like Papa Phil Lane Jr., Rex Weyler, or Ben West— I could see that they knew their stuff inside out. I'd think about how much work it was going to take for me to be like them. But they trained me. They encouraged me to speak at all kinds of different events, and they prepped me for them. I would come at the issues by talking about Indigenous law, which is our culture and spirituality. I wasn't very good at it at first, but I did it over and over again, and I pushed myself to learn and understand the issues. I stuck with it, just as the lessons of the canoe teach us, and by the end of the first year I was doing much better. I think the leadership skills and the teachings of smeńálh I was given by my family really helped a lot too. Now I can talk about the issues for hours on end, at the drop of a hat.

The NGOs did a lot of good work. They were especially helpful when it came to devising strategies, supporting our legal actions, and organizing rallies. But the relationships didn't always go smoothly. Sometimes it felt like the hardest part of the fight was dealing with our own allies. Sometimes it was clear that the NGOs were there to forward their own agenda. One time, when my cousin Will George took action by hanging off the Ironworkers Bridge to prevent oil tankers from entering our waters, people from one of the NGOs asked Will to stop doing so much media because they were concerned that he was diverting attention away from them. There were tensions between NGOs at times as well, because ultimately they compete against one another for funding and attention. A few times I showed up at NGO meetings and after taking a look at the agenda, I said, "I see that there's nothing on your agenda that pertains to what I am doing with Tsleil-Waututh, so I won't be sticking around very long this evening. But I support what you are doing. We are going in the same direction."

Some environmental groups don't seem to understand that many First Nations people and people of colour don't have the luxury of getting paid to focus solely on environmental work the way they do. I understand that the NGO staff are all really busy, too, but when you're a leader in a First Nations community, community members come to you all the time needing help with things that aren't directly related to environmental causes. When we say that we are fighting for our lands, waters, and people, the *people* are a big part of that. We have to take on a lot of additional roles in our communities that folks from outside our communities don't see. For example, I'm a ceremonial Chief, and in that capacity, I have responsibilities to conduct ceremony twice a week and to help my ceremonial family when they need it. As the former director of community development for Tsleil-Waututh, I still have people coming to me for help when they're dealing with certain types of trauma, or when they need counselling, support with addictions, or housing. I also volunteer in the prisons and the Downtown Eastside, because our people need help in those spaces as well. I check in on my brother regularly to make sure that he's doing okay. So, a lot of First Nations leaders in the environmental movement burn out because, for us, it's about so much more than the environment, and we have to do a lot of extra work that remains unseen and unknown by our allies.

To give one example, I do work in the prisons because I saw that some brothers from our communities were caught up in the legal system as a direct consequence of the traumas from residential schools. Some people went straight from residential school into prison, and others had that harm passed down and ended up behind bars. The colonial system that created the residential schools also created the prisons, and it is still locking up our people. You can see the systemic racism in the way that our people are sentenced. One of my cousins was arrested for break and enter. He had to protect himself in prison because it was a really violent place, and because he protected himself, he had extra time added to his sentence. He ended up serving thirty years. This all really frustrated me, and I thought the very least I could do was lead ceremonies in there to help some brothers heal. Some of them had done horrible things, but I did my best to treat them as I would any other human being. I don't think that they are the real criminals: they're the aftermath of a crime that was committed against Indigenous people forced to attend residential schools. They did hurtful things, but those actions came from somewhere. So, I put my heart into helping people heal from the crimes of systemic racism that Canada committed and continues to commit.

What I'm talking about comes back to nəċəmat, the interconnectedness of all things, and our law that states it is our responsibility to care for the lands, waters, and people. We're not one-trick ponies strictly working on environmental issues. We're not working solely as a counsellor, accountant, or scientist. We are a community, and that's what we are working to create. One way we know who our true allies are is by seeing who's willing to take a stand with us not only on the environmental issues that impact us all but also on the issues that specifically impact our people, like the missing and murdered Indigenous women and girls, or the children taken away from our people and placed in care. We look to see who's willing to stand with us on more than just the environment. That's why I'm grateful that a lot of people from the NGOs came to ceremony with us and started to understand the spirit of Tsleil-Waututh, and I'm also grateful that new allies continue to join with us.

I had to focus on the NGO relationships that worked and not get too invested in relationships that weren't working. In some ways, the hardest part of this struggle has been when people who claimed to be our allies tried to fight us on certain things. Whenever these types of dynamics came up, I learned to say, "My fight is with Kinder Morgan, not with you, so I'm not going to work with you because I don't want to waste time fighting with you." It's the same with anyone: you have to set clear boundaries with people, otherwise you end up spending a lot of time and energy on something that is dysfunctional. But I had to learn that lesson. Early on, I was trying to please everyone. If someone wanted to talk or meet with me, I wouldn't say no, even if they were coming to me with issues unrelated to Trans Mountain. I'd try to help them or at least try to connect them to the right people. Sometimes I'd be meeting with people from eight in the morning to nine or ten at night, and I'd have to either drag my kids along or ask my mom to look after them. I was working twelve- to sixteen-hour days almost every single day for four straight years. There was a lot of travel involved, too, which isn't as glamorous as it sounds. At times I was travelling twice a month, living out of suitcases, away from my family, and eating food that is never as good as what you get at home. It was all very exhausting, and I had to learn to be more discerning about where and when I travelled.

You can often tell right away if someone will be a good ally to work with, and if they have the tools and the follow-through to actually do the things they're promising. I still get frequent calls about the terrible things happening to our lands and waters and people. Maybe somebody's missing and the police aren't doing anything about it. Or maybe someone has died in a bad way. Or they are hurting the salmon. Maybe people want me to help them save the trees, stop new building developments, fight the coal plant, stop the toxic spray they're using against invasive species, or do something about the uranium shipments or the cement factory. I get calls all the time because people think if I'm doing this one thing really well, maybe I can do this other thing too. But I've learned that I can't do it all—I just don't have time. So now, unless it's related to Trans Mountain, I have to say, "I'm sorry, but I'm not sure what I can do to help you." I'll still come to their rallies, or speak about Trans Mountain at their events, but I can't do the hard work that is sometimes asked of me. I can't organize for them. It's not that their causes aren't important—they are. But I just can't spread myself so thin. I've learned that I have to pick and choose my battles.

Sometimes when I meet somebody who could potentially be an ally, I look at their social media profiles, because that can say a lot about somebody. One thing I look at is how many of their friends are people of colour, or people from cultures different from their own. I guess I think that if they have friends who are different from them, they might be more open to understanding a little bit about my culture. Maybe they won't see me as a drunken Indian, as many people are conditioned to. When I meet someone, I ask myself if I'd feel comfortable going into their home, and if they'd be comfortable coming to mine. I ask myself if they might raise ridiculous questions like, "Hey, I know this Native guy in Toronto. Do you know him?" I wonder if they will assume that I'm an expert on everything and anything related to Native people, or that I drive around listening to pow-wow music as Native people are sometimes shown to do in movies. I still get people who come up to me and say such weird and racist things.

Being an ally with Indigenous communities is in large part about trying to understand who we are, where we're from, and why we're doing what we're doing. A lot of it comes down to understanding Indigenous law. But some people don't care to try to understand, and if someone isn't open to changing the way they act and think, why would I want to work with them? We're going to do things our way, whether they believe in us or not. The same goes for the NGOs. Some of them didn't understand why First Nations leadership was important, and I wasn't going to waste my time trying to explain that to them. To non-Indigenous people, I would say that even if you think you understand, don't act like you are an expert on us. Every nation is different and has a different culture and a different relationship to the lands and waters. Even if you have learned something about one nation's culture, it doesn't mean that it holds true across the board for all Indigenous Peoples. First Nations literally means that we were here first and that we are many different nations. One thing our nations do hold in common is that we have experienced the genocide of colonization and the residential school system, and despite the efforts of the colonizers to eliminate us, we were somehow able to hold on to our cultures and spirituality. So, we hold in common the hurt and the pain, as well as some of the healing that our people have been through. If you're not First Nations, you haven't experienced what we have. Work with us by

trying to understand our experiences and why we're doing what
we're doing.

Red Cloud once came to my brother's Sweat Lodge. My brother
passed him the water bucket and said, "Uncle, will you pour?" Red
Cloud said, "When you come to my house, I'll pray my way. When
I come to your house, I'll pray your way." I've always remembered
that, and it's just common sense. I'm not going to go into a syna-
gogue, ashram, or church and pull out my pipe and start smoking
it. I'm not going to go there and do my own ceremony. I will go and
be respectful of the ways that people call on their angels and their
ancestors. I will watch how they communicate to whomever they
believe their god or gods to be. And that's what I mean by gaining
an understanding. Many NGOs that we worked with did that: they
came to our ceremonies because they wanted to understand. I call
a lot of them brothers and sisters now because that's what they
became. When we enter our ceremonial home, and when our spirits
are comfortable, they can expand to the size of that home and overlap with one another in a soulful way. When that happens, we do
become family. It creates community. Some folks from the NGOs
are now among my best friends. There are some beautiful people,
some beautiful non-Indigenous Elders, who are happy and healthy.
We became good friends, community, and family in a way, and I
cherish those relationships that came out of our shared effort to
protect what we love.

Although there have been some difficulties working with some
of the NGOs (they can be very passionate about saving our environment to the point of not thinking about human relations), we are
still all going in the same direction, and we need everyone involved.
The NGOs taught us a lot. They helped us with communications,
legal strategies, and event organizing, and they did some really
good research into the issues. I believe that they learned a lot from
us too. We shared teachings from our culture and our law, and we

conducted our own studies that drew on our expertise and contributed to the collective knowledge. My ceremonial door is always open for our allies to come to my home and pray with me, my family, and my nation. And I'll always be open to going to their home and praying their way, when I'm invited. I never say no to a good moment or a good prayer with someone. The environmental fight is not a quick thing. It takes a lot of time and investment of your heart and soul. I got really sick from it, in my kidneys, pancreas, and gallbladder, and it slowed me down for three years. But now I'm more careful, and I encourage others to be careful too.

INDIGENOUS INTERNATIONALISM

From the outset of our fight against Kinder Morgan and Trans Mountain, we started making key allies with other Indigenous Nations across Turtle Island who were fighting pipelines and fossil fuel extraction in their territories. The Haida was the first nation we spoke with, and they've been very supportive of our struggle from the beginning. In Vancouver, there are two iconic mountain peaks that you can see from all over the city, which people refer to as "the lions." But to us they aren't lions: they're two sisters, and they represent a peace treaty that we made a very long time ago with the Haida. That treaty remains in place today, and we help each other stop the oil industry that is harming our lands, waters, and people.

We also connected early on with the Yinka Dene Alliance, a coalition of Indigenous Nations in northern B.C. that came together to fight the Enbridge Northern Gateway Pipelines. We invited them to visit Tsleil-Waututh, and they generously shared all the lessons they had learned from their struggle up north, including the legal and political aspects of their fight, as well as the cultural teachings behind what they did. They invited me on their Freedom Train ride across Canada and asked me speak about our experience with Trans Mountain at every stop between Edmonton, where I joined them, and Enbridge's annual general meeting in Toronto. Some of the rallies along the way were very small, but at other points we were surprised by the big turnouts. Whenever we stopped in First Nations communities, we were welcomed with big feasts, open arms, and lots of singing. People in those communities would tell us that they were experiencing many of the same difficulties. They wanted us to know that we were not alone and that we had their support.

As I started travelling and giving talks in different parts of Canada and the U.S., Papa Phil Lane Jr. connected me with people organizing to oppose the Keystone XL Pipeline in the U.S. Midwest. Auntie Faith Spotted Eagle had this idea of creating an international treaty between all the Indigenous Nations across Turtle Island that were actively opposing pipeline developments and tar sands expansion on their territories. This idea grew into the International Treaty to Protect the Sacred from Tar Sands Projects, which was signed in January 2013 at the Gathering to Protect the Sacred, hosted on Yankton Sioux territory in South Dakota. A lot of really powerful leaders attended that important convergence. Auntie Faith Spotted Eagle was the main organizer with Papa Phil. She and Auntie Casey Camp are powerful matriarchs who have taught me a lot about Indigenous culture and spirituality at Sun Dance. Leonard Crow Dog and Arvol Looking Horse led us all in ceremony for the first two days before we got down to business. Arvol Looking Horse is the nineteenth Keeper of the White Buffalo Calf Pipe, given to the Oceti Sakowin by White Buffalo Calf Woman. Like Crow Dog, he's an iconic spiritual leader. It wasn't until the third day of the gathering that the leaders of the different nations started to discuss the treaty. There was a really smart and talented lawyer there named Jen Baker who asked some pointed questions about how the treaty would work and what its legal implications would be. She was raising insightful considerations, but at the time I was just thinking, Enough with the questions already, let's just sign the damn thing!

Finally, after a day or two of discussions, the treaty was signed. The first two signatories were the Yankton Sioux, or Ihanktonwan Oyate, who are Dakota people, and the Pawnee. This was significant because the Pawnee and the Dakota have been portrayed as bitter enemies in every cowboy movie that I've ever seen, so the fact that they were the first two nations to sign was a powerful message of Indigenous unity. The signing of this treaty corresponded with the 150th anniversary of the 1863 Peace Treaty signed between the Ihanktonwan Oyate and the Pawnee, so it also symbolized a reaffirmation of their enduring peace.

Faith Spotted Eagle had invited some White ranchers fighting Keystone XL to sign the treaty as well. Jane Kleeb from a group called Bold Nebraska brought a bunch of ranchers to the gathering, and they sat in ceremony with us. It was funny because at one point during the gathering, the ranchers were saying things like, "How can the government just come through and take our land and do whatever they want with it? How can this be happening?" An Elder walked over to them and said, "Welcome to the tribe!" After the ranchers signed the treaty with us, we said that we needed to give this new alliance a name. That was the beginning of the Cowboy and Indian Alliance, which ended up getting a lot of press coverage in the years that followed. We called them "the new C.I.A."

INTERNATIONAL TREATY TO PROTECT
THE SACRED FROM TAR SANDS PROJECTS

The representatives from sovereign Indigenous Nations, tribes, and governments, participating in the Gathering to Protect the Sacred on January 23–25, 2013, on the 150 year anniversary of the Treaty Between the Pawnee and Yankton Sioux, have gathered on the Ihanktonwan homelands, and have resolved by our free, prior, and informed consent to enter into a treaty to be forever respected and protected. We agreed upon the following articles:

ARTICLE I

The undersigned Indigenous Peoples have inhabited and governed our respective territories according to our laws and traditions since time immemorial.

ARTICLE II

As sovereign nations, we have entered into bi-lateral and multi-lateral agreements with other nations including the Treaty Between the Pawnee and Yankton Sioux, Mother Earth Accord, the Spiritual Leaders Declaration, the Agreement to Unite to use 16 Guiding Principles, and the Black Hills Sioux Nation Treaty Council Declaration, and all the inter-tribal treaties in the Western hemisphere, among others, which promise peace, friendship, and mutual opposition to tar sands projects and energy development that threaten the lands, the waters, the air, our sacred sites, and our ways of life, and acknowledge other Indigenous Peoples such as the Yinka Dene, the People of the Earth who have exercised their lawful authority to ban tar sands projects from their territories through Indigenous legal instruments such as the Save the Fraser Declaration and the Coastal First Nations Declaration.

ARTICLE III

We act with inherent, lawful, and sovereign authority over our lands, waters, and air, as recognized by Article 32 of the United Nations Declaration on the Rights of Indigenous Peoples which provides:

States shall consult and cooperate in good faith with the

Indigenous Peoples concerned through their own representative institutions in order to obtain their free and informed consent prior to the approval of any project affecting their lands or territories and other resources, particularly in connection with the development, utilization, or exploitation of mineral, water, or other resources.

ARTICLE IV

We mutually agree that tar sands projects present unacceptable risks to the soil, the waters, the air, sacred sites, and our ways of life including:

• The destruction of rivers, lakes, boreal forests, homelands, and health of the Cree, Dene, and Métis peoples in the Northern Alberta tar sands region and downstream Dene communities of Northwest Territories.

• The threat of pipeline and tanker oil spills into major river systems, aquifers, and water bodies such as the Salish Sea, the North Pacific coast, and the Ogallala Aquifer.

• The negative cumulative health and ecological impacts of tar sands projects on Indigenous Communities.

• The irreparable harm to irreplaceable cultural resources, burial grounds, sacred and historic places, natural resources, and environmental resources of the central plains region which is the aboriginal homelands of many Indigenous Nations.

• Greenhouse gas pollution that could lock the planet onto a path of catastrophic climate change.

ARTICLE V

We affirm that our laws define our solemn duty and responsibility to our ancestors, to ourselves, and to future generations, to protect the lands and waters of our homelands and we

agree to mutually and collectively oppose tar sands projects
which would impact our territories, including but not
limited to the TransCanada Keystone XL pipeline, the
Enbridge Northern Gateway, Enbridge lines nine (9) and
sixty-seven (67), or the Kinder Morgan Trans Mountain
pipeline and tanker projects.

ARTICLE VI

We agree to mutually and collectively, as sovereign nations,
call upon the Canadian and United States governments to
respect our decision to reject tar sands projects that impact
our sacred sites and homelands; to call upon the Canadian
and United States governments to immediately halt and
deny approval for pending tar sands projects because they
threaten the soil, water, air, sacred sites, and our ways of life;
and confirm that any such approval would violate our
ancestral laws, rights, and responsibilities.

ARTICLE VII

We agree to the mutual, collective, and lawful enforcement
of our responsibilities to protect our lands, waters, and air
by all means necessary, and if called on to do so, we will
exercise our peace and friendship by lawfully defending one
another's lands, waters, air, and sacred sites from the threat
of tar sands projects, provided that each signatory
Indigenous Nation reserves and does not cede their rights to
act independently as the tribal governments see fit to protect
their respective tribal interests, further provided that each
signatory Indigenous Nation reserves its inherent sovereign
right to take whatever governmental action and strategy
that its governing body sees fit to best protect and advance
tribal interests affected by the pipeline project consistent

with the agreements made herein and subject to the laws and available resources of each respective nation.

This Treaty of mutual defense and support is made on the occasion of the 150 year anniversary of the Treaty Between the Pawnee and Yankton Sioux concluded between the Pawnee Nation and the Ihanktonwan Oyate/Yankton Sioux Tribe on January 23rd, 1863, and the parties thereto hereby commemorate the signing of that historic treaty that has endured without violation for 150 years.

This Treaty goes into effect once ratified by the governing bodies of the signatory nations.

IN WITNESS WHEREOF, the undersigned dually authorized representatives, after having deposited their full powers found to be in due and proper form, sign this treaty on behalf of their respective governments, on the date appearing opposite their signatures.

PLEDGE OF SUPPORT TO THE
INTERNATIONAL TREATY TO PROTECT THE SACRED
FROM TAR SANDS PROJECTS
January 2013

Source: "International Treaty to Protect the Sacred from Tar Sands Projects," Indigenous Environmental Network, January 25, 2013, https://www.ienearth.org/international-treaty-to-protect-the-sacred-from-tar-sands-projects.

Our work fighting the Trans Mountain Pipeline strengthened our ties with other Indigenous Nations also fighting the tar sands and pipeline projects across Turtle Island. Kanahus Manuel and the Tiny House Warriors have been fighting the Trans Mountain

Pipeline in Secwépemc territory since the beginning. Our families have relations going back generations. Kanahus's grandfather George Manuel and her grand-uncle J.D. Manuel were both very close to my grandpa and my uncle Bob. They loved each other very much. George Manuel was a brilliant visionary leader and president of the Union of British Columbia Indian Chiefs. His son Art Manuel, Kanahus's father, was a brilliant and powerful warrior. His daughter Doreen Manuel is a faculty member at Capilano University in Vancouver. Today we stand side by side, and our children are standing up together against the Trans Mountain Pipeline, so that makes at least four generations of our families that have worked together within our laws to defend our Indigenous rights, title, and sovereignty.

Another essential group that has supported us right from the start are our sisters from up in the tar sands—Melina Laboucan-Massimo, Eriel Tchekwie Deranger, Crystal Lameman, and Jesse Cardinal. They are each power matriarchs, fearless leaders, and passionate, eloquent speakers. They hosted the Tsleil-Waututh Chief and Counsel when visiting the tar sands, and we've all travelled around together quite a lot, speaking at different events. We always have good visits when we get to see each other. I've seen how tirelessly they work, and they have taught me a lot, especially at the beginning when I was fresh and they had been doing this work for years. They told me that doing this work as Indigenous people is a lot harder than it is for many of our non-Indigenous environmentalist allies because we're not only fighting a pipeline and then going home at the end of the day. I didn't fully understand what they meant by that at first, but later I started to realize that just because I'm fighting a pipeline doesn't mean that I'm not doing the other things required of me in my community. When you're seen as a leader of a community that has a lot of problems, people come to you with those problems, and in First Nations communities we have a responsibility to help our community when people are in need. A lot of our allies have the luxury of getting to focus strictly on the environmental issues, but we don't get to stop being part of our communities just because we're working on environmental issues— we've got multiple things that we're helping our families and community members with all at once. I see that with those women. For instance, Melina is a big advocate for missing and murdered Indigenous women and girls, so she's really busy taking on multiple difficult issues, not just the tar sands. But they're all so strong and so powerful that they just won't stop.

Winona LaDuke is another powerhouse Indigenous leader. She has a degree in economic development from Harvard and is the author of highly acclaimed books. She's also a former candidate for vice-president of the United States. Winona has been fighting the Line 3 pipeline in Ojibwe territory for many years now. She came to Vancouver for an event in 2018, and it sold out so quickly that a lot of people couldn't get in. The day after, she came to our Sweat Lodge, and some people from our Sweat Lodge family who were disappointed that they didn't get tickets to the event got to sit in ceremony with her, which was pretty special. They got to know her in a way that you don't get to when you see her on stage. It was an honour to pray with Winona like this, and our ceremonial family treated her like the special guest that she was. I enjoy her company very much, and I admire how brilliant she is.

There are just so many beautiful Indigenous relatives from all around Turtle Island who have supported us and stood with us that I couldn't possibly name them all. The amazing people from Wet'suwet'en—like Freda Huson, Na'Moks, and Sleydo', and many others—who fought the Northern Gateway Pipeline and the Coastal GasLink Pipeline, have been big inspirations. Guujaaw from Haida Gwaii is such a brilliant person. After my beloved Uncle Len passed away, Guujaaw stepped up to help me envision the battle to stop

Trans Mountain, and we talk a couple of times a week now. Kirby Muldoe from the Tsimshian and Gitxsan nations has been a big support. I love Jewell James from the Lummi Nation; he's a master carver, and he started these totem pole journeys. He travels to different communities fighting oil and coal developments and honours those communities with the gift of totem poles that he has carved; he gave one of his totem poles to the Tsleil-Waututh Nation. He has many stories of legendary Coast Salish Elders who were true medicine men and healers down in Lummi. He's so brilliant and is always giving me things to read to help me become a stronger and more knowledgeable leader. I remember when I first met him, he had challenged himself to read two hundred books in a year. He's like Kayah in that way, always thirsting for knowledge. Jewell James fought for Lummi fishing rights back in the 1970s with Kurt Russo, who works for Lummi, and Joe Washington, who was a Lummi spiritual leader and close friend of my grandpa. Lummi has always been a huge ally, and so have our other Coast Salish relatives in Washington State, including the Tulalip, Suquamish, and Swinomish tribes; They all stick up for us. JoDe Goudy, chair of the Yakama Nation, is another big organizer. The Yakama have a long history of being warriors you don't want to mess with.

I've also enjoyed the support of brothers like Clayton Thomas-Müller. Clayton is a ceremonial man who always keeps in touch and is always willing to help. We have some good laughs whenever we visit and do events together, and now my son hangs out with him too. My beloved uncle and aunt Grand Chief Stewart Phillip and Joan Phillip are such wonderful people and powerful political and cultural leaders—they are living examples of how we should all be. Adam Beach is another good brother, a famous actor who speaks up for Indigenous rights. I remember one time Adam said to me, "Let's go down to the Assembly of First Nations meeting tomorrow and see which of those Chiefs are fighting the pipeline." So, we go down to the meeting, and all the Chiefs start coming over to Adam, saying, "How's it going, Adam?" acting like they were his old buddies. He asked each one of those Chiefs straight up if they were willing to stand up against the pipeline, yes or no. Then he invited all those who said they were willing to take a stand to a meeting at his house. Something like thirty Chiefs showed up. He really tries to make use of his fame to enhance our people and support good causes, just as my grandpa did.

Russell Diabo from the Mohawk Nation at Kahnawake and Art Manuel from the Secwépemc Nation were always sending me information and telling me that I had to read this or that book or article. I tried my best to keep up with all the good stuff they were sending me. They were both so supportive, and I loved listening to them. Wolverine was another true Secwépemc warrior and Sun Dance Chief who recently passed away. He was involved in the Gustafsen Lake standoff of 1995, where he and other Indigenous land defenders took a stand to reclaim unceded Secwépemc lands used for Sun Dance ceremonies. The state locked him up for five years, but he continued to fight for Indigenous rights and to support front-line struggles for the rest of his life. Then there's Derek Nepinak, former Grand Chief of Manitoba, a brilliant person who leads by Spirit and has always been there for us. Serge Simon, a beautiful friend and brother who served as Mohawk Council of Kanesatake Grand Chief, once told the Government of Canada that if they messed with the Tsleil-Waututh Nation they would be messing with the Mohawks. Shane Pointe from Musqueam is a beautiful Elder with so much knowledge, wisdom, and teachings, and he's such a good person. Same with Robert Nahanee from Squamish and Lee Brown who is Cherokee. I talk with Shane, Robert, and Lee often, and they continue to teach me so much.

Everywhere we went, we found powerful and inspiring Indigenous leaders who believed in what we believed, who stood for what we were standing for, and who were stepping up to put an end to these horrible things that have happened to our communities. Beautiful people who incorporate ceremony and cultural teachings into the work that they do and who put their Indigenous law into practice. Then the actions at Standing Rock happened in 2016, which brought all these inspiring warriors, visionaries, youth, Elders, and spiritual leaders from all the tribes and nations across Turtle Island together in one place to take a stand against the Dakota Access Pipeline and to collectively say, "Enough!" I went to Standing Rock with our relatives from the Lummi Nation and the Affiliated Tribes of Northwest Indians. Jewell James carved a beautiful totem pole and led a totem pole journey to the Sacred Stone Camp at Standing Rock. The Yakama brought two semi-trucks full of supplies. Seeing all these different nations from across Turtle Island standing side by side was a beautiful sight. I asked my uncle Len if this was what the '60s had been like, and he said, "No, this is better."

My grandpa once said, "I don't need anything to travel across our Indian lands because my people will take care of me wherever I go." I witnessed that on the way to Standing Rock. We stopped in a lot of Native communities along the way and talked to them about how we were fighting for Mother Earth. We were guests in some really economically impoverished communities, and they took care of us because it was their teachings to do so. Elders were crying and thanking us for our work. They sang songs in our honour and were so generous, giving us whatever they could. We received more help and donations from the economically deprived Native communities than we did from the really wealthy non-Native communities that we stopped in, and that's because the Native communities knew that by standing up to fight for our lands, waters, and people, we were following our teachings and our law.

When people like Harold Cardinal and George Manuel were fighting the 1969 White Paper, they did it with next to nothing.

They used the little money they had to drive across Canada in a beat-up car, organizing and raising awareness as they went along. They lived hand to mouth while doing that inspiring work, and they persevered. Can you imagine a guy like Harold Cardinal, educating himself at such a racist time, the way he must have been ridiculed and picked on every day in university and college? When my mom left residential school and went to public school, the other students spit on her, pulled her hair, and said bad things about her as she walked down the hall and rode the bus to and from school. But that generation educated themselves and found a way to challenge the forms of oppression they faced, despite being told over and over again that they were stupid or worthless. They said, "That's not who we are," and they stood up to fight for what they believed in.

Today some nations have a lot more resources and are winning in court, but I still think we need another wake-up call. What's sometimes missing is the genuine thirst and hunger to have that spirituality in your life, to pray and connect to Spirit, and to experience that reciprocal relationship to our lands and waters and the things we love. When we have that, it doesn't matter if the government comes along and says, "Your only way out of economic despair is to take this money and sign this agreement." Financially, the previous generation had nothing, and some communities still have nothing. But what they had was their culture and spirituality, and that's what we need to go back to.

What really blows me away is that despite everything that happened, despite the efforts of assimilation and genocide that have been directed against us, we're still fighting. The story that I've shared about my life and my community—the story of all the hurt and the pain and the genocide—is not only the story of me and my people. It's the story of Indigenous communities across Turtle Island. We've all experienced the harms, violence, and traumas of colonization. We've all suffered through the brutality of residential schools and boarding schools. We've all had our lands stolen, our food systems disrupted, and our environments degraded. We've been prohibited from our cultural and spiritual practices, and told that they are illegal and the way of the Devil. And yet we still refuse the money and fight to protect our lands and waters because that's our cultural and spiritual law. Some of those nations are really poor, and they haven't stopped fighting. Sure, some nations negotiate deals, but they're trying to provide basic needs like food and housing for their people. It's a real shame: they're usually forced into a situation where they're offered peanuts for what they have to give up. Nations are told that certain projects or developments are going to happen one way or another, so they might as well get some money out of the deal; along with that money comes toxic infrastructure that makes their people ill. My grandpa would say that you should never go into a First Nations community and tell them how to be or what they should do, because they did what they needed to do to survive, and that's good enough. Some nations are well off economically and don't need to sign—that's where we can lead because we don't need the dirty money they offer us.

Everywhere you look, our people are standing up and saying, "Enough is enough!" They're saying, "You screwed us over for so long, killing and starving our people, forcing them into residential schools, but now we're going to stand and fight. We're going to fight for whatever little bits of land we have left. And we're going to save your asses, too, because you're part of the human race. You drink water and breathe air, so this is affecting you, too, even though you're too stupid to understand that. Enough is enough." It's as if we're taking the last stand, except that turns into a new beginning: the revitalization of our culture that our ancestors held on to, despite everything that the colonial government did to take it away from them. They are our heroes. And just as my grandpa said would happen, through fighting this battle, our nations are waking up and remembering who we are. We're relearning our connection to what we love. The colonial government poked a bear. Now that bear has woken up, and it's not happy. They screwed us over for too long. They tried to take our culture, our language, our identity, and our land. But now we're standing up and taking it all back. We have the most powerful tools to work with—our lands, waters, culture, spirituality, and law. The same tools that they tried to destroy. We work with those tools, and those tools work with us.

CHAPTER 5

Taking It All Back

In 2014, Canada's National Energy Board (NEB) held public hearings on the Trans Mountain Pipeline expansion. The NEB, which has since been renamed the Canada Energy Regulator, is the federal government body tasked with regulating the energy industry. It makes formal recommendations to the federal Cabinet on the approval of new energy-sector developments. Many people see the NEB as serving the interests of the industries that it was set up to regulate. It has a track record of going through the motions of holding public hearings, soliciting evidence and input, and then rubber-stamping every pipeline application. The approval process for the Trans Mountain Pipeline expansion is a case in point. As the public hearings for the pipeline were underway, the federal government appointed one of Kinder Morgan's own hired consultants, Steven Kelly, to the NEB board. Kelly had already written an economic analysis in favour of the pipeline expansion when the government appointed him to the regulatory body tasked with deciding if the expansion should be approved.

These NEB hearings were the primary means through which

the Canadian government sought to fulfill its constitutional duty to consult and accommodate First Nations on the project. We didn't agree that this was sufficient, nor were we ever consulted on the NEB process itself, but we felt obliged to participate in the NEB hearings regardless. If we didn't participate, the government would claim that it had tried to consult us and that we had chosen not to engage. Participating in the NEB process came at a considerable expense to our nation. We had to pay for legal representation, expert analysis, and the preparation of studies and reports, not to mention all the staff time. We applied to the NEB for $766,000 in participant funding and were awarded only $40,000.

The hearings were held in October 2014, in a hotel in Chilliwack, B.C., and there were about twenty-five of us from the Tsleil-Waututh Nation who attended. The NEB set things up so that there could be no protests in the hearings. They said that protests would intimidate the NEB officials and that the officials had to be kept safe. At one point, we were told that the NEB officials had been intimidated by mean looks from our supporters in attendance.

We were given three hours to present our case against this pipeline. In those three hours, we not only had to summarize the 1,200-page assessment report that we submitted as evidence but also had to explain the history of our people and our relationship to our lands and waters dating back to time immemorial. We had three hours to explain how we are the People of the Inlet, how the inlet is our First Mother, how everything has a spirit, the love and connection of nəc̓amat, our law and our legal systems, the history of colonization, and how it continues to impact our people today. The fact that the NEB thinks that three hours is sufficient time to hear from us is yet another blatant example of the broken colonial system. They see us and appear to think: These people won't have much to say; three hours should be plenty of time. They don't understand what's going on, and they don't know what they're talking about. They don't understand the science. They don't understand the impacts that this pipeline is going to have on their lands. They don't understand the national and international importance of this pipeline. When the NEB looks at us, maybe they think all the things they were taught in their social studies classes about how we are primitive hunter-gatherers. Or maybe what comes up for them are all the racist stereotypes about First Nations they've heard throughout their lives. Maybe that's what they are thinking when they say, "We'll give them three hours to speak, then we'll tick some boxes and make a decision for them." As soon as we walked in the room, I could feel their judgment in the way they looked at us and spoke to the representatives of our nation. That's the colonial system.

Well, regardless of what they thought about us, we went in there and we hit them hard. We went in there with Tsleil-Waututh class, style, and pride. Whenever we go to court or attend public hearings, we start by blessing the room that we're in, because we're there to talk about our law, and our law is based on our culture and spirituality. We make it a holy place. We have to fix and clean that space to prepare it so that our law can be enacted and practised within it. Then my brother-cousin Gabe and my sister-cousin Leah spoke on behalf of our nation. Gabe delivered his testimony in our language, which is such a key part of who we are. He took it upon himself to become fluent in our language and earned a master's degree in education so that he could teach our language to others. Leah is a lawyer trained in Indigenous law, and she interpreted what Gabe said. They started off by telling the panel that our participation in this hearing should not be understood as a validation of the process because we did not believe the terms and conditions of the hearing to be fair. They said that we came there under duress. They said that we would share some of our stories, but that we did not consider these hearings as sufficient in fulfilling the government's duty to consult with us as a nation. By saying this, we were setting ourselves up to sue the Government of Canada at a later date, if necessary, for not adequately consulting with us as they are required to do by their own constitution.

After laying out these conditions for our participation, Gabe and Leah gave a beautiful presentation describing who we are as a people and sharing lessons from our cultural and spiritual teachings. They talked about the connections that we've maintained with our lands for many thousands of years. They shared some of our stories going back to the First Man and the First Mother of Tsleil-Waututh, explaining that we come from these waters and that we've been here since the beginning. At one point, Gabe began singing, and one by one, each of the Tsleil-Waututh people in the room stood up and joined him. The NEB staff had no idea what to do. They weren't sure if they should stand up with us or remain seated. They seemed very confused and uncomfortable. Gabe and Leah closed by asking the board members where they were from. Gabe asked the board where their ancestors lived and where their kids live now. He asked them where their connection and ties to the land and the water are based. He explained to the board members that in their recent history, their families were nomadic peoples who moved across the ocean to inhabit new lands. He said that unlike the newcomers to these lands, the Tsleil-Waututh have been here since time out of mind and that we aren't leaving. He said that we've been here for thousands of years and that we will be here for thousands more to come. He told the board that the decisions they made would impact us forever, but that they themselves might end up retiring and moving far away to someplace like the tropics where they wouldn't be affected by those decisions in the same ways that we are. He said that we aren't protestors because we're following our laws, which date back much further than Canadian law. He said that we follow our law, and that Canadian law has only ever caused harm to our people. The idea that the NEB can make decisions affecting the

Tsleil-Waututh Nation staff and members at the National Energy Board hearings, 2014. Image courtesy of John Konovsky.

future of our people, the idea that they can determine what's good for us better than we can, that's the colonial system.

I think that racism and prejudice against Indigenous people is ingrained in White settler Canadians from an early age, starting in school when they learn degrading stereotypes about Indigenous people being hunter-gatherers, drunks, homeless, or criminals. Sometimes I hear people say that First Nations get everything for free, which is bullshit because the people who say that are themselves living on our unceded lands without paying any taxes to us, so we're not the ones getting things for free. There are roughly as many people living in the Maritime provinces of Canada as there are Indigenous people in this county, and these provinces receive billions in federal equalization payments each year, yet people don't go around saying that the Maritimers get everything for free. That's racism.

My doctor told me that my metabolic typing was related to my ancestors having been hunter-gatherers. She was a nice enough person and everything, but this was a racist understanding that she had. It's not her fault personally so much as it's a result of ignorance and miseducation rooted in the colonial system. I had to educate her that our ancestors were so much more than hunter-gatherers. I told her about our sophisticated agricultural practices and how much of the world's food today is derived from plants that were bred and cultivated by Indigenous Peoples of the Americas, and how the same applies to much of the world's medicines. A recent study showed that many Indigenous people avoid the B.C. health care system because they often encounter discrimination, prejudice, and racism from health care workers. As a result, our communities have less access to health care, which ultimately results in worse health outcomes. A lot of people are turning back to our traditional medicines to avoid being treated poorly in health care institutions. I know people who will drive four hours round trip from Vancouver to the Fraser Valley to access culturally appropriate medical care rather than see the doctor in their own neighbourhood, because they don't want to be disrespected and then ushered right back out the door. That's the colonial system playing out right there too.

The colonial system was the backdrop of us sitting there in front of these NEB officials who were just checking the boxes by giving us our three hours to state our case before making a decision on our behalf. It's the colonial system that allows them to treat us that way; otherwise we'd be given however much time we needed to speak, and we would be heard. And if we were heard, there's no way they would have approved that pipeline because our case is based in facts. We submitted a study demonstrating that the pipeline didn't make economic sense for the Tsleil-Waututh, didn't make economic sense for Vancouver, didn't make economic sense for British Columbia, and didn't make economic sense for Canada. We know that the economies of countries pursuing green energy alternatives are thriving. We submitted a spill analysis that showed that an oil spill would be a question of when, not if, and that a spill could place the health of millions of people at risk. We have the facts on our side, but what we don't have is the resources to put people in government who will support our cause, something the oil industry does have.

A little while ago, I was feeling really down about our fight against Trans Mountain. Here we were just trying to protect what we love, and yet it felt like there were huge imposing obstacles in our way at every turn. I needed to clear my head, so I put on my headphones and walked downtown for a meeting I had later that day. As I walked, I thought about how at the start of all this, even some of my own family said we'd never win and there was no point in trying. Neighbouring nations had also said we'd never stop this thing from happening, and that we might as well sign a deal because at least that way we'd get something out of it. We were up against a multi-billion-dollar oil company, backed by very powerful interests. Some of the local municipalities and the Province of Alberta came out against us. The Province of British Columbia, led by Christy Clark, didn't support us. The Government of Canada made it difficult every step of the way. I was thinking about how Stephen Harper's government appointed one of Trans Mountain's own hired consultants to the National Energy Board right in the middle of the public consultation process. Then Trudeau promised that if elected he would require the review process be redone because it was so badly flawed, but after he was elected all he did was order a supplementary review that was also deeply flawed.

So, I've got this rattling around in my mind that morning as I walked downtown, and on top of all that I'm thinking about the other things that keep me up at night, like the reports showing how rapidly species are going extinct; how quickly weather patterns are changing; all the fires, floods, and hurricanes we've been seeing throughout the world; and how many people believe whatever they're told and think everything's just fine. I was thinking about how every creek, stream, and river in our territory had salmon in it when I was a kid and how that has all changed. I was overwhelmed that day. I was walking down Granville Street when I glanced down at the pavement for a moment, and right between my feet I see a bronze star on the sidewalk with my grandpa's name on it—Chief Dan George. It was my grandpa's star from the B.C. Entertainment Hall of Fame. I started to feel better instantly, because I remembered why I was fighting.

The Bronze Star. Image courtesy of Joe Mabel.

Even when it feels like everything is stacked against us, we still have Spirit. We still have the connection to the lands and waters, which are there to help us and to take care of us so long as we love and take care of them back. And we still have prayer. When we put down a prayer, and when we believe in it physically, mentally, and emotionally, then eventually our spirit believes in our prayer, too, which makes the path to our goals easier. So, after my meeting, I went home and I prayed to my grandpa, I prayed to my dad, and I prayed to all those who didn't have a voice and couldn't fight. I prayed for the help of all the ancestors and the Creator. I prayed to the spirit of all those things that are dying, asking for their help too. I prayed that my words would fall into the hearts of the people of colonial society so that they would understand that there's a different path that we can take. I prayed, and then I felt rejuvenated, ready to fight again. Thank you, Grandpa.

WHEN IN TEXAS . . .

I once said a prayer that I wanted to meet the CEO of Kinder Morgan, Richard Kinder, and a couple days later our lawyer Eugene Kung called me up and told me that one of our allies, Lisa Lindsay, had arranged an opportunity for us to attend the Kinder Morgan annual general meeting in Houston, Texas as shareholder proxies. Eugene is a really good brother, and some of my best memories and favourite times fighting this pipeline have been with him. When he asked me if I wanted to go to Houston, I said, "Hell yeah!" He told me that I had to be at the airport in an hour, and the next thing I knew I was on a plane to Texas.

Bryan Parras, a long-time environmental activist based in Houston, picked us up at the airport and gave us a tour of the region's oil infrastructure, which was mind-boggling. Nearly half of the oil refining capacity of the United States is located along the Gulf Coast, and he took us to see miles upon miles of refineries and emissions plants. I saw railway tracks coming in from all directions to deliver oil from across the continent. It looked just as devastating as the tar sands. It reminded me quite a lot of the tar sands because when you're in downtown Houston, you can smell the emissions from the refineries when the air blows a certain way. It reminded me of the smell of the tar in the air in Fort McMurray. It's a smell that makes me feel groggy.

We arrived at the Kinder Morgan corporate headquarters and started taking photos of ourselves in front of the company sign in front of the building. People pulled up in a car and said, "Hey! You can't take photos of that because it's private property." We said, "Since when can you not take photos of private property?" But we stopped taking photos because they were starting to get really upset. Inside, the AGM hadn't started yet, so I started chit-chatting with a group of people also waiting for things to get underway. I didn't really know what to say to them, and somehow we started

Left to right: Lisa Lindsley, Eugene Kung, and Rueben George. Image courtesy of Bryan Parras.

talking about guns. I don't know anything about guns, so I just listed off the names of guns that I'd heard of. As I mentioned each gun, they got all excited and talked about what they liked about that model. They started acting all chummy with me like we were old friends, and once the meeting was about to begin, they came and sat close to me.

Eventually it was my turn to speak, so I stood up and the people around me were all smiling really friendly at me, waiting to hear what I had to say. Once I began to introduce myself in our language, the looks on their faces changed; they knew something wasn't right. I spoke about the Trans Mountain Pipeline and how the expansion project was never going to happen because the Tsleil-Waututh people would never allow it. I talked about our nation's assessment report and our referrals process. I told them that this pipeline was against our law. I also talked about how Canada didn't consult with us as it is constitutionally obliged to do, and how we were going to take them to court for that.

Richard Kinder said, "Rueben, we've been trying to consult with your nation, but you won't talk to us." I replied by saying that any consultation needs to be nation to nation, which means between us and the Crown. I told him, "All you are is a company, and it's not our duty to consult with companies. We consult as a government with other governments." That's when he got incensed and started shouting, "Get out! Go back to Canada! Leave!" He got so mad at me, the way that you might expect to get mad if somebody hurt your loved one. But I suppose his business is his love, and what I was saying was hurting his business.

I kept my cool, turned to the stockholders, and said, "If I was wrong about what I'm saying, then he wouldn't be getting upset like this. The reason he's so mad is that he knows I'm right." I went on to say, "It's up to you to consider what I've shared with you and to make smart choices with your money. This pipeline is not a smart choice." The shareholders must have listened because the company's share prices plunged shortly thereafter. The AGM was in May 2015, and by October, Kinder Morgan's stock had lost about a third of its value; by December, it had lost about two-thirds. We hit them where it hurts them most—their bottom line.

After the meeting, I approached Richard Kinder and gave him a copy of our assessment report. I shook his hand, and it felt cold. I looked into his eyes, and it felt to me like there was no life there. I felt like the greed spirit had pushed his own spirit out, so that his life became centred on extracting oil and making billions of dollars at any cost. Oil is a powerful spirit that can do that to people. When you think about it, there is nothing inherently evil about oil. It's the remnants of ancient plants and animals that gathered at the bottom of the sea a very long time ago, which was gradually buried by sediment, deposited underground. Our ancestors are also buried in the ground, and many cultures around the world return their dead to the earth. Ashes to ashes, dust to dust. Oil has a spirit, just like everything else, and that spirit has its unique character that can be honoured and celebrated.

But our spiritual law tells us that when you overindulge in the unique qualities of something, bad consequences follow. One of my spiritual fathers from Leonard Crow Dog's Sun Dance in Rosebud, South Dakota, once held out some peyote and said, "This can help you if you respect it, but it can hurt you if you disrespect it." Tobacco is another good example of this. It is a plant that's native to North America, and we believe that it was given to us to be offered as a gift of respect and gratitude. It has powerful ceremonial qualities. We use it because when we offer it to the ancestors in love, prayer, and gratitude, they are so grateful that they start dancing on the other side. If you create a good loving relationship with tobacco, it will help you. But when you get addicted to it and overindulge, when you put too much of that smoke inside you or use it for selfish purposes, it's not good for you and it can make you sick. Or think about fire: if you treat it with respect, it will keep you warm, but if you overindulge in it, as the world is doing right now with fossil fuels, it creates havoc and destroys things.

There are some really powerful things that are helpful to us that we shouldn't mess with, like the sun. It's the same with oil. The oil spirit is one of those powerful things that's best to leave alone. It can do really amazing things, but when people get greedy and over-indulge, it can do a lot of harm, create destruction, and kill people. But greedy people become so succumbed by the spirit of oil that they'd move their own mother's grave to get at it. Their intentions become so locked up in that spirit that they can't see that there's more money to be made in alternatives, such as green energy. It's like drug and alcohol spirits, which can start to control your life and make decisions for you. People become so taken by those spirits that they care about it more than their own family's future. They don't care that there are better choices to be made. The spirit runs through them so powerfully that they can't imagine a brighter future. They're overwhelmed by the oil spirit, but for what? It's sad to think that they might spend their whole lives pursuing money and then die before they have a spiritual awakening, because that's something that money can't buy. Money can't make you feel as good as being in a reciprocal relationship with Spirit. It can't make you feel as good as all the things we love and are a part of in nə́c̓əmat.

When I met Richard Kinder, I got the sense that he was so taken by the greed of the oil spirit that he didn't care that he was making really bad decisions that were harming a lot of people. He must not have cared because there's no way he doesn't know about the impact that tar sands extraction has on the people who live in that region. There's no way that he doesn't know about the toxic tailings ponds that are contaminating the Athabasca watershed, or the high rates of rare cancers that people are suffering and dying from in the communities there. There's no way that he doesn't know about the effect his industry has on people's drinking water, or that communities can't hunt or fish the animals that have sustained their people since time immemorial. There's no way he doesn't know about fish found with strange deformities, or flocks of birds that die when they land on the toxic pools of sludge created by the tar sands industries. Something is horribly wrong when we become so disconnected from other people and other living beings that we allow them to get sick and to die. When Kayah was only twelve years old, she said in a news interview that the people who do these things must be psychopaths, because a psychopath is someone who does horrible things and then justifies their actions because they don't have the ability to feel empathy.

As I looked into Richard Kinder's eyes, I felt pity for him. I felt pity because he may never have an opportunity to heal from his wounds. These wounds might be related to his parents, his family, his upbringing, or the communities that are being devastated by the construction of his pipeline, or the plant and animal spirits that are getting sick and dying from the tar sands industries that he is part of. He may never have an opportunity to experience the healing that we experience in Sweat Lodge and in our Coast Salish ceremonies. He may never get to experience the heavenly feeling that we do when we're out on our waters; it's what drives us to do what we do to protect the inlet, restore the salmon counts in the streams, and reintroduce elk to our territory. I felt bad for him because I thought that he may be so overcome by the spirit of greed that he may never get to experience the love of nəc̓əmat. The same could be said about many people in North America. Even many people who claim to practise spiritual beliefs continue to tread forward in the dysfunctional society we live in. But I know that deep down, they are part of nəc̓əmat. I know that deep down they must love somebody. I know that they were born without prejudice, anger, hate, or judgment. At one time, before the greed spirit took over, they were a true human being. Whether they know it or not, they have Spirit, and that's what we want to tap into.

Our spirit is our strength, and that's what Richard Kinder lacks. My uncle Len used to say that a car has four tires, and if you take one of those tires away, the car can no longer run. If we think of ourselves as a car with four tires, one of those tires is physical, one mental, one emotional, and one spiritual. These are the four aspects of our being that need to be nourished and taken care of. If you take one of these tires away, how is that car going to run? When you take away Spirit and replace it with the greed spirit, people no longer make responsible choices for future generations. How many more billions of dollars do the world's wealthiest people need? Some of the richest people in the world could end starvation forever, but when you're not connected to Spirit, you don't think that way. In my community, we've strived to heal and bring our four tires back into balance. Our strength is in Spirit and our prayer, our ancestors, and our ceremonies. They are what get us up when we feel tired, and they are why we know we will win. Richard Kinder may be a rich guy, but that's all he is. He's puny when compared to the spirit of the Tsleil-Waututh Nation. We know that we will win because the ancestors are on our side—even his ancestors. And he knows this, too, which is why he got so upset at me when I told the truth at his AGM.

KWEKWECNEWTXW: THE WATCHHOUSE

In the winter of 2017, some Elders from our local nations decided to construct a traditional watchhouse on our territory, directly along the path of the Trans Mountain Pipeline. We had already been fighting Kinder Morgan and Trans Mountain for years in the courts and at public hearings. Tsleil-Waututh Nation staff couldn't risk getting arrested by participating in civil disobedience actions because that could undermine all the legal work that we'd invested in. It's typically not our style as the Tsleil-Waututh Nation to put blockades up, but we have a saying, "We are all going in the same direction," which means that we are all headed toward our shared goals even if we approach them in different ways. Some people are willing to risk arrest and do whatever it takes, whereas others can't; that's why going in the same direction as our allies is important. So, even though I couldn't get arrested because of my role within the nation, there was nothing stopping my mom from doing that. She has placed her body on the line to shut down the work of Trans Mountain three times. The first time was in 2014, and she was arrested. Someone took a photo of me standing face to face with an RCMP officer that day, and it looks like we are about to strangle each other. That image was published in the news and made things look like there was a really serious standoff going down, but I was actually saying to that cop, "You better take care of my mom!" and he was telling me, "We heard she's diabetic, so we have sandwiches and juice and apples waiting for her in case she needs them."

Rueben George's mom about to cross the line to be arrested. Image courtesy of the Union of British Columbia Indian Chiefs.

Rueben George's mom Amy George and Grand Chief Stewart Phillip. Image courtesy of the Union of British Columbia Indian Chiefs.

Rueben George, Ta'ah Amy George, Grand Chief Stewart Phillip, and other Elders about to be arrested. Image courtesy of Marnie Recker.

Another time, my mom chained herself to the fence outside of the Trans Mountain tank farm in Burnaby and said, "Nobody's going to work here today because what you guys are doing is wrong." We need to approach things from all angles, and we're all going in the same direction. My friends, my family, my allies, my mentors, my teachers, my colleagues—we're going in the same direction.

The idea of the watchhouse arose when some of the Elders in our communities decided that we needed something out on the land to demonstrate that this was our territory and that we were present on it. It could have been an artifact, a totem pole, or anything that signified who we are and that this is our land, but the Elders decided it would be a watchhouse because these structures have been used by our ancestors for thousands of years to monitor and protect our lands, waters, and people. Kwekwecnewtxw is the Halkomelem word for "a place to watch from." Traditionally these structures were placed at key vantage points to see who was entering or leaving our territory. If enemies were seen entering the territory, the community would be notified so we could then take appropriate measures to protect ourselves.

Some people wanted to call it a longhouse, but a longhouse is something very different. Years ago, we lived in longhouses. Our Elders explained that this building was a watchhouse because it was put there to protect from anything that might bring harm to our people or territory. So, the Elders built a watchhouse right beside the Trans Mountain tank farm, to keep a careful watch out for our enemies and make sure that no harm comes to our First Mother.

Our Elders explained that building a watchhouse is a very serious undertaking of great cultural and spiritual significance that must happen in ceremony. The structure itself was designed by Shain Niniwum Selápem Jackson, a lawyer and artist from Sechelt Nation. His art is so beautiful because he puts his spirit and his love into everything he does. Everyone he works with carries a good heart and a good mind, and that's expressed in the art they create. So, from the moment that Shain began to design the watchhouse, it was invested with really strong spiritual energy and good intentions.

A site was selected directly adjacent to the tank farm on Burnaby Mountain, and before the structure was built, the Elders visited this site and put down traditional medicines to bless the ground. As they did this, they shared teachings about how everything has a spirit, including the trees that became the posts for the four corners of the watchhouse. Our Elders blessed those posts because the spirit of those posts would be watching over the land and water, helping to protect us. Those posts are like ribs that cover the spirit of that house, and the spirit of that house is the heart that beats the love and courage of our Indigenous law. Traditionally a watchhouse would have dirt floors, and that dirt would connect us to who we are each time we set foot on it, reminding us that we're rooted down into the earth and this place we call home.

The Supreme Court of Canada ruled in the *Delgamuukw v. British Columbia* decision that under Canadian law, Indigenous title can be proven by demonstrating that nations have continuously used and occupied their territory from pre-colonial times up to the present. Following from this ruling, a structure such as the watchhouse on the ground is an important way of affirming our rights and title in Canadian law. But the significance of the watchhouse was so much more than that. By blessing the ground and blessing the poles, and by building the watchhouse in ceremony on our territory, our Elders were enacting Coast Salish law, snəẃeyəł, in this space. They were affirming a legal system that is not grounded in the Canadian constitution, Canadian legal rights, or the state's claims to sovereignty and political authority. The Elders were enacting a legal system grounded in the Coast Salish concept of nəćəmat, which we've been practising for many thousands of years, before Canada even existed. The watchhouse was governed by Coast Salish law and

Tsleil-Waututh law, which is the foundation of our culture and our spirituality. We're the descendants of that water, and it's the basis of our law. Our law is how we conduct ourselves and how we carry ourselves. And on the grounds of this law, the Canadian state had no right, no legal authority, and no jurisdiction to remove the watch-house. Nor did they even dare try.

On the day that the watchhouse was built, we held a march in partnership with many of our key allies. More than ten thousand people walked with us up Burnaby Mountain that day. Shain had designed the structure to snap together quickly, in a way that required very few fasteners, so that it would pop right up before anyone even realized what was happening. With the help of a few of our allies, the structure went up so quickly that by the time the march arrived at the site, it was already nearly complete.

The march on March 10, 2018, was led by Chiefs and Elders from across Turtle Island. At the very front were prominent Indige-nous leaders, including Grand Chief Stewart Phillip and Joan Phillip, Chief Bob Chamberlin of the Union of B.C. Indian Chiefs, Sun Dance Chief and Squamish Elder Robert Nahanee, Musqueam Elder Shane Pointe, Chief Na'Moks of the Wet'suwet'en, Chief Phil Lane Jr., Guujaaw of the Haida, and my mom, Ta'ah. They were joined by family and friends from all of our local nations—Tsleil-Waututh, Squamish, Musqueam, and Stó:lō—as well as many of our closest Indigenous allies from far and wide. Chief Darrell Bob from the St'at'imc marched with us. Eriel Tchekwie Deranger, Melina Laboucan-Massimo, and Jesse Cardinal were there—powerful Indigenous women from communities on the other side of this pipeline, where tar sands extraction has been devastating their homelands. Kanahus Manuel of the Secwépemc Nation, who is a leader of the Tiny House Warriors, was right there with us. Clayton Thomas-Müller of the Mathias Colomb Cree Nation walked with us as well. People from many Indigenous nations across

Kwekwecnewtxw, the watchhouse. Image courtesy of Louise Leclair.

March up Burnaby Mountain, March 10, 2018. Image courtesy of Brian Kahn.

Turtle Island marched with their drums. Following behind our Indigenous leaders and allies were political leaders, including Gregor Robertson, mayor of Vancouver at that time, and Kennedy Stewart, who became Vancouver's next mayor. Many other notable figures marched with us, including renowned environmental leader David Suzuki. People came by the busload, travelling from throughout British Columbia and as far away as Alberta and Washington State, to march in solidarity with us.

Midway through the march, my uncle Shane called me over and said, "Nephew, come with me, you've got to see this!" As we walked back through the crowd a little ways, people were stopping to greet us and saying, "We stand with you. We want to do this with you!" I saw so many people that day whom I knew from years of organizing, but even people I'd never met before were thanking me. Uncle Shane said, "Now, Nephew, I want you to stand here and feel the love. Feel the energy pass by you; just feel it. None of this would have happened if it wasn't for you. Sure, you've had lots of help from a lot of allies and really brilliant people, but this wouldn't have happened without you. This is you!" I probably let about eight thousand of the ten thousand people walk right by me as I soaked it all in. Uncle Shane was right: I could feel the energy, the love, the hope. No more than ten seconds would pass without someone saying hello and offering me a handshake or a big hug. Some people wanted to talk, but I was sort of out of it. I let some tears flow as I watched so many people coming together in such a good way, saying collectively, "That's enough. We're gonna come together and do something about this. We're gonna stop this together."

As powerful as that day was, it was all a bit of a blur because I was in such a spiritual state. One thing that I've learned from ceremony is that when you have a goal, and when you believe in your goal mentally, emotionally, and physically, your spirit will believe in your goal and make your path to that goal easier. During those years of my life when I was fully consumed by stopping the pipeline, eventually all my thoughts around it turned into prayer. Through this prayer, I envisioned our victory, and I envisioned this march years in advance. Standing there watching it go by was the strangest thing because it was something I had pictured over and over again in my prayers. I envisioned exactly what it would look like and who would be there. I envisioned my family, my mom, my cousins, all the Indigenous leaders, the political leaders, all our allies, and hundreds and thousands of people. I had pictured all of that. When it came to that moment of being there, I was witnessing the fulfillment of that prayer. I felt like I was on autopilot, or in a dream that day, but that's because I was in a deep spiritual place. I bet that if you asked some of the Elders who were there that day, they would tell you that they experienced the same sort of thing. The prayer had pushed things so that the right people converged in the right places to ensure that the right things happened. When you realize that you are a part of the land and the waters, the oneness of nəċəmat, how could you not love them? How could you not care for them? How could you not protect them? How could you not do something to save them? We take care of the lands and waters because they take care of us.

RECONCILIATION IS DEAD

On August 30, 2018, Canada's Federal Court of Appeal ruled in favour of the Tsleil-Waututh Nation's legal challenge that we brought forward with our Squamish, Stó:lō, Coldwater, Upper Nicola, and Secwépemc relatives. By ruling in our favour, the court nullified the federal government's approval of the Trans Mountain Pipeline expansion on the grounds that it had not fulfilled its constitutional duty to consult with First Nations on the project. The court affirmed that the duty to consult requires the government to engage in a meaningful two-way dialogue with First Nations, and it concluded that what the government had actually done was merely register our concerns before approving the project without any effort to accommodate those concerns. In its ruling, the court described the government's role in the National Energy Board consultation process as being "essentially notetakers," who recorded First Nations concerns but didn't reasonably address or respond to them in any serious way. The court affirmed that the duty to consult requires the Crown not only to listen but also to make changes to proposed developments in response to what it has heard. Additionally, the court ruled that the NEB did not adequately consider the impact that increased oil tanker traffic would have on the endangered Southern Resident orca population in the Salish Sea.

Much like the day of the march, I had had a vision of what it would be like the day we won in court, and everything happened exactly as I had imagined. I walked into our community hall on the Tsleil-Waututh reserve, and everyone was there. My brother-cousin Justin, who was the Chief when this fight began, and my auntie Maureen, who was the current Chief, were standing up in front of our community at the microphone. When they saw me enter the hall, they called me up to say a few words. I talked about how much we've lost as a people due to colonization, and I talked about what it meant for us to win. I talked about how we were now shedding some of the pain that we have gone through, and how we were taking back what was stolen from us. I talked about how this was a victory for our lands, waters, and people.

The shareholders at Kinder Morgan must have seen the writing on the wall because several months prior to the court ruling, they started to waver on their commitment to the project. The company was looking at the evidence and was wise enough to see that this pipeline no longer made financial sense. The price of oil had fallen steeply in the years since the project was first proposed, and demand for tar sands oil had plummeted. The company was also facing difficulties securing insurers for the pipeline. Studies had shown that

Press conference, August 30, 2018. Image courtesy of Michael Wheatly /
Alamy Stock Photo.

the risk of a spill was too high, and that the ensuing environmental
damage could be astronomical. On top of that, they knew that our
court challenge had a strong chance of overturning the project's
regulatory approval. Kinder Morgan must have been considering all
of this when it came to the conclusion that it needed to off-load
the pipeline and all its associated infrastructure to whoever was
foolish enough to take it. After years of fighting Kinder Morgan, we
finally drove them away, and on their way out we said, "Thank you
very much, goodbye, don't come back."

The problem for Kinder Morgan was that no one was interested
in taking such a toxic asset off their hands. This was Trudeau's golden
opportunity to allow the pipeline expansion to die on its own, but
instead he doubled down. The Canadian government stepped in
and spent $4.5 billion of taxpayers' money to purchase the Trans
Mountain Pipeline from Kinder Morgan. The Trudeau government purchased an asset that no one else wanted at an inflated price
in an act of desperation to ensure that the project didn't die. The

Government of Canada was now the owner, operator, and regulator of this pipeline.

Justin Trudeau came to power claiming to be a climate leader. He signed the Paris Agreement, boldly declaring to the world that "Canada is back" after nearly a decade of climate obstruction under Stephen Harper. That was a proud moment for a lot of Canadians. Trudeau also made repeated claims that he was committed to reconciliation between Canada and Indigenous Peoples. He affirmed that the Government of Canada's relationship with Indigenous Peoples was its most important relationship, and many believed him. Some people in my own family voted for him because they believed he was committed to making change. But it's actions that count. None of those pronouncements mean anything if Trudeau is investing billions to expand fossil fuel industries and infrastructure that even the oil industry itself is unwilling to invest in, and ramming a pipeline through our lands and waters without our consent. There can be no reconciliation when you don't even recognize that you are doing something wrong.

The Trudeau government responded to the Federal Court of Appeal ruling by announcing that it would engage in additional consultation measures and seek reapproval. Since the government had already purchased the pipeline, this essentially meant that public consultation and adjudication of the pipeline would be conducted by the owner of the pipeline. Trudeau's Cabinet proceeded to reapprove the project in 2019, less than a year after the court had negated the government's initial approval. We had to take them back to court, but this time the judges sided with the government. Once again, we told the courts about how the increased oil tanker traffic would jeopardize our food systems and kill the endangered Southern Resident orcas. We told them how a spill could make millions of people sick and how there was no strong economic case for this project. We told them about all the negative impacts that this pipeline would have. And ultimately they agreed with us, but they determined that the pipeline expansion was nevertheless in the best interests of Canada. So even when we win, we lose.

On February 4, 2020, when the second Federal Court of Appeals decision came down, I stood in front of the national and international media and said, "Reconciliation died today." The Trudeau government throws words like *reconciliation* around while they work to keep us down and keep us silenced. The colonial system continues to retraumatize our communities. Today there are more Indigenous children who have been taken from their families by the government and placed into care than there were kids in the residential schools at the height of that system. Children continue to die in government care. Canadians should be up in arms about this, saying we cannot continue to allow these Indigenous children to be taken from their homes and allowed to suffer, but most people remain silent. In 2019, the Canadian Human Rights Tribunal ruled that the Government of Canada had engaged in "wilful and reckless" discrimination that breached fundamental human rights by unnecessarily removing tens of thousands of First Nations kids from their homes, families, and communities since 2006. The Tribunal ordered the maximum possible compensation to be paid to victims, a ruling that is reserved for only "the very worst cases" of racial discrimination. Rather than acting to correct this systemic racism and offering the compensation that the court ordered, Trudeau's government chose to invest time and resources in appealing this decision.

To see how colonialism continues to operate in this country, you can also look at all the Indigenous communities in Canada that remain under boil-water advisories with no access to clean drinking water. You can see it on the streets of Vancouver, where a third of homeless people are Indigenous despite comprising only two percent of the city's population. Look at all the incidents of anti-Indigenous police violence, or the fact that thirty percent of inmates in Canadian prisons are Indigenous. As I've said, my cousin served thirty years for break and enter, whereas the guy who murdered Colten Boushie was let off the hook. Tell me that is not systemic anti-Indigenous racism. Trudeau says he's committed to reconcilia-tion, yet his government spends billions of dollars forcing a tar sands pipeline through our territory without our consent. We spent years fighting the Government of Canada at great expense to our community. They lied and cheated the entire time, and they arrested our people when we stood up in accordance with our law to protect the fish, elk, moose, and everything that is there for our future generations. So, when you look at the reality of the situation, it becomes clear that *reconciliation* is just a bullshit word that the gov-ernment uses to try to paper over the travesties committed against our people in the past while it continues to uphold the colonial system in the present.

Meanwhile, the genocide continues. Look at the numbers of missing and murdered Indigenous women and girls in Canada. Again, Canadian society should be raising hell in the streets over this. Do you think they'd be silent if it was their daughters who were stolen? The people who don't give a shit about the missing and mur-dered Indigenous women, girls, and Two-Spirit people today are the descendants of those who didn't give a shit about little children being starved, molested, and murdered by nuns and priests in residential schools in generations past. Trudeau set up a national inquiry to investigate the missing and murdered Indigenous women and girls, and at one point the inquiry asked if I would moderate some of its hearings in several key cities. But some lawyer friends of mine told me that the only reason they were asking me to do this was because a lot of people had resigned from the inquiry and they needed to regain credibility. My friends said that the inquiry was hearing testimony from the victims' families, and that was a good thing, but what they weren't doing was interrogating the police who failed to investigate the murders, the judges who let offenders off lightly, or the coroners who said that the victims had died of natural causes when they had actually been murdered. These are the people who need to be investigated because they're the ones who let this happen. They are the ones who uphold the structural racism that allows violence against Indigenous women, girls, and Two-Spirit people to continue. Once again, Canada wanted to avoid investigating itself, and I was disgusted by that. The inquiry did a lot of good work in the end, but it also received a lot of criticism for the approach that was taken, and quite a few people resigned midway through the process.

We lost a lot to colonization. Our communities were decimated by disease. The Tsleil-Waututh population declined from around fifteen thousand prior to colonization to no more than a couple dozen in the early nineteenth century. Our lands were stolen, and we were removed from our villages, forced onto reserves, and told we couldn't leave without permission. We were prohibited from selling our reserve lands, and we still are today. Our children were taken away and abused in the residential schools. We were punished for speaking our languages and given English names. We were banned from practising our ceremonies. The Indian Act banned us from forming political organizations and prevented us from accessing legal representation to defend ourselves in Canadian courts. We were prohibited from voting. Every single one of the treaties signed by Indigenous Peoples with the Crown was broken, and when we defend our treaty rights, we have to do so in Canada's courts rather than our own legal systems.

Colonization has been devastating to our communities, and it continues to be. A lot has been taken from us. One thing that's consistent across our communities is that we've lived through a lot of pain and hurt. But through all that, we never lost our spiritual connection to our lands and waters. Even when we were prohibited from practising our culture and spirituality, our Elders still talked about the importance of that connection, and they passed on our teachings. They still taught us the lessons of giving back to the earth and respecting the water, like when my mom taught us to return shells back to the ocean after we harvested clams and crabs. We were always taught that you can't own that which you're a part of. When everything else was taken from us, the ancestors and knowledge-keepers held on to that spiritual connection to our lands and waters, and we used that connection to build ourselves back up when we had nothing else. It has helped us pick ourselves up, and we drew on these teachings to help us find our way. Today we draw on the lessons of our ancestors to heal, and as we heal, we're standing up. The more connected to our lands and culture we become, the healthier we are; the healthier we are, the stronger we are. That's why the colonial governments are still trying to keep us disconnected from our lands and culture—because when we do connect with them, when we do find our strength, when we do abide by our teachings, we find the power to stand up and create change.

When we're connected, we want to live and celebrate the life of trees and the water and the air and the sky, and to live how we've been living for thousands of years. The colonial harm continues, but we're reconnecting with our lands and culture, and as we do, we get better at healing and protecting what we love. We're waking up and recreating things as they have been for thousands of years. That healing is growing and spreading throughout our communities, and I pray that it will touch the hearts of all human beings so that non-Indigenous communities can also learn to love the spirit that they carry inside themselves and to love their ancestors, their Creator, and one another, recognizing that they're interconnected with something bigger, nəȼəmat.

What's happening now is not reconciliation. What's happening now is that we're gathering strength from within our own communities and saying, "Enough is enough!" The government is not coming in to fix us—we're fixing ourselves, and we are fixing them too. We're not going to ask for permission any longer. We're not going to wait for their funding or payouts any longer. We're going to make decisions for ourselves—decisions that benefit not only us and our future generations but everyone. We don't need help: we need sovereignty. Governments in Canada do things like adopt the United Nations Declaration on the Rights of Indigenous Peoples, but not because they want to or because they care about Indigenous nations. Never in the history of Canada has the government ever wanted to talk with First Nations, and they still don't want to today. They are only doing it now because we've forced their hand and the tides are shifting. They're doing it now because we're winning.

Across Turtle Island and all around the world, Indigenous nations are drawing on their connections to their lands and waters and using the resources they have to create something better. Just look at what the Mohawk did in Kanehsatà:ke in 1990, or the Nlaka'pamux in the Stein Valley, or the Mi'kmaq in Burnt Church, or Grassy Narrows. Look at the work of the Haida, and the Wet'suwet'en, and the Tiny House Warriors, and all our relatives near the tar sands. The Lummi, Swinomish, Tulalip, Suquamish, and Yakama down in Washington State are doing amazing things, as are tribes all the way down the coast to Southern California. You can look to Oklahoma, where a 2020 U.S. Supreme Court ruling acknowledged that tribes hold legal jurisdiction over half the state. Or look to the amazing work that the Seminoles are doing to rehabilitate alligators in their territory. The Yankton Sioux are fighting. The Indigenous Peoples of Panama and Brazil are taking a stand. I visited Australia and witnessed how Indigenous Peoples there are also winning. And then there was Standing Rock, which was a huge statement from the nations across Turtle Island, telling the world that colonial governments are ruining everything and that we aren't going to take it anymore. Standing Rock was a moment when the world saw what Indigenous Peoples are doing to protect what we love. It was an important step toward taking back what is ours.

Another important moment came during the #ShutDownCanada actions in 2020 following the RCMP invasion of the Wet'suwet'en yintah, their unceded territory. Indigenous nations and their allies across Canada responded by blockading railways, highways, ports, and other infrastructure, demanding that the RCMP get off the yintah and that Canada honour the rulings of its own Supreme Court, which had affirmed Wet'suwet'en title and the jurisdiction. A lot of settler Canadians complained that the #ShutDownCanada blockades inconvenienced their lives, but I'd say that colonialism is the real inconvenience. It's an inconvenience how we're still being treated by the police, by the courts, by the prison system, by child and family service departments, by the health care system, and by the extractive industries polluting our territories. To those who see the blockades as an inconvenience, I say, "I'm sorry that you can't make it home for dinner right away—that is an inconvenience. But we've been inconvenienced for hundreds of years now, and that has to come to an end." The #ShutDownCanada actions were a very important moment, and even the premier of Alberta, Jason Kenney, said that this was just a warm-up for future actions against projects like Trans Mountain. That might be one of the only things that Jason Kenney and I actually agree on.

At the start of 2020, Indigenous youth occupied the steps of the B.C. provincial legislature building for a month, in solidarity with the Wet'suwet'en, and they created such a welcoming, loving, and gentle environment around that space. I visited them during that action, and I was blown away by how brilliant and articulate they all were, speaking with such confidence on the issues. There were so many powerful Indigenous youth there who reminded me of Cedar and Kayah. I wanted to sit back in awe and listen to them speak all day long. I was so impressed and so proud of them. I just loved what they did.

All across Turtle Island, Indigenous people are healing and standing up to protect what we love. They're standing up and saying you can't put a price on the sacred. Sure, the money and the payouts we're being offered could help us in certain ways, but imagine if you had a loved one who was hurting and someone offered you a million dollars so that they could continue hurting them—would you take it? We say no, not a chance. We're going to heal our loved ones, and we're going to fight those who harm them. That's what our nations are doing.

I have some trading beads that were given to me by Chief Shellbone Williams with whom I Sun Dance. They're the only jewellery I wear. Some of those beads are over four hundred years old. It's been said that we traded our lands and waters for beads, which is complete bullshit. But the reason I wear these trading beads is because to me, they represent all that we lost to colonization and how we're now taking it all back. We're taking back our language, our culture, our spirituality, our ceremonies, our lands, our waters, our rights, our governance, our way of life. That's why I wear those beads. Reconciliation is dead. We're gathering strength, and we are taking it all back. All of it.

So, there is hope, and it has to start somewhere, which is why we're choosing to stand up and put a stop to this damn pipeline. And we need lots of help. The pipeline expansion would kill the orca whales of the Salish Sea, and the government says it's in the interests of Canada—killing those majestic whales! In 2018, the orca Tahlequah carried her dead calf around the Salish Sea for seventeen days, showing the world that this is what's going to happen to us all if that pipeline is built. We're going to start with this pipeline and then fix everything else. You don't have to be asleep and have this country of Canada telling you how to be. There are alternatives. Look beyond all the dysfunction of colonial society to see yourself as a crystal-clear human being, just as you were when you were born. We can break all these barriers that prevent us from celebrating who we are, and I will do that with you. I will love you as a human being, no matter who you are or what you look like.

CHAPTER 6

We Will Take You with Us

My grandfather said that like the Thunderbird of old, our people would rise up and build ourselves into the proudest and strongest segment of society, and that's exactly what's happening. He said that our lands would be governed by our own people again, and that's happening too. Not long ago, there tended to be two types of people in Indigenous leadership: those who were cultural and spiritual leaders, and those who were well educated. What I see now is a new generation of Indigenous leaders who are cultural, spiritual, and also very well educated, and that's significant. We need all the different skill sets within our communities if we want to build our communities up. Jewell James says, "Go get an education, then come back and I will decolonize you." Well, that's happening now too. People are getting educated *and* decolonizing themselves by learning the tools and teachings that have worked for our ancestors for millennia. That's how we flip things. We can't live exactly how we used to, but we still have to remember where we come from. We have to remember both the good things about where we came from and the hard times that we've lived through. We draw on all of this to find the motivation to try harder. I'm sick and tired of fighting, but I will continue because if our Indigenous culture and spirituality die, then what hope is left for the future of the Americas? There's too much at stake to allow Canada to continue to do what it's been doing.

When Uncle Len was Chief of our nation in the 1990s, he had a vision that in order for us to be sovereign and govern our lands, we required financial independence. When he started out as Chief, the only people the nation employed was himself and one administrative assistant. But Uncle Len saw that in order to protect ourselves, we would need to build up a big war chest, and one of the ways to do that was with economics. He used to say that since we can't go hunt and provide for our families in the traditional ways anymore, we have to adjust by bringing our tools to the society we live in today. So, he talked about economic sovereignty and came up with a vision for our community. Uncle Len developed an economic strategy informed by our cultural teachings to help us reclaim all the key things that were taken away from us and to support our healing. At one point, the Tsleil-Waututh Nation had zero unemployment, and that was achieved because of Uncle Len's vision. Of course, we have to be careful because money doesn't solve social problems on its own. In fact, when money comes into a community it can accentuate existing problems, making them even worse. Our economic development plan ensures that when resources do come in, they don't benefit only one person or family. It ensures that our resources take care of everyone, especially those most in need, just as a hereditary Chief becomes a higher Chief by making sure that everyone in their community is taken care of. Our plan was to reinvest our resources where they matter most by supporting healing and language revitalization, by bringing back our culture and spirituality, by cleaning up the inlet and all the pollution that's been dumped into our sacred waters, and by reclaiming the lands that were stolen from us. We would base the economic direction of our nation on the fundamentals of our being; our law; our medicine wheel of truth, family, health, and culture; and everything that encompasses the past, present, and future generations. That's our way. That's our teaching. That's what Grandpa spoke of.

Guided by this vision, Takaya Developments was created as a Tsleil-Waututh-owned company, and we found partners willing to invest in our nation. To this day, it remains against the law for First Nations in Canada to sell our reserve lands, which is total bullshit, but we are permitted to sign long-term leases. In 1993, our community voted to lease some of our lands to develop the Raven Woods community. Our reserve is already such a tiny fraction of our traditional territory, so the decision to lease our lands for real estate development was scary, but this development continues to provide a source of wealth for our community today. By developing and leasing out some of our lands, we've been able to buy back other land cheaply and we've acquired way more land than we would have dreamed of back in the 1990s. Revenues from these investments support the community in important ways, helping to pay for initiatives such as our language programs and our fight against the Trans Mountain Pipeline. Every department at the Tsleil-Waututh Nation is supported by our economic development initiatives in one way or another. There are still things that we need to work on to improve economically in our community, such paying our people more for the work they do, offering complete coverage for medical and dental care, and providing higher living allowances for our members pursuing post-secondary education. But we're getting there.

Back in the 1990s, our Elders told the leaders of our nation that what they wanted more than anything in the world was for us to be back out on our lands and waters. They said that they wanted their children and grandchildren to experience what they had experienced. So, the nation did what the Elders asked for. Supported by our amazing staff, we began to reclaim and rehabilitate our

territory, cleaning up the polluted waters of the inlet and making
them beautiful again. We're enhancing our clam beds, and in 2016
we harvested clams for the first time in decades. We are bringing
back that crystal-clear water from which our ancestors ate an abundance of clams. We brought our salmon count back up from six
thousand to millions in one decade. And when we do that, we don't
tag those salmon before they swim out into the Pacific and say,
"Don't touch this—it's a Tsleil-Waututh salmon!" All people will
benefit from the abundance of salmon that we've created. All people
benefit from the work that the Tsleil-Waututh Nation and our allies
are doing. We've reintroduced elk to our territories, and with the elk
came grizzlies and wolves, which is very significant because we are
the Wolf Clan. So, the inlet is regenerating itself and we are helping
it—helping to complete that ecosystem, which gives back to other
species. We're protecting what we love and saying no to industry
infringing on the beautiful things in our territory, which everyone
benefits from. And we are bringing our children and youth out onto
our territory, accompanied by our Elders, so that the next generations can experience what it means to be Tsleil-Waututh.

Hand in hand with that cultural growth is the strengthening of
our self-esteem as we take our rightful place in society and became
a powerhouse nation. We're growing healthier and stronger; we're
connecting with the land again; and as we do that, we're taking back
the power of who we are as Tsleil-Waututh people, stewarding our
lands and governing ourselves in accordance with our own law.
Jewell James once told me, "When you win back your land, do ceremony with it, celebrate with it. You will feel it, you'll understand it,
and you'll see how this uplifts your people." I'm so proud of our
people for what we've accomplished.

Much like our nation and its economic development plan, I'm
in business because I want to have the resources to uplift our people
and hammer the colonial government. Inspired by the vision of

Uncle Len, Uncle Bob, my mom, and Grandpa, I want to create change and do right for our lands, waters, and people. I got into business because companies approached me to ask if I could provide them with consulting services. I thought it was a little weird that people would want me to consult on their business practices. I was living in my mom's basement at the time, and I told myself that I didn't need money because I'm a spiritual person. Then I was visiting with one of my spiritual teachers, Oscar Moreno, and his beautiful family in Baja California, and he told me to take these opportunities. He said, "You have a good heart, and you are a good person. Money won't change who you are, but it will allow you to help more people." I thought about his words and they made sense to me. So, with the encouragement of Oscar, I started to do a little consulting work here and there in the evenings or on weekends while still working for Tsleil-Waututh Nation.

After I did some consulting work for this one company, the owner asked me what I wanted to do with the money I made in business. I told him I wanted to build an environmental centre and a healing centre for my people. He said, "Those would be really good things, but why are you thinking so small? You're capable of doing so much more than that. You're holding yourself back. How can you dream bigger?" I was a bit offended because I thought this was a great vision. When I went home that night, his words stuck with me. I kept asking myself, why are you thinking so small? How could I create change on an even larger scale to help Indigenous people across Canada and around the world? I kept thinking about it, and I went to talk to Uncle Len. He had been thinking about similar things and was working on a plan for what he called a governance model— a system based on our cultural law. Uncle Len always found time to teach me about how to approach business with integrity and in accordance with our cultural and spiritual teachings. He used to say that if you want to fly with the eagles, don't play with the pigeons.

We sat down together and thought about how we've put so much energy into stopping Trans Mountain—compiling numerous assessments, reports, analyses, and legal submissions, all based on our own law—and we imagined what could happen if we applied our law and confronted the colonial system in everything we did as a nation. We thought about how Indigenous children are taken away from our communities and placed in the child welfare system. We thought about the police and the prison system locking our people behind bars. We thought about the missing and murdered Indigenous women and girls. We thought about the disproportionate number of Indigenous people living on the streets in the Downtown Eastside of Vancouver. We talked about how the colonial system that created residential schools is the same colonial system that we're still dealing with today.

We were thinking about all this, and we asked how we could use the tools that we have to fix these things ourselves. That's when we began to conjure up these beautiful ideas of how we could apply our law, our culture, and our spiritual beliefs to things like housing, raising children and youth, education, employment and training, economic development, and all that we are as the Tsleil-Waututh people. We began to imagine what it would be like if we had enough resources to open our own schools, where we could educate our children in culturally appropriate ways, or if we had enough resources to support our people who live in the Downtown Eastside. We thought about how we would be much more successful at healing our people if we took care of the problems we face rather than leaving it to the colonial government to take care of things for us. And that's how we came up with our governance model, which is a vision where everything that happens within our territory must abide by Coast Salish and Tsleil-Waututh law. We already have protocol agreements and a referrals process, which require projects within our territory to be assessed and permitted by our nation. The vision of our governance model is to make this not only a protocol or agreement but also the law of our territory. At present, more than a half-billion dollars of goods move through the Port of Vancouver and Tsleil-Waututh waters each day, and we don't see any of that. Canada and the big multinational corporations are milking resources from our lands, and we want to get to the point where if they are operating within our territory, then they must abide by our law and governance policies, which can be stricter than those of any federal, provincial, or municipal government. Trans Mountain says that it has gone through the most stringent approval processes of any pipeline in Canadian history. Well, that may be true, but that's not saying much considering that the Indian Act prohibited our people from even having legal counsel when the pipeline was first built in the 1950s. But in a way they're right: those weak-ass regulations from the past aren't enough anymore. We're going to make them abide by our law, and that scares the shit out of government and industry. I said to Uncle Len, "This is big. This is good. This would really change things."

With that vision in mind, I approached my brother-cousin Justin about going into business together. Justin is Uncle Len's son, and he is very well loved in our community. He's a gentle but strong warrior who has a big, beautiful heart, but he can be fierce when he needs to be, especially if someone disrespects our family or nation. He's less than a year older than me, and we did everything together when we were kids. Later in life, he served as Chief of the Nation while I was the director of community development. When I approached him about going into business together, he held the economic development portfolio for the Tsleil-Waututh Nation, but he was slowly starting to step away from that. We each shared our visions of going into business to make some money that we could use to implement our governance model and support Indigenous struggles worldwide, not only here in British Columbia and across Canada but also in places like Brazil and Panama. Justin had similar dreams to uplift our community and our people as I did. He had a vision of helping the youth in our community excel at sports because he played NCAA Division I hockey for Northern Michigan University and later played professional ice hockey in Europe, so he wanted to set things up for other kids from our community to have the same opportunities that he did. We have a lot of natural athletes in our community, and with proper training and coaching they could go really far.

Justin and I went into business together because we're passionate about the things we love, and we want to be able to support those things in our community. When we meet with potential business partners, the first thing we ask them is if they know the story of First Nations in Canada. Even if they say they do, we share a bit anyway. Justin explains the ugly story of colonization, residential schools, and intergenerational abuse that we have lived through. We tell them that we're in business because we're motivated to create change, and we explain our vision of economic sovereignty. We tell them that we want to help not only our nation but also nations across British Columbia, Canada, and the world. Their response dictates whether or not we work with them. If they show some understanding and support for our vision, we're happy to continue talking, but if they don't show interest, we pass because we only work with people who share our vision for change. We start by praying on our vision, then we work hard, and we never compromise who we are or what we stand for. We've been taught to never compromise our ceremonies, so why would we compromise who we are as we work to protect and enhance our lands, waters, and people? That's what Uncle Len wanted for the Tsleil-Waututh people, and that's what he wanted for Indigenous Peoples across Canada.

We started consulting on some cannabidiol, or CBD, businesses. CBD is a medicinal and non-psychoactive chemical extracted from cannabis. I had taken it after getting major operations on my organs, and it did amazing things to help me heal. I'd been tired for three years, and the exhaustion got so bad that just getting up and going to work became really difficult. It felt like having the flu for three years straight. I thought it was burnout from working so hard against the pipeline while continuing to help people in my community. After years of experiencing all the stress that came from that work, I got sick. One night, around four a.m., I felt this acute pain and I went into the hospital thinking I was having a gallstone attack. The doctor gave me some pain medication, and I said, "Thanks—can I go now?" That's when they told me that they were going to operate in about two hours. I said, "Oh, well, I better go extend my parking permit then, because it sounds like I'm gonna be here a little longer than I thought!"

They operated on my kidneys and pancreas, and I don't know what order they did it in because I was all drugged up. I went in on a Friday and then I slept through until the following Monday. When I woke up, I told them that I was feeling better and again asked if I could leave, but they told me that they needed to operate again, this time I think it was to remove my gallbladder. By the end of it all, I had five incisions, one of which was right across my stomach. You don't realize how much you use your stomach muscles until something like that happens; after the operation, it took me about twenty minutes to walk across the room to go to the bathroom. I went home and my muscles were cramping up. The pain was excruciating, and I felt so much discomfort. I didn't know what I was going to do, but someone told me to try CBD. I tried it and started to feel better within twenty minutes. I started taking CBD regularly, and even when I did get cramps, they went away more quickly. Over time, my blood pressure and protein levels dropped. I had been really close to having to go on dialysis, but over time my kidney function improved. I also rubbed CBD on my back, and that helped with my back pain too. So, I really started to believe in the medicinal properties of

CBD because it had helped me, and I gave it to my mom and others.

Now Justin and I consult for a company called All Nations, founded by Darwin Douglas, who is a childhood friend from Cheam First Nation. Otis Jasper, former Chief of the Soowahlie First Nation, is also a director of the company. Both are brilliant guys. We introduced the company to Serge Simon, former Grand Chief of the Kanesatake Mohawk, and Derek Nepinak, former Grand Chief of the Assembly of Manitoba Chiefs. Like Justin and me, they all want to create change, help their communities, and support Indigenous Peoples' struggles across Canada. I'm excited about the direction we're going, and I think we'll do really good work. All Nations has already built a large grow facility and six dispensaries. We want to branch out right across Canada, and wherever we build dispensaries, we will give half of what we make to the local First Nations on whose lands the dispensaries are located. That's our deal with the Creator. We have a brotherhood and sisterhood of good, smart, cultural businesspeople from nations right across Canada who share our vision, and we work with them regularly. It's a breath of fresh air, because even in the business realm we need people with stronger values who want to create change.

SACRED CIRCLE

During the COVID-19 pandemic, some of the guys at the men's treatment centre where I volunteer fell off the wagon. It was really bothering me, so I did some research to figure out what we could do about it. I knew that people like Gabor Maté were doing good work with Indigenous people to treat addiction, and I had heard that there are some plant medicines that can heal people's addictions without withdrawal. I came across this story about the healing powers of ayahuasca and other psychedelic medicines. Not long after that, I got in a long conversation with my friend Dr. Rae St. Arnault, who's a naturopath and environmentalist. We talked about how different cultures around the world use psilocybin for healing purposes. I read up on this some more and eventually phoned Darwin Douglas to tell him what I'd learned. Darwin said, "I'm already on this, bro—I've been reading on this for three months already!" That's when we decided to do something.

I got together with Justin, Darwin Douglas, Francine Douglas, Otis Jasper, Katy Gottfriedson-Jasper, and others to create a program called Sacred Circle, which would administer psychedelics for healing purposes in accordance with our law. We teamed up with Papa Phil Lane Jr., who helped lead the ceremonies, which we conduct within our sovereignty and the law of who we are. Psilocybin and other psychedelics are ceremonial medicines. We know our ancestors used them because they knew every inch of our territory, and they knew the medicinal uses of every plant that grows here. They knew the benefits of this medicine, and they knew it was a gift given to us to help our people heal. We work with a team of medical professionals on our protocols before and after the ceremonies.

My first ceremony with these medicines was a very difficult one. I hadn't done any psychedelics since I was a teenager because I found them to be a bit scary, so I didn't want to go first. But in our teachings, you can't ask somebody to do something unless you do it yourself, so we knew we had to try this. It took us six months to decide that we were going to it. During the ceremony, I wanted to focus on remembering some of the traumatic events that had happened to me during my childhood, because they still affect me. I wanted to work on this trauma in ceremony to help scar over and heal the wounds from the bad things that happened. I knew this would be a scary thing to face, but I wanted to do the work—I wanted to deal with the trauma.

As with our other ceremonies, this medicine helps people reach a higher state of spiritual consciousness and experience a little bit of heaven—the oneness of everything. During the ceremony, when you close your eyes and look far into the darkness, you can eventually see the spiritual realm. That first time, when I closed my eyes, all I saw was a dark orb preventing me from seeing anything beyond it. I believe that it was the spirit of my trauma that I don't remember. I couldn't see past it. It encompassed all my vision when my eyes were closed. I could get little glimpses of heaven beyond the orb, but all I could feel was anguish. I literally had to hold on to two other people. I brought their hands to my heart and asked them to tell me I was okay, because I sure didn't feel okay! I told them, "I think I took too much!" But the intensity I was experiencing wasn't from taking too much of the medicine. It was from facing the spirit of sexual abuse, physical abuse, mental abuse, emotional abuse, alcoholism, and drug addiction. I was facing the spirit of all those things that were passed down from the Church—the starvation, the murders, and all those intergenerational wounds over multiple generations from my grandparents to my parents to me.

There are studies that show that a person can experience the effects of their parents' trauma without having experienced the trauma themselves. Characteristics of anxiety and depression can be passed on through generations if traumatic wounds were never healed. Some studies say that traumatic impacts can be felt for up to three generations, although our cultural ways tell us that they can persist for seven generations. What I was experiencing in that moment was an open wound of my grandpa, an open wound of my mom and dad, an open wound that was passed on to me, which I passed on to my kids. That's the spirit that I carry from the trauma I don't even remember—not only my own trauma but that of my family and my ancestors. In that moment, the spirit of all this trauma felt overwhelming, and I couldn't take it. I yelled out, "I don't want to see it! Go away! Push it away, push it away, push it away!" But when I tried to push it away, it only got worse. I asked for help, and my friends held me closer. They said, "You're okay,

Rueben. You're dealing with it, and you're processing." The whole time they were telling me to surrender, but I couldn't. I pushed it away, as I had for many years of my life, pushing the trauma so deep into the back of my mind that I couldn't even remember it. I was now facing it head-on, and I tried to push it back to where I wouldn't have to deal with it. Four hours later it still wouldn't leave me alone, and I tried to push it away once again. My friends reminded me that I had prayed to see my trauma; I had prayed to deal with it, and now I had to face it and surrender. They told me, "We love you. We support you. Just surrender." So, I finally surrendered, and then I got what I prayed for. I said, "There's the spirit of my pain, I see you. I see you!" And as soon as I did that, it disappeared and I could see the spiritual realm that had been blocked out by the orb. That wound that was carried from my grandparents to my parents, and from my parents to me, had begun to heal and scar over.

Thousands died in those residential schools. The nuns and priests beat, molested, raped, starved, and murdered little children. My mom witnessed that and wondered if she was next. How could my mom not have passed down that hurt and pain to my siblings and me? Each and every time one of those children was hit, or abused, or witnessed violence, or heard about someone dying and not coming back, a trauma spirit was born. How could that pain not have been passed down to Indigenous Peoples across Canada? Tsleil-Waututh is such a beautiful community, but we are not immune to the traumas of colonization. Our whole community felt it, and although we've healed together, we still have open wounds. That pain was passed down, and it wounded me too. The physical abuse wounded me; the sexual abuse wounded me; the mental and emotional and spiritual abuse wounded me.

So, I prayed in that psychedelic ceremony, and I said, "No more! No longer will I be a prisoner of the horrible things that happened to me!" When I did that, I felt freedom. I celebrated myself and I felt freedom. I breathed deeply, and I felt freedom. I hollered, and I felt freedom. I heard my brothers in the ceremony dealing with some similar stuff. I heard my brother scream, "No more! We are taking it back! No more! We are free! We have freedom!" We take those open wounds of hurt and pain that we have carried for seven generations, and we think forward to the next seven generations, and then we close those wounds of my grandfather, and we close those wounds of our parents, and we close those wounds of ourselves, and we find our freedom. That's what our people deserve, and that's what this medicine gives us. And this time, we're not asking permission from the government or anyone else to help my people to heal. No colonial government is going to tell us how to heal, especially after what they created with the residential schools.

I did many more ceremonies after that first one—I now do them, on average, about once every six weeks or so. I started working on all the hurt and pain that I caused my kids, women whom I disrespected, and men whom I fought with, and I said, "I'm sorry. I'm deeply sorry." I've been healing in ceremony for twenty-eight years, but I still carry guilt for the pain I've caused to others. When I was younger and still hurting, I passed that pain on by hurting other people. That spirit of guilt was also an open wound that needed to scar over and heal. Doing that healing work doesn't mean that I can move on, or that I don't need to continue to work at it anymore, or that I won't stand up and recognize the wrongs I've done if somebody needs me to. But it does mean that I'm sorry. It means that I no longer have to be a prisoner to all the horrible things I've done. I can let it scar over and heal.

We each have mental, emotional, spiritual, and physical parts of our being, and as Uncle Len would say, the four tires on a car need to be in balance in order for it to run. A society can't run without its spiritual tire any more than it can run without its physical, mental, or emotional tire. Our hope is to put that spiritual tire back on each individual across Canada, the United States, and the rest of the world. We will open this medicine up to everybody living in our territories because we want to show them a higher state of spiritual consciousness. We want to show them heaven. We want them to understand that they carry a spirit inside themselves. We want to give them a right to heal and change their life. We want them to learn how they can love their children more, love their partner more, and love the Earth more. I'm so happy to say that because of ceremony I love my kids even more, I love my mom even more, I love my partner even more, and I love everybody more. My partner, Olivia, was already a beautiful person, and since she started doing these ceremonies, she has blossomed into an even more beautiful being and I love her even more! That's what I want for people. The freedom that I experience is the freedom all people deserve. And when they experience that, their lives will be better, and they will make better choices. Then collectively we will create change.

FINDING A WAY

Our people lost so much to colonization, but we're picking ourselves up and healing. When you consider where we came from as a community, I'd say we're doing pretty well. Disease wiped out our population from many thousands to seventeen people or fewer. Our lands were stolen and multiple successive generations of our people, including my brothers and cousins not much older than me, were forced into abusive and genocidal residential schools. Those experiences caused severe harm and trauma that were passed on from one generation to the next. We continue to face systemic racism to this day. But I'm so proud of my people for the healing we've done and continue to do. Despite all the hurt, pain, and trauma that our ancestors, parents, grandparents, and siblings experienced with residential schools and the devastation of Canada, we still managed to hold on to the spirit of our ceremonies, and our Elders taught us the tools that we use to heal those traumas today.

It started with my grandpa and my aunties and uncles finding a way, envisioning what a better future for our people would look like and showing our people what they could achieve. My grandpa sang the "George Family Prayer Song," which was later adopted as the Coast Salish anthem. I say to my kids that Grandpa must have been in such a holy place for such a beautiful song to be gifted to him from the ancestors. Uncle Len also found that beautiful place. He would sit in his spiritual room dedicated to ceremony, where he was surrounded by all his winter and summer artifacts, and bring himself to that holy place where Grandpa was when he was given the beautiful "George Family Prayer Song." They found a way for our community, and they inspired us to find a way too. That's what my grandpa did, and that's what my uncle Len did; that's what my uncle Bob did, that's what all my aunties and uncles taught us to do, that's what my mom does, and that's what we still do today. The nuns and the priests tried to beat all the hope and faith right out of them, but amazingly they were able to find a way despite all the abuse they endured in the residential schools. Grandpa had a vision and a goal, and he pursued them despite the abuse. Uncle Len had a vision and a goal, and he pursued them despite the abuse. My mom had a vision and a goal, and she pursued them despite the abuse. She let go of all her prejudices, hate, and anger from being abused, and today when people come to our ceremonies, our home, and our territories, no matter who they are, she welcomes them in and says, "Call me Ta'ah."

I implore people to understand that they, too, have the spirit within them, and that they can have that beautiful relationship with Spirit, with their ancestors, with the Creator, and in turn with everything. If you carry yourself in a good way and sit in a beautiful holy

Amy George was nominated for the YMCA Women of Distinction
Award in 2018. Pictured with two of her children Rueben George
and Cecily George.

Amy George (centre) with her children (left to right) Damian George, Rueben
George, Nathan George, and Cecily George.

place, if you pray for a vision to guide you in the direction you need, you can open that spiritual doorway to the ancestors and receive messages that will help you in the future. If you sit and meditate on that vision, it will guide you in the direction you need to go. If you listen to Spirit, and if you believe in that vision mentally, emotionally, and physically, your spirit will believe in that vision, too, and the path to your goals will become easier. That's what Uncle Len did, sitting in his ceremonial room, praying and meditating on the questions of what our people need and how we can make things better, drawing on all the spiritual lessons and teachings of the ancestors, until a vision for lifting our people up came to him. He found a way. I miss him, and I love him, and now I do what he did. I find my way. Like I said, I'm not the best or the smartest, but I have the drive to create opportunity. I ended up working in many different fields in my life. I have no educational background in environmentalism or business, but I pray, and I work hard, and I find a way, just like my uncles did. And I pray to my uncles, my dad, and my grandpa—they are my ancestors now. I pray to them to help me find that way.

My mom is now an Elder in our community. She still shows up at rallies or comes to my house and says, "Okay, what work do you guys have for me to do today?" She's always willing to give. Her grandchildren visit her regularly, and she sits with them and passes on the teachings. She talks with them about her experience in residential schools. The discovery of the unmarked burial sites of children at the Kamloops Indian Residential School, and then other residential schools across Canada, opened a lot of eyes and raised a lot of questions, but my mom's been speaking out fearlessly about all the horrible things that happened at residential schools for over thirty years. Some people were not happy with her for talking about these things, but she did it anyway because it was the truth. She told my kids the truth about the abuse, and she also told them how she healed, and by doing that, she helped them heal. When my kids look at my mom, they see their beautiful grandma, just as I saw my beautiful grandpa. They see someone who has done the work of healing, and now we all see her that way. She still comes to Sweat Lodge and prays hard for all of us to heal. When it gets really hot in Sweat Lodge, people often bring themselves closer to the earth where it's cooler; sometimes I look over and see that my mom is the only one still sitting up straight. She's so happy now, and she has an amazing sense of humour—she reminds me of Grandpa in that way. One time, she poked her head inside the Sweat Lodge and everybody there looked at her, expecting her to offer one of her profound teachings or a prayer, as she usually does. We stared at her in silence for a while waiting, until she finally said, "What are you all doing in there?" We burst out laughing. To live through what she's been through and then turn out as beautiful as she has, to be as strong as she is, to be the matriarch that she is to our community, is such a beautiful thing to witness. As my son says, "Ta'ah is my hero."

When I was a kid, many of the adults in our community drank, and sometimes with the drinking came harm. But today, around eighty percent of our people have quit drinking, and most of those who do, don't have problems with it like I did. We're learning to deal with the trauma. We're building ourselves up economically. Our businesses are thriving, and we're acquiring our lands back. We've become an environmental powerhouse, cleaning up the inlet, reintroducing elk to our territory, and raising the salmon counts in our streams and rivers. We work with a lot of really good people who share our vision of creating change and who are happy inside themselves. My sister, Cecily, has been a consistently bright star with the biggest heart despite everything we went through. She's such a good and kind matriarch of our family who we can always rely on to be there and love us no matter what. Cecily and her husband, Chad, are leaders in our ceremonial family. My big brother Damian has always been a spiritual leader. My brother Nathan has the most charisma of us all—people always loved him when we were younger. He could sing just like Bono from U2, and he could dance, and he was such a beautiful happy, funny person. The colonial system and all the intergenerational pain, it all ruined him as it did so many people living in the Downtown Eastside. But when I visit my brother, I still see his beautiful crystal-clear spirit. Just like the inlet—we know that it has been polluted, we know that all these horrible things have happened to it due to colonization, we know that you have to be careful going into that water now, but if you go down there on a nice day, it still looks crystal clear and shimmers.

My sister-cousin Charlene and my brother-cousin Justin are incredible leaders of our community. I'm proud of what all my brother-cousins and sister-cousins and my nieces and nephews have accomplished spiritually and through their education. We are lawyers, educators, business leaders, anthropologists, and much more. My partner, Olivia, highly respects our culture. She learned to love First Nations cultures early on in her life when she had the opportunity to be included in the Squamish language program in high school. Later on, before we met, she started praying with my sister-cousin True Thomas in Sweat Lodge for many years, and that's where she became more involved in ceremony. She has three wonderful kids, Moya, Kin, and Teo, who carry the respectful teachings that their mom has taught them. In some ways, spirituality is about being good people, and the Lohan family are definitely good people. Olivia carries her good teachings and incorporates them into everything in her life—in her parenting, in her work as a therapist, and in her community engagement work. I'm lucky to have such a beautiful and inspirational partner. My kids are doing really well, and I'm so proud of them. Cedar and Kayah have both travelled the world speaking out against injustices. They're really powerful warriors and talented at what they do. Cedar is taller than me now and can

Left to right: Rueben George, Cedar George-Parker, and Kayah George.

lift me up on his shoulders. He is a brilliant young person and does really good work spreading positive messages. Kayah is finishing university, and she's a strong, intelligent woman. They live with no spiritual doubt or boundaries around the miracles that they're capable of, just as our Tsleil-Waututh ancestors did. They know they can achieve anything they set out to do. As my son says, their generation is the first in a very long time that wasn't told their Indigenous culture and spirituality is evil and that they would burn in hell if they practised it. This upcoming generation has come to understand things at a much younger age than I did, and they're already surpassing me in so many ways. What they did standing up for Wet'suwet'en was just amazing. By the time this generation gets to be my age, they'll be unstoppable.

As the manager of the Sacred Trust, I've often been the spokesperson for the Tsleil-Waututh Nation in our fight against Trans Mountain, but what blows me away is thinking about how every single one of my brothers and sisters and cousins and nieces and nephews could do what I do. They're all super-intelligent and well-educated spiritual leaders who are articulate speakers and who incorporate our law and culture into everything they do. They tell me that they're proud of what I do, but I know they could do the exact same thing because they all have the same good teachings from the Elders that I have. Despite the brutally harsh things that our parents went through at residential schools, they were able to hold on to their teachings and pass them on to our generation. That makes me proud to be a George. That makes me proud to be Tsleil-Waututh. And I'm proud to be a Baker and Squamish on my dad's side for the same reasons.

So, I raise my hands to honour my community, the Tsleil-Waututh people. We're a small nation that worked with our allies like the Tiny House Warriors, the Elders at watchhouse, and all the NGOs, to take down a multi-billion-dollar oil giant and send it back to Texas. We built ourselves up, and we did it as a community and as a nation with a unanimous vote of support from our people. We spent a lot of time and money defending our rights in court—time and money that could have gone to other things. But it's been ten years and that pipeline is still not built, so that's a victory right there. In addition to the oil and bitumen, there's also coal and uranium transported through our waters, as well as the chlorine plant on our shores. There are few old growth cedars left in our traditional territory due to all the industrial logging. The bitumen and the pipeline are only one part of the story of how colonization has impacted our lands and waters, but we had to take a stand somewhere, and we did it as Tsleil-Waututh because we are the water people. The water is our mother. It's who we are and why we protect and monitor and give back to the water. We've been doing this for thousands of years, and we will do it for thousands more. We'll do whatever it takes to win because that's our law, and we've said over and over again that we work within our law. That's what we told Trudeau, and before

The George family.

Trudeau, that's what we told Harper; we've been telling this to Canadian society for many generations, trying to teach them a better way. We talked with the Government of Canada in good faith, but the officials had their minds made up even before we sat down to talk. So, we're not going to wait for them any longer because they've proven themselves incapable of making good decisions for future generations. We're not reconciling with the Canadian government because it doesn't even understand what the problem is to begin with. We're taking back our integrity. We're taking back our connection to Spirit. We're taking back our way of life and our beliefs. Because we love the connection that we have, which is nə́čəmat.

This is just the beginning. With our governance model that we developed in conversation with Uncle Len, we're affirming the Coast Salish teachings of truth, family, health, and culture—the foundations of our existence. We're asserting our law and solidifying our hereditary right to be the stewards of our lands in a reciprocal connection to nə́čəmat. We're protecting what we love without compromise. Our people are educating themselves and stepping into important leadership positions in our community. We're building up our capacities, which the colonial system and the residential school system tried to suppress. They tried to take away our voice, but the spirit of the Tsleil-Waututh people will always prevail, and that spirit is only getting stronger.

This next generation will be the voice for all those ancestors who had no voice. Like my dad, who died from colonization. Sometimes I think that he'd be really proud of me. I always wanted to tell my dad, "I love you." The closest I ever got was when my kids said those words to me. That changed my life. My dad was robbed of the opportunity to be a father and a grandfather, and we were robbed of a dad and a grandpa. He didn't have the opportunity to draw on our culture and spirituality, to shed the harms of colonization, and he overdosed and died because of that. He never got to experience Sweat Lodge, Sun Dance, smudge, or our Coast Salish ceremonies as I have. Same with my stepdad, Philip Gurney, my uncle Donny, my uncle Clyde, my auntie Corrina, and so many others. They didn't have a voice, and they didn't have a chance to heal themselves with our culture and spirituality. So, we do it for them, and we ask for their help in prayer because they are in the spiritual world. We do it for all those people like my brother-cousin Isaac, my brother Nathan, and everyone on the Downtown Eastside who deserves a better opportunity. Enough is enough. So much injustice has been done to our people, and as my mom says, that's why we fight to create change, to make things better, and to be in a reciprocal relationship with our lands and waters as our ancestors were. No longer will we work in this broken system that's degrading us, hurting us, and harming us. We're going to fix it ourselves. We're no longer going to be stuck. We're going to unite, and heal, and fight, and move forward for all those people like my dad. A lot of our people died due to colonization, but we're still here and we still fight. My grandpa fought until the day he died. Uncle Bob and Uncle Len and my other aunties and uncles fought until the day they died. And as my son says, we will not be the generation that stops fighting.

We still face difficulties and challenges in our communities. I'm not naive, and I'm not oblivious to the things I see around me. As an Indigenous person, of course I see the challenges that we continue to face. We still have trauma in our community; we still have people who suffer; we still deal with addiction in our community; and we still have people who die in tragic ways. We're not perfect by any means. Unfortunately, trauma is still consistent and constant in our Indigenous communities. I still struggle at times; I'm definitely not perfect. I will continue my healing. In ceremony, I'm constantly seeking the freedom to let go of that hurt so that I am no longer a prisoner to the bad things I did, or to all the bad things that happened to me. I pray for those I hurt, and I forgive those who hurt me and my family. I pray with my mom to make that happen, I pray with my kids to make that happen, and I pray with my community to make that happen. Canada and the Church are responsible for inflicting so much hurt and pain, for perpetrating so much abuse and murder of our people. And we work together as a family to forgive them too.

We've come a long way as a family, and I have come a long way as an individual. But we still have a long way to go. So much more work needs to be done. I will continue to help others heal, especially those who have been hurt from the wrongs that I've done. Some of the traumatic things that happened during my childhood, which I pushed so deep down inside that I couldn't feel them anymore, still rise to the surface at times. When they do, I suffer from bouts of anxiety and low self-esteem. But the difference is I'm now better equipped to deal with those problems. We're better equipped to draw on our culture and spirituality to heal and to deal with environmental issues in our territory. We're better equipped to govern ourselves as a sovereign nation and to deal with the colonial government and the systemic racism of Child and Family Services, the court systems, and the police. We're better equipped to stand up for our lands and our waters and our people. We're better equipped to stand up for our Indigenous rights. We work toward a better way collectively. We work to forgive the horrible things that happened to us, and we work to apologize for the harm we created when the oppressed became the oppressors. By healing the generational pain that was passed on like an open wound, we reclaim our freedom, which was taken from us by the colonizers—Canada and the Church. I heal the hurt and pain of my dad. We heal the hurt and pain of our parents and our grandparents.

We will take you with us. We will take anybody with us who wants to learn a better way. It's clear that what we need globally is more love and Spirit—connection to our individual spirit, to our ancestral spirit, and to whatever you believe your god or Creator to be, which in turn connects us to the spirit of all things that are good. The world is losing its connection to the land, the water, the air, the energy from the sun—all those things that we need to live—and that's rooted in trauma. That people don't love the Earth or others enough to stop the harm and make things better is itself a sign of trauma. As Tsleil-Waututh people, we're healing from our trauma. We are healing from our hurt and our pain, and we will do this with you. We open our doors to you, and we will help you recognize the trauma that you also carry, which prevents you from caring about the harm that is being done to you, to other human beings and living creatures, and to the Earth. When you come into my ceremonial lodge, our spirits will expand to the size of that space and overlap with one another in prayer. When that happens, we become brothers and sisters and family in ceremony, and that's where the healing takes place. So, we will take you with us, and we will heal together.

Jedi. Image courtesy of Cliff Vestergaard.

My grandpa is smiling down upon the Tsleil-Waututh people right now. He's smiling down upon his kids, his grandkids, and his great-grandkids. He's smiling because this next generation will be the strongest yet. He's smiling because we haven't forgotten his teachings. We haven't forgotten our culture, our spirituality, or our ceremonies. Some of our ceremonies haven't changed for thousands of years. That's the medicine that's healed us, and that medicine will continue to be our strength. That medicine will help us continue to love one another and make our circles bigger and stronger for future generations. We know we will win because the ancestors are on our side. Canada is too puny to stand up to the spirit of the Tsleil-Waututh people. We will no longer allow Canada to treat Indigenous Peoples the way it has. It stops here. And there are even bigger changes to come. We will find a way.

by Michael Simpson

I heard of Rueben George long before I met him. His name was spoken among activists working to stop the Trans Mountain Pipeline expansion with the deference and admiration reserved for the most revered leaders. Like thousands of others, I flocked to Burnaby Mountain on the south shore of the Burrard Inlet in November 2014 to stop Kinder Morgan from conducting geological tests related to its proposed pipeline. I knew that the company was planning to twin the Trans Mountain Pipeline, though admittedly I didn't know much else about the project at the time. Nevertheless, like many others who converged on the mountain that autumn, I found the thought of pouring billions of dollars into building new pipeline infrastructure to facilitate the expansion of tar sands extraction at a time of compounding climate and environmental crises to be utterly unacceptable. Over the course of the month, an ever-increasing stream of people ascended Burnaby Mountain to make their opposition clear. Many were arrested for acts of civil disobedience. It was an inspiring moment of people coming together to take a stand against the powerful fossil fuel industry and their accomplices in government. Although this convergence appeared to have materialized rather suddenly and spontaneously, Rueben and his allies had been working relentlessly to oppose Trans Mountain for several years, patiently building up the grassroots support and awareness that make moments like that one possible.

In the years that followed, the movement opposing Trans Mountain continued to gain momentum, buoyed by people elsewhere across North America taking similar stances against fossil fuel pipelines, from Keystone XL to Northern Gateway and Dakota Access. A new federal government of Canada, led by Justin Trudeau, came to power preaching climate action and Indigenous reconciliation, offering momentary hope for change that quickly yielded to further disappointment. In March 2018, ten thousand supporters marched behind Rueben and Indigenous leaders from across Turtle Island back to Burnaby Mountain, where Elders from local Coast Salish nations built a traditional watchhouse structure, Kwekwecnewtxw, directly in the path of the proposed pipeline. The erection of this watchhouse was a powerful assertion of the legal jurisdiction of Coast Salish nations over their unceded lands and waters. It was clear that this was more than just another movement seeking to protect the environment. This movement sought to upend a colonial system that has been the root cause of environmental harms, and it would do so by asserting Indigenous legal obligations to protect their sacred lands and waters. As Rueben says, the goal was not only to defeat Kinder Morgan and the pipeline but to defeat them in accordance with Coast Salish law. As I write these words at the close of 2022, the watchhouse remains in place, the Trans Mountain Pipeline expansion has not reached tidewater at the Burrard Inlet, and the project has proven to be a massive boondoggle riddled by cost overruns.

After getting a taste of this opposition, I wrote a PhD dissertation on the expansion of fossil fuel extraction and its associated infrastructure. However, upon completing my studies I was reluctant to take the typical next step in academia, which is to develop the dissertation into a book. I struggled with the question of what authorized me, as a White settler academic, to write a book about a topic such as the resistance to the Trans Mountain Pipeline expansion, which was largely an Indigenous-led movement that many people had devoted their lives to over the preceding years. I grappled with the question of to whom I was accountable in doing this work, and I was keenly aware of the danger of doing more harm than good by imposing my own narrative upon this story, regardless of how well intended I may have been. After dwelling in this uncertainty for some time, I worked up the courage to approach Rueben, seeking guidance. Rueben's immediate response was to say, "Let's write a book together." I had not expected this, and I think this invitation to collaborate speaks to the trust and generosity with which Rueben and his family are always inviting people to join them. For me, this came as a dream opportunity—one that would change my life.

In the summer of 2019, Rueben and I met up at a small deli on Commercial Drive in East Vancouver to discuss what the nature of this collaboration might be. I still had in mind that we would be writing a book about the Trans Mountain Pipeline, and I arrived with printed documents outlining potential themes we might explore. I talked nervously through these ideas for some time, and only when I finished did Rueben begin to tell his story. As I listened, it quickly became clear that this was a story about so much more than a pipeline. Rueben's story is the story of the Tsleil-Waututh people and their ancestral connection to the lands and waters in which their legal and spiritual systems are grounded. It's the story of the founding of Vancouver through colonial acts of violence and dispossession, and how these acts continue to animate the city today. It's also the story of how this colonial violence is passed on laterally and intergenerationally within families and communities. Most of all, this is a story of great strength of spirit. It's a story about the work of healing from colonial harms, both personally and collectively. Linked to wider movements of Indigenous resurgence across Turtle Island, this is the story of an Indigenous nation drawing on their laws and culture to reclaim their lands, waters, and food systems to bring a decolonized future into being. While the struggle against Trans Mountain was a very prominent matter of public concern in Canada, for the Tsleil-Waututh people and other Indigenous nations along the pipeline route, this was only the most recent chapter in a much longer history of how their people have experienced and resisted colonialization. It became clear that the story to be told here was Rueben's story, and my role was to facilitate the telling of this story as best as I could.

Rueben often says that when two spirits come together, a new spirit is born. In many ways, I see this book as having been created through the coming together of our two spirits. This is a book that was written in friendship and in ceremony. As Rueben shared his stories and teachings with me, we were often doing things together, often out on the land. Rueben took me to sites of great cultural and spiritual significance to the Tsleil-Waututh people. We spent time with his relatives, who generously shared the bounty from their territories. We fished, harvested crab, and swam in sacred waters. We built ceremonial drums, shared meals, and attended legal proceedings. Most significantly, we sat in ceremony. In this book, Rueben recounts how Indigenous Elders told non-Indigenous environmental leaders at the outset of the struggle against Trans Mountain that if they wanted to work with the local Coast Salish nations, they would first have to learn about Coast Salish law by attending ceremony. The same applied to our collaboration.

The invitation to sit in ceremony with Rueben and his family has been nothing short of transformative for me. I knew from the start that working on this book with Rueben would be a very special experience from which I would learn a great deal. What I perhaps didn't quite realize was how profoundly healing this experience would be. As Rueben introduced me to ceremony and shared stories about the healing journey that he and his family have been on over the past decades, he was also gifting me powerful tools to use in my own healing process, and he regularly encouraged me to use these tools to face the discomfort of my own personal wounds. He would remind me that even those who have been the beneficiaries of colonialization have been harmed by these structures, disconnected from the spirit shared by all beings. When Rueben says that settlers are harmed by colonial structures, the intention is not to portray White settlers as victims, nor is it to equate their harms with the violence that has been perpetrated against Indigenous Peoples. The point that I understand Rueben to be making is that colonial violence continues to manifest and reproduce itself in part because those who perpetrate colonial violence have not owned up to the harms that they have directly committed or indirectly benefited from, nor have they acknowledged their own pain and taken up their responsibility to do the work they require to heal. I think that this conviction that we all have to heal is a big reason why Rueben, his family, and his community are always so willing to invite people to do this work with them in ceremony. As Rueben always says, despite all the harm that has been inflicted upon their people by White settlers, the George family will always welcome people into their ceremonies, no matter who they are. His mom will always say, "Call me Ta'ah." I will always be grateful to Rueben and his family for the generosity with which they have welcomed me into their homes and lives, and for helping me along in my own healing journey.

The responsibility of being entrusted with the stories shared in this book—some of which belong not just to Rueben but also to the George family and to the Tsleil-Waututh people—is not lost on me. Nor is the long history of problematic collaborations between Indigenous people and White settler academics. With this in mind, I approached this project with the intention of ensuring that Rueben's voice would come through the text to the greatest extent possible. Nevertheless, it would be dishonest to say that I have not influenced the shape of this text in any significant way. The stories that are shared in this book were initially spoken as part of many different conversations over the course of several years. At times, these conversations may have been prompted in certain directions by questions that I asked or comments I made. They were, after all, a dialogue. These conversations were then transcribed, shaped, and reordered into a manuscript, with distinct sections, chapters, and a narrative arc. A lot of this work was done together, as Rueben and I read over the manuscript and made additional edits and modifications. Rueben also read over the manuscript with members of his family and community to help with accuracy, and to ensure that we were not sharing stories that should not be shared. But, inevitably I made certain editorial decisions along the way, and consequently my fingerprints are undoubtably found on the finished product. I think it's important for me to both acknowledge and take responsibility for this role that I played in shaping how this story has been told and arranged. I can say with sincerity that I approached this work with as good a heart and as good a mind as I knew how, but I'm also aware that despite my best intentions, I will have made mistakes and errors of judgment along the way, many of which will be a reflection of my own positionality and the limitations of my understandings.

Projects such as this unavoidably require multiple acts of translation. Most obviously, there is the linguistic translation of words and concepts from one language into another—in this instance from Halkomelem into English. But such acts of linguistic translation are not necessarily as straightforward as substituting out words with their equivalent in another language. Given that concepts gain meaning in relation to the cultural and intellectual systems from which they are derived, they don't necessarily have a direct synonym in other languages. This presents the risk (some would say, the inevitability) that nuance will be lost and meaning distorted when translation involves removing concepts from one cultural-linguistic context and placing them in another. For instance, when Rueben discusses Coast Salish concepts such as nəċəmat or smeńálh, which are core to the teachings of this book, they are translated not only linguistically but also across distinct intellectual (one might say ontological and epistemological) traditions.

This book has also required translation from oral to written forms. The dialogues in which Rueben and I engaged over the period of three and a half years were modified to read as though they were narrated by a single voice. The informal tone of our spoken conversations was edited to conform with the more formal written style and conventions that one might expect of a book. The context in which these conversations were had—the places we visited, the things we did together, the precise moments in time and space when these stories were told—have also been largely lost in the text. While I hope that the power of Rueben's voice comes through, the intonations, passion, and emotion in his voice as he shared these stories have proven difficult to capture with the written word.

Books are also products of the systemic conditions in which they are created—even those that are the most critical of prevailing power structures. In the context of a capitalist economy, books become commodities—legal objects that are bought, sold, and circulated for profit. While the book began with just two of us, before long there were agents, contracts, and publishers involved. This being said, our publisher, Nick Garrison at Penguin Random House Canada, and our agents, Stephanie Sinclair and Ron Eckel at CookeMcDermid, have been great supports throughout the process. At Penguin Random House Canada, I would also like to thank

Zainab Mirza for work on many different aspects of this book's production, Crissy Calhoun for attentive copyediting, Kelly Hill for the powerful cover design, and Dan French for work promoting the book.

I feel fortunate to have had supportive work environments at the University of British Columbia and the University of St Andrews where I've been surrounded by colleagues and mentors who saw the value in this project and allowed me the space to do this work. I would like to thank Philippe Le Billon and Trevor Barnes for supervising my PhD studies, and Jess Dempsey and Deb Cowen for supervising my post-doctoral research. At the University of St Andrews, I would especially like to thank Dan Clayton and Jo Sharp for their support. When this project began I was supported by a Social Sciences and Humanities Research Council post-doctoral fellowship, and in the later stages I was supported by a fellowship from the Royal Society of Edinburgh, both of which enabled me to do the patient work that a relational project like this requires.

I would also like to thank Ruth Ozeki for guidance navigating the world of publishing, Benjamin Kao for help with transcription, Celina O'Connor for editing, and Eugene Kung for legal fact-checking. Finally, big thanks to all my friends, family, and mentors who have supported and encouraged me while working on this book over the past years. I can't possibly name everyone who has helped me along the way, but I would especially like to acknowledge Bobby Arbess, Oliver Kellhammer, James Rowe, Dave Segal, James Tully, and most important of all, Celina O'Connor and Cedric Tay Barclay-O'Connor.

I think it's important that I make clear that I have not received any direct financial compensation for my role in the making of this book, and I requested that Rueben direct any share of the proceeds that I might have otherwise received to support Coast Salish and George family cultural work in ways that he deems most appropriate.

I'm disclosing this not because I think it deserves any praise or recognition, but because I think this is the way it should be: these stories do not belong to me, and I feel it is therefore inappropriate for me to benefit monetarily from them.

Collaborating on this book with Rueben George has been one of the most profound and meaningful experiences of my life. Rueben is unquestionably one of the kindest, most loving, and beautiful people I've ever met. He is an important visionary of our time. I will forever be grateful for all that he has gifted me over these past years, and I'm honoured to call him my friend and brother. His stories and teachings have inspired me on my own healing journey, and I hope they will do the same for others who read this book and listen carefully to his words.

Michael Simpson
Fife, Scotland
December 2022

Rueben George and Michael Simpson.

INDEX